QMW LIBRARY
23 0934625 6

KV-636-038

EDWARD THOMAS
A Critical Biography

EDWARD THOMAS

A Critical Biography
1878–1917

WILLIAM COOKE

FABER AND FABER
London

First published in 1970
by Faber and Faber Limited
24 Russell Square London WC1
Printed in Great Britain by
Latimer Trend & Co Ltd Plymouth

SBN 571 08494 x

ACKNOWLEDGEMENTS

I am indebted to the late Professor W. D. B. Grant for his continuous support throughout this book, which originated as a short research exercise at Leeds University in 1966. For reading it, in whole or in part, prior to publication, I should also like to thank Mr. Geoffrey Hill of Leeds University, Mr. A. J. Gilbert of Lancaster University, and Mr. Richard de la Mare, who also spoke with me of his memories of Edward Thomas. Finally, I should like to express my gratitude to the late Mrs. Helen Thomas and to Mrs. Myfanwy Thomas, who answered many questions in the course of this study, supplied photographs for illustrations, and freely allowed me to quote from innumerable manuscripts and letters.

My thanks are also due to the following, who helped in the search for material, lent correspondence, or otherwise supplied help and information: Mr. Conrad Aiken, Mr. Christian Berridge, Mr. David Garnett, Sir Geoffrey Keynes, Mr. F. W. Oser, Mr. Harold Owen, Dr. Arundel del Ré, Mr. A. V. G. Richards, Mrs. Patricia M. Rogers, Mr. Stanley Snaith, Professor R. G. Thomas, Professor Lawrance Thompson, Mrs. Renée Tickell and Mr. Rowland Watson.

Mr. Edward Connery Lathem of Dartmouth College Library, New Hampshire, generously supplied me with copies of the unpublished file of Edward Thomas—Robert Frost correspondence, and Mr. David Posner of the Lockwood Memorial Library of the State University of New York at Buffalo very kindly lent microfilm of an important MS notebook. Acknowledgement is also made to the following libraries which readily made available their books, manuscripts and other relevant material: the Academic Center Library of the University of Texas, the Henry W. and Albert A. Berg Collection of the New York Public Library, the Bodleian Library, the British Museum, the Brotherton Library, the Jones Library, Marquette University Library, the Harriet Monroe Modern Poetry Collection at the University of Chicago, the library of the University College of South Wales and Monmouthshire, and Yale University Library.

ACKNOWLEDGEMENTS

For permission to quote from copyright material, I should like to make acknowledgement to the Trustees of the Hardy Estate and Messrs. Macmillan and Co. Ltd. for 'In Time of "The Breaking of Nations" ' from *The Collected Poems of Thomas Hardy*; to Sir Geoffrey Keynes on behalf of the Brooke Trustees for extracts from two letters by Rupert Brooke to Edward Thomas; to Mrs. H. M. Davies and Jonathan Cape Ltd. for the last two stanzas of 'Killed in Action' from *The Complete Poems of W. H. Davies*; to the Executors of the Robert Frost Estate, Jonathan Cape Ltd. and Holt, Rinehart and Winston Inc. for extracts from Lawrance Thompson's *Selected Letters of Robert Frost*; to Holt, Rinehart and Winston Inc. and Jonathan Cape Ltd. for quotations from *The Complete Poems of Robert Frost*; and to Mrs. Myfanwy Thomas and Faber and Faber Ltd., for quotations from *The Collected Poems of Edward Thomas*.

For information not otherwise available to me, I have drawn on the two earlier biographies, Mr. R. P. Eckert's *Edward Thomas: A Biography and a Bibliography* (London, 1937) and Mr. John Moore's *The Life and Letters of Edward Thomas* (London, 1939), and on Miss Eleanor Farjeon's *Edward Thomas: The Last Four Years* (London, 1958). I wish to express a general debt to all three books.

Lastly, I should like to make acknowledgement to Mr. Jon Silkin, editor of *Stand*, who first published part of the chapter entitled *Roads to France*.

CONTENTS

ILLUSTRATIONS

INTRODUCTION

'One day,' recalled H. W. Nevinson, 'after I had been staying with him in his cottage above Steep, I ventured to ask him, "When are you going to give us your poems?" and he answered, "Poems! I have never written a line of poetry in my life!" I glanced at him, but said no more, knowing how shy poets are of their verse. Of course, I thought it was not true. The strange thing was that it *was* true.'[1]

Edward Thomas's story is one of the strangest in literature. When he died in 1917 at the age of thirty-nine, he was known to his contemporaries as an influential reviewer, the writer of occasional *belles-lettres*, and the author of more than thirty prose works ranging from nature books to historical biography. Not until after his death were two slim volumes of poetry published, all of which had been written in the last two years of his life. For his admirers they were an unexpected bonus which his prose continued to overshadow. H. G. Wright in *Studies in Contemporary Literature* (1918) declared: 'However much we may admire Edward Thomas's poems, his claim to fame will rest on his prose. For this no praise can be too high.'[2] For his detractors Thomas's poetry must have seemed suspiciously like the product of a hack writer who could turn his hand to anything. 'Once in so often,' Robert Frost recollected, 'men of other cliques would say to me, "Why did you start Thomas off writing poetry? God knows his prose was bad enough." '[3] For friend or foe, the poetry was unusual and somewhat disturbing. John Freeman described it as 'singular without making any effort to be singular; his poems attract because they are written for the ease and activity of his own changing spirit, and without a thought of how it strikes a contemporary.'[4] Edward Shanks found them 'disconcerting in content and form, and unlike anything ever written by anyone else.'[5] Harold Monro refused to publish them under the imprint of the Poetry Bookshop; Edward Marsh excluded them from his *Georgian Poetry* anthologies. A reviewer for *The Times Literary Supplement* pronounced what they all felt: 'What is uncustomary, especially in art and literature, must slowly win its way. So perhaps it may be with these poems. But whether they have few readers or many, they are among the rarest fruits of these strange years.'[6]

Today Thomas's poetry is likely to be looked on as the culmination of his literary career, expressing economically, freshly and directly all that he had tried to express over the years in prose. Certainly this is how Thomas himself regarded it. Always rigorously self-critical, he had no illusions as to the quality of those books he wrote solely for money. Throughout his life he had been the slave of publishers' contracts, producing merely what was asked and paid for. And despite his apparent diffidence, he grew more conscious than any of his friends that he was working against his own nature, that such an existence robbed him of every opportunity of realizing his innermost ambition—to become a poet. His hack work turned out to be hard labour, and it was almost lifelong. The war was a macabre blessing in disguise, allowing him a brief moment of fulfilment before it killed him.

This book attempts to portray the artist in his diverse (and often incompatible) roles of reviewer, hack, and poet, before considering in depth his search for self-expression and self-discovery. In the course of eradicating several current misconceptions which have distorted the true nature and significance of his poetry, it is hoped that Thomas will emerge as 'a very original poet who devoted great technical subtlety to the expression of a *distinctly modern sensibility*'[7] rather than the Georgian 'nature poet' whose dismissal is still too often summary in recent criticism.[8] The discussion of his prose, much of which has gone out of fashion and out of print, will be severely restricted to the light it throws on the poems. Ultimately it was upon their resilience that Thomas wished to stake his reputation. In 'Words' he made this plea with characteristic humility:

> Let me sometimes dance
> With you,
> Or climb
> Or stand perchance
> In ecstasy,
> Fixed and free
> In a rhyme,
> As poets do.

'His last word to me,' wrote Frost, 'his "pen ultimate word" as he called it, was that what he cared most for was the name of poet.'[9]

Thomas has survived rejection by the Georgians and rejection with the Georgians to become one of the most popular of twentieth-century poets. He, if anyone, has earned the title of that name.

Part I
BIOGRAPHICAL

I

HOW I BEGAN

1878–1897

Everyone begins by talking, stumbles into writing, and succumbs to print.

'How I Began', *The Last Sheaf*

I

Philip Edward Thomas was born at Lambeth on 3 March 1878 and his boyhood and youth were spent largely in London.

In spite of his 'accidentally cockney nativity', he was of mainly Welsh origin. His father, Philip Henry Thomas, was born at Tredegar, the son of Henry Thomas of Glamorgan and Rachel Phillips of Gwent, though he derived some Devonshire blood from a mariner family named Eastaway.* His mother, Mary Elizabeth Thomas, was the daughter of Edward Thomas Townsend of Newport, Monmouthshire. She was partly English and partly Welsh, with an admixture of foreign blood from her mother, Catherine Marendaz.[1] She was a fair-haired, blue-eyed, undemonstrative woman whose looks and temperament were visibly reflected in her eldest son. The same air of melancholy prevailed over her features, possibly as a result of the foreign strain in her blood, but more likely the result of her upbringing by a repressive maiden aunt after she had been orphaned at an early age. With her Thomas felt the strongest possible affinity; with his father he felt none at all.

His parents had settled in Lambeth after their marriage but moved to Wakehurst Road, Wandsworth, when 'Edwy', the first of their six sons, was nearly two. The road suited a lower middle-class family of small means, and their neighbours included doctors, clerks, and a court usher who lived next door. His own father was a staff clerk for light railways and tramways at the Board of Trade—an 'officer' in the Civil Service Thomas would tell his school-friends. He was a short, stern, dark man who had struggled from a poor background to a position far

* The name Thomas used as his pseudonym when he came out as a poet.

above that of his relations. He was therefore determined, and perhaps over-anxious, that his sons should succeed after him. In the fragment of autobiography published posthumously as *The Childhood of Edward Thomas*, he appears as a strict, unsympathetic figure who inspired fearful respect rather than affection. 'He was eloquent, confident, black-haired, brown-eyed,' wrote his son, 'all that my mother was not. By glimpses I learnt with awe and astonishment that he had once been of my age.'[2]

One such revelation has survived in a MS notebook entitled 'Addenda to Autobiography' which contains eleven sketches, some of which were incorporated into his *Childhood*. This genial glimpse of his father was, unhappily, omitted:

> Father had a few songs and comic speeches that he used to treat us to in turn when we were six or seven. He used to put on an artificial voice and expression and say 'Walk up. Walk up and see the show! Strike up, Joe! Walk up and see the live lions stuffed with straw and Napoleon crossing the Alps in an open boat.' When we were younger he had us on his knee to sing
>
> Paddy from Cork he had never been
> A railway train he had never seen,
> He's off to catch the great machine,
> That runs along the railway. Whoop!
>
> (It ended in a high whoop and a wrinkling grin of delight from my father as he tossed us up.)[3]

The Childhood rarely admits as much attachment as those few lines. In general the thought of his father seems to have aroused only a bitter hostility, the quintessence of which is found in the poem which simply bears his initials for its title, 'P.H.T.' It begins:

> I may come near loving you
> When you are dead
> And there is nothing to do
> And much to be said.

Its conclusion, however, is inexorably rooted in the present:

> But not so long as you live
> Can I love you at all.

With great aunts at Newport, Caerleon and Swansea, Thomas spent many holidays in Wales from the age of four onwards. Although he never spoke or understood the language, he always regarded himself as Welsh, and his visits there were visits home. The kindling of his passion for the land of his ancestors is the subject of another extract from the 'Addenda to Autobiography', which is headed 'at ten':

> My early feeling for Wales culminated in my singing of Moore's 'Minstrel Boy', was clinched and fostered by it. I knew only of Welsh harps. I supposed the minstrel boy with his wild harp slung behind him was Welsh and as I sang the song I melted and trembled with a kind of gloomy pleasure in being about to die for Wales, Arthur's and Llewelyn's Wales, the 'land of song'. While I shivered with exaltation repeating his words
>
> though each man else betrays thee
> One sword at least thy rights shall guard,
> One harp at least shall praise thee,
>
> it might have been my harp and my sword.[4]

Thirty years later when he was a serving officer in the British Army, he told one close friend that he had discovered a new understanding and joy in Milton's line about the Welsh people—'An old and haughty nation, proud in arms.'[5] And though, as a poet himself, he became more English than many an Englishman, the 'land of song' was not forgotten or unpraised:

> Make me content
> With some sweetness
> From Wales
> Whose nightingales
> Have no wings,—

he asks in 'Words', the invocation to his art.

His other lasting passion was for the country. 'Almost as soon as I could babble,' he wrote, 'I "babbled of green fields" '.[6] Two or three times a year he went to his aunt's or grandmother's in Swindon, whose homely cottages were for him 'the corner-stone of the universe'. There he was free to roam the countryside to his heart's content, often in the company of boys who might be considered too 'low' for him in London, more often in the company of David ('Dad') Uzzell, an ancient ex-poacher and militiaman whose colourful life outdid anything he had ever read. Uzzell delighted the boy with his knowledge of wood-craft and wild-life, a debt the poet repaid years later when the old English peasant was remembered—'He sounds like one I saw when I was a child'—and immortalized in 'Lob'. At Swindon too he became aware of a character and rhythm of life he had never seen in the city:

> The slower thinner weekly procession to market was the other great sight. Curious wizened old men with old hats, enormously stout women with shawls and black bonnets, smiling rosy ones with feathers, drove by. Their little carts were laden with eggs, butter, fowls, rabbits, and vegetables, from Lydiard and Shaw and Parton and Wootten Bassett. One or two always stopped at our gate, and the woman came to the door with a broad flat basket of eggs or butter under a cloth, and, very rarely, some mushrooms. She said, 'Good morning. How are you this morning? Got your little grandson here again. Nice weather we're having. Musn't grumble. Yes, the butter's one-and-two now . . .' While my grandmother went for her purse I stood at the open door and looked at the shrewd cheerful woman or at her dog who had come for a moment from under the cart. She with her cheerful and shrewd slow way was as strange and attractive as any poet's or romancer's woman became afterwards, as far away from my world. I never knew her name, nor did she use ours.[7]

Most of his hobbies were connected with the country and he took home collections of moths, butterflies, and birds' eggs, and stories of fishing expeditions. In turn his early reading, after a period of 'Indians, cowboys, and Mexican greasers mounted on fiery mustangs',[8] began to centre round the naturalists. His father's taste was for the directly philanthropic and progressive in literature (which meant Longfellow and Tennyson as far as poetry was concerned), yet he kept a library of several hundred books, among them Shakespeare, Chaucer, Shelley, Keats, Byron and Browning. Thomas, though he early devoured Scott's poems, came to the rest more slowly and he believed that he was fifteen before he really began to read poetry for pleasure. (The discovery of Gray's 'Elegy' was, he felt, a significant turning-point.) Until then the staple of his reading diet had been Thomas Edward, Buckland, Wallace, Izaac Walton, and above all Richard Jefferies. Before long he was copying out in each of his books the last words of

The Amateur Poacher: 'Let us get out of these indoor narrow modern days, whose twelve hours somehow have become shortened, into the sunlight and the pure wind. A something that the ancients thought divine can be found and felt there still.' It was 'a gospel, an incantation'.[9] And when he first began to write seriously in his teens, it was in a style as close as possible to that of Jefferies. With one essay he won a botany book at the Sunday School of the local Unitarian chapel he attended, and the minister was so impressed that he persuaded the editor of a children's paper to print it. Within a few years Thomas would 'succumb' to some of the leading periodicals of his day.

However, according to *The Childhood*, 'nothing I ever heard at home attracted me to literature or the arts.'* His father's interests, apart from his work, tended to be mainly religious (he was a leader of the 'Positivists') or political. For him poetry was nothing compared with the question of Home Rule. His Liberal sympathies—unlike his religious beliefs—were even communicated to his son:

> I used to go with my father to the Washington Music-hall on Sunday evenings and hear John Burns, Keir Hardie, and the Socialists. Once there I saw Michael Davitt standing by an iron pillar, dark, straight, and austere with his armless sleeve dangling. I think I knew that he had then just come out of prison, and this probably helped him to a place in my mind with the Pathfinder and Milton's Satan. John Burns was another glorious, great and good man. I honestly admired his look and voice and was proud to shake hands with him and also to have my middle stump bowled clean out of the ground by him once on Clapham Common.[10]

A visit to Kelmscott House to hear Grant Allen and William Morris further enhanced their reputation in his eyes. Out of school he distributed political handbills, sang a Liberal parody of 'Men of Harlech', and with the help of a *Daily Graphic* penny 'Election ladder' followed

* This again seems summary rather than exact. His brother Julian, in the introduction to the same book, remarked: 'To my father he owed more than he would ever admit, in especial the art of reading aloud, and through this the appreciation of poetry.' And Anthony Davies in an article entitled 'Edward Thomas and his Father' wrote: 'I discussed the family with an old friend who knew Philip Thomas and Edward, both at their London home and during their visits to Wales. Philip was described as a quiet intellectual type; a Nonconformist of fine character who, far from wishing to suppress his son's writing ambitions, sought only to give him anchorage in a secure job.' *John O' London's Weekly*, 28 October 1949.

the elections as keenly as he did the cricket scores. In school, despite his intense shyness, he declared himself a Liberal in a class dominated by Conservatives. And when, at the age of fourteen, he was faced with an essay on 'Bicycling' or 'The General Election', he chose the latter without hesitation, beginning: 'The General Election of 1892 was a great political crisis—a struggle between privilege and reform . . .'.[11]

Such activities were part of his father's policy for broadening his son's education, as were the evening classes on Botany, Sound, Light and Heat, and the special lessons in Latin and Greek to which he was sent. For Philip Thomas had decided that his eldest son should go to a Public School before following in his footsteps into the Civil Service. But his son felt otherwise. He was beginning to discover Shakespeare and the other poets, who were to convince him that 'there was something for men besides eating and drinking and getting a living or having it got for you.'[12]

2

Frederick Walker, High Master of Manchester and afterwards High Master of St. Paul's, Hammersmith, was a remarkable man. He was not unlike Dr. Johnson in his startling volume of voice, heavy figure, creased florid face and creased black clothes, and in a certain tendency to explode at odd moments. Generally, however, his wit was not misplaced and had about it the homely and popular flavour of the north country. When a fastidious lady wrote to ask him what was the social standing of the boys at his school, he replied: 'Madam, so long as your boy behaves himself and the fees are paid, no question will be asked about his social standing.'[13] On another occasion he met one of his pupils in the street whom he recognized as the author of some Swinburnian imitations in the school magazine, and roared at him that he had a literary faculty that might come to something if somebody could give it solidity. The startled schoolboy was Gilbert Keith Chesterton.

From 1892 to 1895 he had at least three notable writers in his school—and all in the same form. History VIII was a special branch of the highest class which had been created so that one or two promising pupils might study for history scholarships at the Universities. One of its founder members was E. C. Bentley, the author of *Trent's Last Case*, who was soon joined by Chesterton, his lifelong and closest friend. Chesterton left for the Slade Art School in 1892, and Thomas, then sixteen, entered the form in 1894.* Bentley remembered him as 'an exceptionally reserved and quiet boy who usually had in his pocket a rat or so, and a few snakes, which he would shut in his desk with his books, and occasionally peep at stealthily.'[14] Reserve was not characteristic of either himself or Chesterton, and the broad humour and gusto with which they chose to portray their school-days—Bentley in *Those Days* and Chesterton in the chapter 'How to be a Dunce' in his *Autobiography* —are in marked contrast to the pages that Thomas devoted to 'Public School: First Impressions' in his *Childhood*. Unlike the other two, Thomas had not grown up through St. Paul's, and the rootlessness of his own school-life (he had been to five schools in all, varying from board to grammar schools) resulted in few lasting friendships. As he came to be surrounded by boys who were more and more his social superiors, his self-consciousness deepened. He was alarmed and impressed by the other boys' apparent independence, not realizing as Chesterton had that the convention of independence fostered by St. Paul's was to a certain degree false, since it was a false maturity. 'The boy really is pretending to be a man; or even a man of the world; which would seem a far more horrific metamorphosis. . . . We had begun to be what no children are; snobs. Children disinfect all their dramatic impersonations by saying "Let us pretend". We schoolboys never said "Let us pretend"; we only pretended.'[15]

Most of them wore men's clothes of a material different from Thomas's black or grey ready-made ones; they carried their books in bags like clerks and seemed grimly earnest, thinking only of work and success; they read many books, saw many plays, and held strong opinions about them. 'What are you reading, Thomas?' asked one, soon after he arrived. '*The Gamekeeper at Home*,' he replied. 'The gamekeeper's place is in the woods,' said the former, and Thomas kept silent, not venturing to remark that the woods were his home. More often he was ignored. What he chiefly remembered of this period was his own misery and isolation:

Many others looked well off, spoke in more refined voices than I was

* Robert Vernède, author of *War Poems* (London, 1917), was also a contemporary of Chesterton's and preceded Thomas to Oxford. They were killed on the same day in 1917. Leonard Woolf entered the school in the autumn of 1894, and though he soon met G.K.C. through the school's societies (even though he had left), he never met Thomas.

> used to. I came alone in the morning, and in the afternoon I went home alone, often in a railway carriage containing three or four schoolfellows, but alone, in a state of discomfort which I imagined would have multiplied if they had taken any notice of me, which they never once did, in spite of my morbid looking out for signs that they noticed my discomfort. During the middle of the day I was alone: I stood alone watching Rugby football or practice for the sports. For most of the boys in my form went home to lunch; the rest also disappeared. If I had lunch at school I sat alone and was spoken to only once. . . . When I was not reading or watching games I walked along the far side of the river watching the gulls and swans, sometimes in such wretchedness that I wanted to drown myself.[16]

Everything at school was an aimless task performed to the letter only. His father had urged him to try for a history scholarship, but it seemed to him that he had never come across duller books than Bright's *History of England*, Kitchin's *France*, Lodge's *Europe*, and Marshall's *Political Economy*. The only time he took part in the weekly debating society he opposed the motion that 'Elizabeth was a Bad Woman and a Bad Queen'. In preparation he did nothing but look up relevant sections in the school's text book, supposing the matter had been settled long ago. His opponent immediately began by complimenting him on his 'admirable summary of Bright', and Thomas sat blushing under his cleverness.[17] Only in English did he make any showing, watched over by the form-master of History VIII, Mr. R. F. Cholmeley. The minister of the local chapel had also kept up his interest in the boy, and now he began to look round for someone to give his literary faculty 'solidity'.

James Ashcroft Noble, a new member of his congregation, had recently moved with his family to Wandsworth from Liverpool. At fifty he was established as a literary critic for *The Spectator*, *The Academy* and *The Daily Chronicle*, and he had edited the weekly literary supplement of *The Manchester Examiner*. Among his works he had published a collection of reminiscences and reviews, *The Pelican Papers* (1873), a book of poetry, *Verses of a Prose Writer* (1887), a critical study called *The Sonnet in England* (1893), and he was then completing what was to be his last book, *Impressions and Memories* (1895). The minister (with the consent of Thomas's father) sent him one or two essays for an opinion, and soon after school broke up for the summer of 1894, Thomas was invited to call and discuss them at 6 Patten Road.

In Noble he had found a sincere and kindly mentor who patiently criticized his work, suggested and lent him books, and generally instilled the image of the successful man of letters in his mind. Their first meeting was short but congenial. As they were concluding, one of his daughters, Helen Berenice, just eighteen, 'plain, with a round healthy face and small nose, rather serious in expression, but not entirely unattractive', [18] entered the study to ask him to stay for tea. He refused. Soon afterwards he was gone. After several of his visits Helen wrote to tell her best friend Janet Aldis of the attraction they seemed to have for each other. But she felt that nothing would come of it since they were both so shy.

3

Thomas left St. Paul's in April 1895, ostensibly to read for his Civil Service examination under the direction of his father, but in fact reading and writing with Noble's encouragement. He saw to it that Thomas's sketches were published (and paid for) by *The Speaker* and *The New Age*, and he must have been instrumental in consolidating his protégé's 'faint ambition, both definite and indefinite, to do something in connection with learning or literature.'[19] Consequently, as soon as he left St. Paul's, Thomas began to concentrate on several essays and a diary, which were to be published in book form two years later. The diary allows us to trace his movements from 1 April 1895 to 30 March of the following year. On the first day he was at the heronry in Richmond Park; on the twelfth he went to Wimbledon; next day he was on Wandsworth Common in fine blue weather, watching the return of swallow and house-martin. On 15 April he set off to walk to Marlborough Forest and then on to Swindon, putting up at inns and cottages on the way. There the blackthorn was steeped in blossom, the chaffinch was building, and on 2 May he saw orange-tip butterflies for the first time, threading the copse like blown leaves. In June he visited Coate Farm, where Jefferies had lived and worked, and spoke to the old housekeeper who used to prepare the cheese-room as his study. To all eyes, particularly his father's, he seemed to be listless and lacking in application. Yet his true state of mind is perhaps best revealed through his description of that of Jefferies at the same age.

In his later critical biography, it is evident when we read of Jefferies' 'taunting' father, his 'tender, restless, melancholy' mother, that Thomas's youthful admiration had advanced to self-identification. His explanation for Jefferies' apparent 'idling' might therefore have been his own: 'He was in a ferment of undivined and growing powers which isolated him, of ambitions, of needs, which presents of books from his aunt could not satisfy. His father was not a man of books, though far from illiterate. . . . But however bitter the days of poverty, loneliness, misunderstanding, and constraint, the time when he was sixteen and seventeen had probably as great sweetness as bitterness, since the two go together in the extremes at least as much at that as at any other age.'[20]

As summer passed he returned to read desultorily for his examination and continue writing his essays. That autumn he was a frequent caller at Patten Road, though no longer for purely literary reasons. Early in the New Year Helen told Janet: 'I and the Thomas boy are very slowly making way. He wrote and asked father if I might go out with him on one of his long walks. To my great surprise he said I might. So I was in a great state of elation. But to my disappointment Edward never turned up for me. And when he came last night and was asked the reason, he said he had never dreamed I would be allowed to come.' To make up for it he asked her to visit his home the following afternoon, but Mrs. Noble refused to let her daughter go unchaperoned. 'Mother says what would Mrs. Thomas think?' Helen reported. 'I say if she thought till she was tired, she could not possibly think of any wrong. I feel so cramped in. . . . Why we may go walks together, and not go to his home where there is all his family, I simply cannot imagine. It is too deep for me. . . . I am going to ask Edward what his views on the subject will be. I rather think he will be very broad-minded. He looked awfully amazed when mother said I could not go with him to see his books.'[21]

Despite these setbacks they were gradually being drawn together in a bond which was more than friendship, and when Thomas left for a spring visit to Swindon they wrote to each other nearly every day. While he was away, Helen went impulsively and introduced herself to his mother. If Mrs. Thomas was surprised by so unconventional a visit, her own mother was furious. She had never shared her husband's affection for the boy and now she insisted that Helen break with him completely. As a result their correspondence became secret, Thomas's letters reaching her through a school-friend who went to enquire after her father's health. Noble had long suffered from tuberculosis of the throat, and his health deteriorated to such an extent in the early months of 1896 that when Thomas arrived back suddenly on 30 March he was too ill to be seen. He died two days later after an emergency operation. 'Edward is a dear boy,' wrote Helen, 'and helps me wonderfully to keep up under the first fearful trouble in my life.'[22]

Her distraught mother took advantage of the situation to demand that she stop seeing Thomas, while his own father repeatedly urged him to commit himself to the Civil Service. In the end both parents had to give way. Helen left home to become a nursery governess in Margate. Thomas, after a protracted struggle, persuaded his father to allow him to try for a place at Oxford. For once, both were perfectly happy. Thomas worked hard to catch up on his reading at the same time as he prepared his first book for press. Helen adored her work with the children, though they were 'a handful and more' sometimes. 'Baby is getting on splendidly and looks very bonny,' she informed Janet. 'He knows me quite well now, and we spend all the morning together. Amusing, and nursing, and putting him to sleep makes me feel quite like a mother, only the sense of great responsibility and possession is wanting. Good training for my future ambition isn't it? When I am walking up and down with him lying in my arms, perhaps half asleep, looking so well and sweet, I think to myself and wonder will the joy of bringing another being into the world ever be mine. How glorious, how heavenly if it is someday. Too good for the likes of me. I am not half good enough to be called "mother". I must improve before I shall think myself half good enough.'[23]

The Woodland Life, dedicated to the memory of James Ashcroft Noble, appeared in the spring of 1897 when Thomas was nineteen. Helen, after a temporary reconciliation with her mother, had returned to work in London as governess for a Mrs. Andrews. They could again meet every day and, as Helen has frankly related in *As It Was*, they were soon lovers. Throughout that summer, evenings and week-ends were made idyllic by leisurely walks to their favourite spots on Wandsworth or Wimbledon Common where they re-read those poems of Shelley which held so profound a significance for them—'Love's Philosophy', 'Prometheus Unbound', 'The Revolt of Islam', 'Queen Mab', and—most important of all—'Epipsychidion'. Taking pride in their rebellion against social conventions, particularly against the institution of marriage, they agreed with Shelley that it was immoral to be bound together if love failed. They needed no ceremony themselves, and Thomas simply gave her an antique ring in his possession as a token of their wedding. In September, under the threat of impending separation, he told his parents that he had to go to Oxford for a few days, but instead took Helen for a 'tiny honeymoon' to Swindon where they stayed with David Uzzell and his wife. When they returned, Helen went back to her duties as governess and Thomas went to his own home. Shortly afterwards, with *The Woodland Life* going into a second edition, he went up for his first term at Oxford

2

THE DIVIDED SELF

1898–1904

Which way shall I go?
A voice says: You would not have doubted so
At twenty. Another voice gentle with scorn
Says: At twenty you wished you had never been born.
'The Sign-Post'

I

He matriculated as a non-collegiate student and spent his first year in a lonely room at 113 Cowley Road. Making little contact with the university world, where he felt as much out of place as he had at St. Paul's, he would often wander for miles in the Oxford countryside in order to alleviate his appalling sense of isolation. For what seems the first time—and the last for many years—his anguish was sharpened into poetry:

O Nature! let me love thee more:
For friendship[s] fail
And life is frail:
I love—I hate: but as of yore
I love thee—let me love thee more.

O Nature! whereso'er I turn
I find no heart
The counterpart
Of mine; though hearts of men to learn
Long strive I whereso'er I turn.

As early as this, his 'melancholy' began to express itself as a longing to escape, an adolescent flirtation with death itself:

I gaze: the sun is low
And lucid breezes blow:
The trees are blank;

The sward is green
Liquidly like the green of happier climes:
I think that I
At last am there
Where I have dreamed but never hoped to be:
Exalted and
In purer air
Dead, gazing on the azure plains of heaven.[1]

Having failed a scholarship at Balliol, he studied hard for one at Lincoln which he took in March 1898. In the examination the alternative subjects for the essays were 'Vox Populi, Vox Dei' and 'Might is Right'. Thomas combined them and came top. He took up residence at Lincoln in the autumn term of his second year, choosing rooms on Staircase 12 immediately above those once occupied by John Wesley. Thereafter he was able to play a more active part in the life of the university among some of his distinguished contemporaries. Bentley, who had preceded him from St. Paul's, had become President of the Union; John Buchan was Librarian; Hilaire Belloc and Raymond Asquith frequently spoke there to a house that 'believes or disbelieves, and applauds'. Later that year he became friendly with Ian MacAlister, a future secretary of the Royal Institute of British Architects, and E. S. P. Haynes, the well-known lawyer and author. To Harry Hooton, who that year had married Helen's childhood friend Janet Aldis, he gave this account of his undergraduate experience: 'I can topple into bed *off* the verge of drunkenness; swear; use slang creditably; howl the usual foul choruses . . . also I can be heartily sick and well rid of it all.'[2]

His holidays were spent partly in Wales, partly at home, and partly with Helen. She was then working for the Logans, a Hammersmith family which led a Bohemian 'progressive' life within its own circle of young artists and poets. She admired and imitated their apparent freedom from conventiality, but Thomas was unimpressed and during their discussions on beauty and art, morality and 'the new woman', he sat among them like a 'judging Sphinx'. However, he was always made welcome and that Christmas he often spent the night there with Helen. 'We are happier now than ever before,' he told Hooton. 'It is a happiness so mild and cool that it is like a kind of Saintliness after passion; yet it is not satiety.'[3]

At the beginning of the spring term of 1899 he rowed for his college in the Torpids and was sufficiently established to deliver several papers to the Davenant, Lincoln's literary society. Norman G. Brett-James recalled one in particular: 'I remember a very illuminating paper which he read to the Davenant Society on the birth of the Nineteenth Century, the wave of Revolution, the break-up of Europe and the threatened destruction of society, and the genesis of a new literature as exemplified in the poems of Coleridge and Wordsworth.'[4] With Haynes he walked all round Oxford, usually to Shotover, Cumnor, and Bagley Wood. Sundays were spent on the Isis and Cherwell, bathing, sculling, talking, and eating as the mood came. Together they planned a novelette called 'Olivia Patterson', which was begun the following year but never finished or published. In its first chapter (a social evening at Balliol) there is a half-mocking portrait of a character named Borlase, who is seized with the idea of sending a 'prose poem' on Celtic melancholy to the *Briton*. It is in Thomas's hand:

> 'No one understands the constitution of a man of genius. The psychological moment flashes on him; he is aflame with creative fire and then in another instant he is a mere ash. And here above all other places he is daily crucified—with wretched health and pedantic overseers.'
>
> 'My dear Borlase,' began Langton, 'you won't pull yourself together. Have a good drink like a Christian and sprint round the quad till you have some decent air inside you.'
>
> The man of genius eagerly adopted the former suggestion with a zest that soon put the latter rather out of the question.[5]

Despite asides about 'pedantic overseers', Thomas accepted Oxford with equanimity after the disillusion and loneliness of his first year. It gave him his first real intellectual and social companionship, and a period of leisure he would never know again. It also gave him the opportunity to indulge his pleasure in literature rather than the history he was supposed to be reading under Owen Edwards. 'His talk was in those days much of books,' recorded Haynes. 'He seemed to known Aubrey's Lives almost by heart and he could invent passages of seventeenth-century prose the authenticity of which was never suspected.'[6] The occasional essays he contributed to *The Speaker*, *The Academy* and *The Literary World* (from which he derived an income of about £80 a year to supplement his father's allowance) had themselves become precious and over-elaborate. The influence of *The Yellow Book* had superseded that of *The Amateur Poacher*; Pater, Wilde, and Beardsley had taken the place of Shelley and Keats. 'No one,' Thomas wrote of the shade of Pater's influence in the 'nineties, 'was too proud to have a soul "with all its maladies" '.[7] But their influence was relatively short-lived and afterwards scrupulously exorcized. 'On paper,' he was to write in reviewing Wilde, 'he seems often not affected but incapable of sincerity. Thus, literature is made a craft rather than an art, related to wall-paper and carpets more than life. It is a literature of the idle classes, for the idle, by the idle.'[8]

His own idle days at Oxford were rapidly drawing to a close. In May Helen told him that she was pregnant.

2

They were officially married at Fulham Registry Office on 20 June 1899 without a word to their parents. Afterwards he returned to Oxford and Helen went to live with the Hootons. During the vacation he went to Swindon as usual, but found no peace of mind there and left for Wales. It seemed extremely probable that his father would withdraw his allowance and force him to leave the university when he learnt of the 'catastrophe', yet Thomas was restless until he was told. Finally it was agreed by all concerned that Hooton should break the news. On 12 August Thomas received a letter from his father which was short and to the point. 'Mr. Hooton has made some revelations,' it read. 'What are the facts?'

'So here I am,' he wrote to Haynes from Ammanford, 'in a pretty state, with no letter since Tuesday from Helen, and not a notion of my father's attitude; tho from what I can judge the above laconism is worse than a tirade. There's not a human being here I can talk to; or if I did, they would reply in the neo-Baptist vein. All my mock-heroic position is upset. I was looking forward to my garret in Carshalton, with more or less lyrical work, interspersed with pot-boiling; I even thought I should alter pot-boiling rather than let it alter me: and now it looks as if my father is going to play the long-suffering saint. The present obvious remedy is laudanum. Of the future I can't make anything. One thing is certain: I can't live at home.'[9]

However, when all was said and done, Mr. Thomas allowed him to stay on for his last year, hoping no doubt that fatherhood would bring him to his senses—and to the Civil Service. Mrs. Noble, on the other hand, would have nothing further to do with her daughter, and in the early autumn Helen went to live with the Thomas family. On 15 January 1900 their son was born, whom they named Philip Mervyn. Two days later his young father—a hero of his college—was back at Oxford studying for his finals. In the third person, generalizing from his own experience, he subsequently described the end of his university career:

> He has begun to pay his smaller bills and to find out what books he must read for a degree, when the examination day arrives. Then he borrows his old dignified look of indolence in the sultry schools, while he writes hard, and secures a second class by means of a legible handwriting, clear style, and amusing irrelevance. He goes down, alone, still with a fascinating tongue, desperate, and yet careless of success, ready to do anything so long as he can escape comfortable and conventional persons, and quite unable to be anything conspicuous, but a man who has been to the garden of the Hesperides and brought back apples that he alone can make appear to be golden in his rare moments of health.[10]

Retrospectively he portrays an aplomb which he scarcely felt at the time. In a frenzy of worry and indecision he had worked badly, and his second-class degree was a bitter personal disappointment. For his father it was the last straw. Only his friends took it lightly. As he went down they at least were confident that he was destined for a brilliant literary future. In the words of Mr. T. Russell, a retired college servant who could still remember Thomas in 1949, 'if anyone looked a poet, he did.'[11]

3

'After leaving Oxford . . . he lived in English villages, as far as he could get away from any railway; he made and cultivated his gardens, and tramped about in the open air in all weathers as recreation from his studies and labour in literature.'[12] With this flicker of Voltaire, Philip Thomas summarized the remainder of his son's life. After a final break in their relations, Thomas moved with his wife and child—'a fat ludicrous optimist' of eleven months—to a slum in Earlsfield and then to one at Balham. 'I am romantic enough to think I am probably far more fitted to be a family man than a very minor "prose poet" ', he informed MacAlister in November.[13] But it was only a gesture, and he knew it. He had signally failed in nearly every attempt to get literary work, and his income then was less than it had been as a student. Immediate necessities crowded upon him. After paying the rent he had to live on soup for several weeks while he made fruitless rounds of editorial offices, meeting with vague promises, condescension, or contempt. His only major success came with the literary editor of *The Daily Chronicle*, H. W. Nevinson, who recalled their first encounter in *Changes and Chances*: 'When he first came to me, I said to myself, "Yet another poet!" . . . He was tall, absurdly thin, and a face of attractive distinction and ultra-refinement was sicklied over with nervous melancholy and the ill condition of bad food or hunger. Almost too shy to speak, he sat down proudly and asked if I could give him work. I enquired what work he could do, and he said "None". . . . I asked whether he would like some reviewing on any subject, and on what. He replied that he knew nothing of any subject, and was quite sure he could not write, but certainly he did want work of some sort. . . . Of course, he at once became one of my very best reviewers, and soon one of my closest friends.'[14]

Reviewing, however, was ill-paid and exhausting, and it brought him no sense of achievement. 'I now live—if living it may be called—by my writing,' he told one friend, ' "literature" we call it in Fleet Street (derived from "litter"). . . . It's a painful business, and living in this labyrinth of red brick makes it worse.'[15] Sometimes he took on as many as fifteen assorted books a week, yet as soon as the pace slackened he started worrying and searching for more. In the ten months from August 1900 to June 1901 he earned £52, out of which £20 went to clear old debts. There were signs that he was even prepared to consider a secure job of some sort. He was turned down for several sub-editorships; Haynes tried to get him a librarianship at the House of Lords; his father was allowed to enquire after openings in his department. Nothing materialized except the offer to work as an unpaid probationer with the Charity Organization Society. He stood it for a week. 'I might as well work with my nails cut to the quick as with them,' he assured MacAlister.[16]

In the autumn of 1901 he and Helen decided on the country at any price, and before the year's end they had moved into an ugly, red-brick house, misnamed Rose Acre, a mile from the village of Bearsted in Kent. The building looked raw and naked on a little hill, its garden overrun with weeds. A door with a stained-glass panel gave entry to a narrow passage and two downstairs rooms, bare except for cheap red wall-paper. The rent was £32 a year. All the following spring, in the intervals from work and worry about work, he 'cultivated his garden'. To Jesse Berridge, a poet (later a clergyman) whom he had met and reviewed in London, he wrote to sympathize with illness in his family: 'We can't conceive of illness here where we make as much of this fine weather as the crocuses, the rooks and the willow trees. In a superior way of course—having one acre of our own—we congratulate you on your garden; we may even be able to help you, though our own experience has been slow and dearly bought. I only hope you haven't got a lot of new brick dust and mortar instead of loam to work upon. But in a London garden, there is one good rule; when in doubt, sow *sweet peas*. A penny packet will make a score of ladders as rich in dreams as Jacob's. I have unfortunately had to vary my gardening with selling my books. Until last week I had earned nothing for a long time and had to get nearly twenty pounds by selling books. Now I hope I may have peace for a while. But my peace of mind returns rather slowly and since I sent you my last letter I have written little.'[17]

All he had produced were a number of essays which he published as *Horae Solitariae* later that year and *Rose Acre Papers* in 1904. They were the distillation of his Oxford experience, and the earlier volume was fittingly dedicated to Owen Edwards, his former tutor. The second was dedicated to another protégé of James Ashcroft Noble who had continued to write to Helen after her father's death—the poet Gordon Bottomley. Thomas had introduced himself by enclosing a note with one of his wife's replies, and although the two men did not meet until 1903 they were soon fast friends.

These two slim volumes held all the work that Thomas would publish voluntarily until 1910. For in March Helen discovered that she was pregnant again. Despair drove all happiness from his mind.

4

For the only time in her life Helen became a victim of that despair. To Janet Hooton, who sensed that something was wrong, she poured out her soul:

'Since I received your sweet letter I have made at least two attempts to answer it, but have never had the heart to finish either letter. For it is just because you *are* so sympathetic that I have hesitated to tell you what is troubling me so now. It seemed cruel and unnecessary to give you pain when you were the happiest little [wife] in the world. But since you seem hurt that I have kept silence about things which I know however sympathetic you are you will never quite understand . . . I will tell you, tho do not talk of me to people: I never in my life desired solitude, complete isolation of body and mind as I desire it now. Two great facts are always before me. First as I expect you know I am to give to the world another baby in October. This alone is terrible for no one wants the poor wee thing; no one looks forward to its coming, and I least of anyone. I know I shall love it when it lies in my arms, perhaps all the more because I know it will have only me to depend on for love: but now I cannot have any happy thoughts of it. I think of it only with tears in my eye and a fierce pain in my heart, an intolerable aching which wears me out body and soul. It is terrible to me more than to most people perhaps for down crash come my purest ideals. I feel accursed because of this sweet thing lying near my heart. You ask why I do not want it? Because we are very poor; because it means more anxiety for Edward and more work for him. Home will become unendurable to him. Even now poverty, anxiety, physical weakness, disappointments and discouragements are making him bitter, hard and impatient, quick to violent anger, and subject to long fits of depression. . . . You see Edward is at home all day. If he were not I could manage even the two babies with ease, for it is the knowledge that the little worries of domestic life are irritating him that drives me to despair. He cannot have the quiet he needs, and anxiety and discouragement are no fit fortifications against the little worries and irritations that occur where there are young children. How then will it be with two? We cannot afford any extra help; there are no prospects of being less poor. He is selling some of his dearest books to pay for baby clothes and doctor, etc. and as he packs them up I know how he is rebelling at fate, how hard life seems to him, how he regrets it all. But on me who love him more than my life the burden falls doubly. I can no longer be . . . the one he looks to for all his joy, for all the sweetest things of life. He cannot love, Janet, he cannot respond to my love. How can he when all is so dark, and I, I have deprived him of it all, the joys of life and love and success. If he would only begin life again without me my heart would rejoice. I should be very happy, for his happiness is all I care for. But you will not understand, you cannot you sweet happy creature. How can you know what it is to feel the love of your dearest one being torn from you by fate and evil days. I have prayed that I and my babe may die, but we shall not, tho this would free Edward. I am as strong as ever. I pile work on work till my body can scarce move for weariness, but nothing lifts the darkness from my soul.

Edwy tells me you want to come here. O come and let me cry and cry till all my tears are gone, and then I will make you happy here in this perfect country.'[18]

Throughout their lives they blamed themselves for each other's misfortune. Helen saw herself as the cause of her husband's entanglement in uncongenial work; Thomas blamed himself for having condemned his wife to a life of extreme poverty and hardship wherein her proud ambitions of motherhood could not be realized. In his poem 'And You, Helen', written fourteen years later when their situation was just as precarious, he wished he could offer her

> As many children as your heart
> Might wish for

and a similar release as she had desired for him:

> I would give you back yourself,
> And power to discriminate
> What you want and want it not too late,
> Many fair days free from care
> And heart to enjoy both foul and fair,
> And myself, too, if I could find
> Where it lay hidden and it proved kind.

'There was never any pretence between us,' wrote Helen in *World Without End*. 'All was open and true. Often he was bitter and cruel, but I could bear it because I knew all. There was nothing left for me to guess at, no lies, no falsity. All was known, all was suffered and endured; and afterwards there was no reserve in our joy.'[19] During their marriage there were frequent periods of estrangement when Thomas would find family life as unbearable as Helen had feared. At other times only the power of her faith and love stabilized an existence fraught with anxiety and uncertainty. Thomas summarized his feelings towards his wife in a letter which is contemporary with his other poem to her,[20] 'No One So Much As You': 'Nobody but you would ever be likely to respond as I wished. I don't like to think anybody but I could respond to you. If you turned to anybody else I should come to an end immediately.'[21]

There never was anyone else, for either of them.

5

Rachel Mary Bronwen—'the genius of smiles'—was born on 29 October 1902, and in the New Year they could not pay the rent. For several months Thomas had done nothing apart from a painstaking edition of the poetry of John Dyer and his ordinary *Chronicle* reviewing. At a very low ebb he had once admitted to Berridge that all he possessed in the world was 1s 8½d. So critical was their position that he was forced to go and stay with his parents in London and seek work there. He left Rose Acre on 11 February, and for a week Helen waited in suspense for news. On the sixteenth a telegram arrived. It said: 'Am writing a book on Oxford for £100 by arrangement.' It was momentous news. 'I scribbled a reply,' Helen noted in her diary, 'being far too excited to collect my thoughts, but could do nothing but kiss the children as some way of letting out my delight, and spent the rest of the day in wondering how it all came about. Took the children to Maidstone in the afternoon. Had a lovely walk; came back to find the fires out, and the coals not here. However, just as I was starting down to the village the coals came, and we soon had a fire and tea. All the evening I sewed.'[22]

The windfall had come through H. W. Nevinson who had been approached to write the text of a book to accompany a series of coloured pictures by John Fulleylove. Nevinson had turned down the offer but suggested Thomas in his place, who readily signed the contract. By it he undertook to provide no less than 60,000 words in four months (on top of his reviewing) at the rate of 30s a thousand.

He made a quick trip to Oxford to refresh his memories, spent precious days at the British Museum prospecting for material, and then wrote every day, seven days a week, for three months. When he handed the manuscript in to the publishers a week early in June he was sick to death of it. 'It is neither good hackwork nor good Edward Thomas,' he lamented to MacAlister. 'It will hurt me very much to see it in print. Day after day I had to excite myself and write what I could; and of course I shall be judged as if I had chosen the subject freely and had done my best at it. It has left me dried up, and I feel that I shall never do good, slow, leisurely work again.'[23] To Berridge, he was even more contemptuous: 'Most of it is either dull or drivelling,' he wrote.[24]

Yet for the first time *Oxford* left them with money to spare, and on the strength of an advance on royalties they moved into Ivy Cottage in the village of Bearsted itself. The ivied, half-timbered house with a dormer window in the tiled roof was altogether superior to Rose Acre. An upper room ran the entire width of the house, narrowing at one end where an old-fashioned hobbed fireplace stood. Under its low beamed ceiling Thomas stacked his books and prepared to work amid the pleasant sounds from the wheelwright's next door and from a farmyard at the back.

However, having won a breathing-space from immediate financial pressures, he found himself in no condition to enjoy it. He had completely written himself out. 'I can't write even a short review without an effort before, exhaustion and dissatisfaction after,' he told Berridge. 'An essay is inconceivable.'[25] In such a state of helpless frustration his notorious melancholy would descend to blight the lives of everyone around him. Helen saw that mood as a dark streak inherent in his nature which would have recurred no matter how different their circumstances. 'Many of the days were saddened for us by [Edward's] anxiety,' she wrote, 'and by that melancholy *which had its roots in no material circumstances but came to cloud his spirits and our life, unbidden and uncontrollable.*'[26]

Thomas, likewise, though he described himself as 'a miserable sinner in journalism', never blamed his involvement in hack work entirely for his disposition. In his letters to friends he offered several alternative 'causes' to explain his proneness to melancholy. The following were three of the most persistent:

> Only just now such friendship as yours [Berridge's] makes me feel the bitterness of my isolation more. It is that as well as my poverty I suffer from . . .[27]

> I live for an income of £250 and work all day and often from 9 a.m. until 1 a.m. It takes me so long because I fret and fret. . . . My self-criticism or rather my self-contempt is now nearly a disease.[28]

> Oh, my self-consciousness, it grows and grows and is almost con-

> stant now, and I fear perhaps it will reach the point of excess without my knowing it . . .[29]

He seems to have had enormous difficulty in experiencing himself 'together with' others ('with me,' he once told Bottomley, 'social intercourse is only an intense form of solitude')[30] and 'at one' with himself ('I must believe in myself or forget myself and I cannot').[31] Instead he could experience himself only in despairing aloneness which accentuated his introspection to the point of acute self-torment. His predicament—that of being isolated without being self-sufficient and without being able to muster any normal sense of human solidarity—would have been scarcely tolerable in any circumstances. In the circumstances in which he existed for the greater part of his life, his melancholy was constantly exacerbated beyond measure.

MacAlister wrote of him: 'He seemed to be a born poet. He loved and understood poetry as few men of his time did. He longed to write it himself. But it would not come. It was, I think, the conditions of his life that made it impossible. There was no peace, no rest.'[32] Helen herself referred to the 'hateful hack-work books . . . which though he did them well did not at all satisfy his own creative impulse, *the damming up of which contributed largely to his melancholy*.'[33] There is sufficient evidence in Thomas's own books to substantiate both of these suppositions. The time and energy drained by his bread-and-butter work brought him little money and less satisfaction. Indeed, the more his responsibilities increased and the harder he drove himself, the more he thwarted his own fulfilment as a poet. Nothing could have been worse for a writer who began by looking forward to 'more or less lyrical work, interspersed with pot-boiling', and ended by looking back over pot-boilers interspersed with lyrical work. He was never less than competent. None of his books is unreadable. Yet when he did glance back over his life's work in 1913, his chronic self-contempt amounted almost to a 'disease'. Mr. Torrance in *The Happy-Go-Lucky Morgans* is a portrait of the Edward Thomas whom he expected would be remembered—if anyone ever remembered him:

> He wrote what he was both reluctant and incompetent to write, at the request of a firm of publishers whose ambition was to have a bad, but nice-looking, book on everything and everybody, written by some young university man with private means, by some vegetarian spinster, or a doomed hack like Mr. Torrance. . . . His books

> are not the man. They are known only to students at the British Museum who get them out once and no more, for they discover hasty compilations, ill-arranged, inaccurate, and incomplete, and swollen to a ridiculous size for the sake of gain. They contain not one mention of the house under the hill where he was born.[34]

It was one of Mr. Torrance's pains that 'seldom more than once or twice a year came the mood for doing what seemed to him the highest he could, namely, write verses.'[35] For Thomas that mood had not come since his undergraduate days, and in 1913 he must have despaired of ever satisfying himself in that direction. Only a year later Frost would tell him: 'You are a poet or you are nothing.'[36]

Whatever the cause, his melancholy was acute during the last months of 1903. In desperation he consulted the first in a long line of doctors, who told him not to exhaust himself, mentally or physically, to be more 'social', and to take a holiday. He wandered aimlessly around Swindon, Warminster, and London, returning to Bearsted in March, homesick and penitent. 'You know that I tried to live in London, to escape the noise of the children?' he asked Bottomley. 'I escaped the noise and fell upon horrible silences, where people talked abundantly indeed to me, but said nothing to break the silence of my soul. I was the victim of a score of kind acquaintances and even persons I had called friends for years. Work abounded: I could have doubled my income. But I fled....'[37]

Just as he was beginning to write again—for the first time since *Oxford*—Helen fell ill and went to the coast at Walmer. Thomas never liked being left alone in an empty house, especially one which was usually noisy with children, and so he had Arthur Ransome down for company. The advice he gave to him on this occasion was equally applicable to himself if he had been in any position to take heed of it. 'Ransome is a remarkable boy,' he agreed with Bottomley. 'My only fear for him is that he may become merely five years older than he actually is; that he may become merely old for his age. For he seems to be working as hard as if he liked it, at pure journalism, though it is quite clear that he has in him things which can never be expressed in pure journalising, and may even be suppressed by it, at his age. I told him so. But of course there is no reason why he should listen to me, who am an obvious failure. I am.'[38]

He was just twenty-six.

6

After Helen, Bronwen fell dangerously ill and nearly died. The picturesque old house was condemned as hopelessly insanitary, and Thomas decided to leave immediately. He saw an advertisement in the local paper of a farmhouse to let on the Weald, near Sevenoaks, and in May 1904 they moved to their fifth home in four years.

Elses Farm was a large square farmhouse standing in its own fields. Oasthouses, cow sheds, and stables were grouped around it on two sides with an orchard and a large garden on the other. Inside long flagged passages led to dairies, store-rooms and an immense kitchen and scullery. About a mile away Thomas rented a small cottage as a study. The site was congenial, but the move had left him 'very badly off' with only 5s in hand and the prospect of £1 from his work in July. He resorted to his habitual remedy of taking as much reviewing as he could and selling his books. 'I have the usual dull books to review and I do the usual dull reviews and worse,' he informed Berridge in September. 'Nothing else. I am sick of books and am selling many old possessions now (prose; never poetry, I hope). Ruskin is the first to go. I want to begin again and this is my frantic and vain protest.'[39]

If this was his intention, he was doomed to failure. Later that month he went back to town, looking for more of the same work. J. C. Squire confirms Nevinson's picture of his typical approach, guaranteed to create little impression (or the wrong sort of impression) on the editors who received him: 'He would appear, very quietly, as though he had come through the wall, in the office to discuss contributions, and particularly reviews; a tall spare man with violet eyes in a long beautiful face, evenly gilded by the sun, and strong hands; he took suggestions in a sad and fatigued way; had all his ideas been scouted, one felt that he would have been completely resigned; the world had, it seemed, finally beaten him, though he had patiently to continue the similitude of a struggle.'[40]

Thomas hated the work; worse still, he hated begging for it. Consequently editors saw only indifference and lack of energy instead of the enormous reserves of strength and determination of which he was capable. He was, observed one friend, 'too gentle and not blustering enough to compete with others who were less able to do the work'.[41] According to Norman Douglas he lacked 'a little touch of bestiality'.

'He was too scrupulous,' Douglas commented in *Looking Back*. 'Often . . . I told him that it was no use trying to be a gentleman if you are a professional writer. You are not dealing with gentlemen; why place yourself at a disadvantage? They'll flay you alive, if they can. Whereupon he would smile wistfully, and say that another pint of Burton would be my ruin.'[42]

In the face of such advice he accepted a commission for a book called *Beautiful Wales*. Like *Oxford*, it was on a subject he might have enjoyed given his own length and his own time. But again the publishers wanted it in a hurry. With Helen he spent a few 'immortal days' at Ammanford in order to 'abuse' (as he put it) one or two of the notebooks he always carried with him. Then he hastened back to his tread-mill, for sixteen hours a day from November to March. 'Wales!' he gasped. 'I suffer as Jonah did.'[43]

'There were many dark periods while we were here,' wrote Helen, 'many days of silence and wretchedness and separation.'[44] There were also some of the best moments of their lives, when work was abandoned and the whole family sang and picnicked and tramped for miles in the country. The harmony of that life is beautifully evoked in *World Without End*: 'Of course haymaking on the lovely slope of Blooming Meadow was a festival for us all at the farm, and we learnt how the ricks that rose like a town in the rick-yard were shaped so symmetrically, and thatched as carefully as a house. It is this full life of homely doings that I remember chiefly at the farm—the early morning expeditions with [Edward] to a large pond about three miles away to fish for perch and roach and even pike; the walks to Penshurst and Leigh and Ightham Moat; the picking and storing of apples; the making of quince jam; the finding of an owl's or a nightingale's nest; the woodpecker which cut the air in scallops as it flew from oak to oak; the white owl which brought its young to the roof ridge to be fed; the beautiful plough-horses with their shining brass ornaments; the cows going into their stalls like people going into their pews in church . . . the woodcutting and faggot-binding by men whose fathers had done the same work and whose fathers' fathers too . . . the lovely cycle of ploughing, sowing and reaping; the slow experienced labourers, whose knowledge had come to them as the acorns come to the oaks, whose skill had come as the swallows' skill, who are satisfied in their hard life as are the oaks and the swallows in theirs.'[45]

When Thomas's poetry came to him as naturally as leaves to a tree—

an aspen tree—he revived some of these memories with a sureness and delicacy long denied him:

> that day
> When twenty hounds streamed by me . . .
> In Blooming Meadow that bends towards the sun
> And once bore hops . . .
>
> ('Tears')

> Every time the horses turned
> Instead of treading me down, the ploughman leaned
> Upon the handles to say or ask a word . . .
> Scraping the share he faced towards the wood,
> And screwed along the furrow till the brass flashed
> Once more.
>
> ('As the Team's Head-Brass')

> It was a perfect day
> For sowing; just
> As sweet and dry was the ground
> As tobacco-dust.
>
> I tasted deep the hour
> Between the far
> Owl's chuckling first soft cry
> And the first star.
>
> ('Sowing')

'Perfect'—not a word that Thomas would use lightly—reminds us that he knew such days.

3
PROMISES TO KEEP
1905–1912

The woods are lovely, dark and deep,
But I have promises to keep.

ROBERT FROST:
'Stopping by Woods on a Snowy Evening'

I

'My great enemy is physical exhaustion,' he wrote to Bottomley in the throes of *Beautiful Wales*, 'which makes my brain so wild that I am almost capable of anything and fear I shall some day prove it. . . . Shall I ever have the relief of true and thorough insanity?'[1]

With the help of laudanum the book was finished by March and was, he conceded, 'infinitely worse even than *Oxford*.' Its completion brought him no release for he at once enlarged the scope of his reviewing. John Moore compiles this astonishing list of books which he reviewed in one week in July:

Tchaikowsky's *Life and Letters*,
A folio Chaucer,
A new Keats,
Thomas Moore by Stephen Gervyn,
The Grey Brethren by Michael Fairless,
William Bodham Donne and His Friends,
The Heptameron,
The Decameron,
Peeps Into Nature's Ways,
A Country Diary,
Travels Round Our Village,
A German on *The Development of the Feeling for Nature*,
A Frenchman on Charles Lamb.[2]

'I can't read anything but review books,' he complained to Berridge. 'I am in a horrible state. You are too kind and hopeful to believe me if

I try to explain, and I know you are misled by my jesting, my apparent good health, and the many things that ought to make me happy (as you think).'[3] Berridge, like Norman Douglas, felt that he was being too scrupulous, as may be guessed by Thomas's reply: 'Of course I know books and reviews are not important, but vanity prevents me from treating them quite lightly as well as badly.'[4] He was a perfectionist (as well as a gentleman) in a world of expediency, trying to give his best to order in the most impossible conditions. Douglas said bluntly that he would sooner have been blacking boots.

Yet even reviewing occasionally had its rewards. In *Beautiful Wales* Thomas talks of the sheer delight in reading the work of a 'fresh modern poet, straight from the press, before anyone has praised it, and to know that it is good.'[5] His criticism kept him in touch with the latest developments in poetry and helped him to slough off the scholarly aestheticism which Oxford had encouraged. It also brought him the friendship of many of those poets whom he distinguished with 'timely and untimely praise'. 'His recognition of new talent arising in any quarter,' wrote Ashley Gibson, 'was forthcoming instantly and without stint. . . . English poets and not a few prose-writers of this century owe much to him, some of them everything.'[6] In the autumn of 1905 he spotted the work of one such poet. It was *The Soul's Destroyer* by W. H. Davies.

On 12 October Thomas called to see him at the address given in the book—The Farmhouse, London—and discovered a cheap lodging-house for tramps and down-and-outs. Davies was a small, dark man, rather Jewish-looking with a strong Welsh accent. He was one-legged, desperately poor, and, apart from a spark of genius, illiterate. 'If you have any spare copies of even the most elementary poetry I should be glad to transmit them,' Thomas wrote to Bottomley. 'When I saw him he had only a 6d Wordsworth and a Shelley—which it must have been fearful to read by the light of a coke fire . . . I have given him a Wordsworth, a Sturge Moore, and I forget what else: I am taking him a Byron and a Cowper.'[7]

Davies had spent his life's savings of £19 to cover the printing costs of his first volume of poetry, copies of which he had then sent to one or two literary personalities, asking for the price of the book or its return. Bernard Shaw, who received a copy in this way, was immediately attracted to the poetry's 'freedom from literary vulgarity which was like a draught of clear water in a desert.' He not only bought the book but sent money for eight additional copies to be distributed among 'such critics and verse fanciers as he knew of, wondering whether they would recognize a poet when they met one.'[8] Thus a copy arrived for Thomas, whose generous review in *The Daily Chronicle* soon after his visit 'must have done a great deal towards making Davies's budding reputation secure.'[9] He began:

> Mr. William Davies is a Monmouthshire man. He has been active and passionate. He has been poor and careless and hungry and in pain. 'I count us,' he says, in his 'Lodging-House Fire', which is as simple as a cave man's drawing on bone, and yet of an atmosphere dense with sorrow:
>
> I count us, thirty men,
>   Huddled from winter's blow,
> Helpless to move away
>   From that fire's glow.
>
> He has travelled: he knows Wales, London, America, and Hell. These things and many more his poems tell us; and to see him is to see a man from whom unskilled labour in America, work in Atlantic cattle boats, and a dire London life, have not taken away the earnestness, the tenderness, or the accent, of a typical Monmouthshire man. I have often wondered idly how I should meet the apparition of a new poet—it was so easy to praise small or middling writers of verse—and now all that I can do is to help to lay down a cloak of journalists' words, over which he may walk a little more easily to his just fame.

The review goes on for more than half its length to copious quotations from the poetry with Thomas's comments. He ended:

> It is to be hoped that such a poet of experience will not suffer for his inexperience in the selling of books. He wants to go back to Monmouthshire.[10]

Instead Davies accepted Thomas's invitation to stay at a real farmhouse, and in February 1906 he took up residence in a tiny two-roomed cottage in Egg Pie Lane, not far from Elses Farm. It was furnished with only the bare necessities the Thomases could spare—a camp bed, table, chair, cupboard, lamp, and a few crocks. Davies, however, spent a good deal of his time at the farm, becoming a great favourite with the children (to whom he was always 'Sweet William') and almost one of the family. 'Since his early boyhood,' recalled Helen, 'he had had no experience of a "home", and he found the family atmosphere and the domestic intimacy very congenial. I used to mend his clothes, but he used to wash them. . . . He was very neat and clean always—nothing at all of the tramp in his appearance and his speech was the soft sing-song Welsh [which] was very pleasant.'[11] In the evenings, over beer and tobacco in front of the fire, he related the unusual story of his wanderings which outdid many picaresque romances. Thomas gave this résumé of it in a later review:

> He was apprenticed to a picture-frame maker, but soon grew tired of regularity and confinement in a town, and so went over to America, where he lived off and on for nearly ten years, chiefly as a tramp who begged his bread (or rather cold turkey and fried oysters), but with intervals of fruit picking, and of work on cattle boats between Baltimore and Liverpool. In the cold weather he sometimes enjoyed the luxury of prison life—warmth, good food, tobacco and idleness. . . . He was to have gone to the Klondyke, but missed his footing on a train that was to have given him a free ride, and so lost one leg. He then returned to England and learned a good deal about 6d lodging-houses and humanity. . . . He is, on the whole, a favourite of what used to be called Providence, and what Mr. Shaw calls the Life Force. He survives; he enjoys; he does good work which no one else has done or could do. He has solved the most difficult questions without knowing it.[12]

In the peace of the Kentish Weald, Davies was persuaded to write down his narrative and prepare it for publication. That summer Thomas and Edward Garnett, a publisher's reader living at Edenbridge with whom he had only recently exchanged visits, considered many of its details with him. They both felt that the book would stand a better chance if it contained a foreword by a well-known author, and Shaw was again approached. Before it eventually appeared in 1908, the latter had added a sprightly preface and an original title—*The Autobiography of a Super-Tramp*.

Soon after he arrived Davies broke his wooden-leg and nearly precipitated a financial crisis. Apart from his income of 8s a week, he was living entirely on the charity of the Thomases. They paid his rent and gave him his meals (which never, alas, rose to 'cold turkey and fried oysters'), but any extras were luxuries. Thomas could not afford the £5 necessary to purchase a new peg-leg and had to ask his friends to subscribe. In the interim, knowing Davies's morbid dread of any of the villagers learning about it, he drew a sketch of a makeshift appliance which he gave to the wheelwright without disclosing its purpose. The finished article was sent to Elses Farm with a bill stamped 'Curiosity Cricket Bat—5s'.

Such a story is a sad comment on Thomas's own fortunes, for he was approaching the time when he would often need to write two hack books simultaneously. In 1906 he had accepted commissions to edit a popular natural history called *British Country Life*, to compile an anthology of *Songs For the Open Road*, and to write another 60,000 words on *The Heart of England*. As soon as this last book was finished in June he started to prepare an edition of Borrow's *Bible in Spain*, allowing himself no respite whatever. He was getting used to living in a state of perpetual mental strain, which he graphically described as 'a feeling in my head as if a bullet had got into each temple'.[13] Considering his circumstances, his action in taking Davies under his wing at this time is even more magnanimous.

The period of their closest association was brought to an end when the Thomases were given notice to leave the farm in September. Davies regarded their going as a personal tragedy, especially since they were moving to Hampshire where he would see them only infrequently. Nevertheless, Thomas supported him as before, helping with selection,* proof-reading, or reviews, and the surviving correspondence between the two men is its own tribute to his infinite kindness and patience.[14] They still met fairly often in town, for Thomas had made a practice of going to London on business on alternate Tuesdays, when he would meet a number of literary acquaintances for lunch and tea. Often Davies had accompanied him until, at last, he was sufficiently recognized as a member of the company that he could turn up whenever he pleased. Lunch was held at the Mont Blanc, a restaurant in Gerrard Street, Soho, and was presided over by Edward Garnett. Here Davies might meet Norman Douglas, Hilaire Belloc, W. H.

* James Guthrie remembered one instance of Davies's absolute confidence in E.T.'s judgement: 'Thomas told me that in early days D. used to send him poems to read and approve. When he found that D. destroyed those he had not cared for, he stopped criticizing them, as his opinion was, after all, only personal.' Quoted in Lawrence W. Hockey, 'Edward Thomas and W. H. Davies', *The Welsh Review*, vol. VII, no. 2 (1948), 87.

1. Helen Thomas

2. Edward Thomas

Hudson, Percival Gibbon, Muirhead Bone, John Masefield, occasionally John Galsworthy, and rarely Joseph Conrad. Some of these writers and artists would reappear for tea at the St. George's, a vegetarian restaurant in St. Martin's Lane, over which Thomas himself presided. Regular attendants included Ralph Hodgson, Charles Dalmon, John Freeman, and Arthur Ransome; Bottomley and James Guthrie when they were in town; and later Walter de la Mare (another of Thomas's 'discoveries'), Rupert Brooke, D. H. Lawrence, and Ford Madox Hueffer. 'All sorts of current and old literature would be discussed,' wrote Helen, 'no doubt gossip about publishers and "log-rolling"* and fun poked at this writer and that poet or reviewer. W.H.D. would often I think be out of his depth in this talk, for he was not in the least intellectual, but he had a pretty shrewd grasp of people and would no doubt put in an effective comment now and then. Everyone liked him and he was at home with everyone.'[15] With Ralph Hodgson he preferred to talk not of poetry and art, but of dogs and prize-fighters.

He continued to publish at regular intervals, *New Poems* in 1907 (dedicated to Helen and Edward Thomas), *Nature Poems* and *The Super-Tramp* in 1908, and *Beggars* in 1909. After the publication of his autobiography he refused further financial aid from Thomas, knowing that his benefactor was never far from penury himself. As a result his complaints about money became more vociferous. He began to imagine himself 'the sport of fame', receiving good reviews and remaining penniless at the same time. (When *The Soul's Destroyer* went into a second edition he was sent the 'magnificent sum' of 14s 1d by the publishers.) 'He is genuinely unlucky, I think,' Thomas wrote to Garnett. 'I mean I don't consider myself unlucky, because I can't hope to attract attention. But a man with a wooden-leg in one hand and a preface by Shaw in the other—! But luckily Davies though he has a little childlike conceit does not know how good his work is, or I don't think it would be so good in that kind.'[16]

Davies's dejection expressed itself forcefully in his premature *Farewell to Poesy* (1910). Fame in England, he decided, was not as profitable as begging in America. The book's reception, however, somewhat restored his spirits. Shaw told him privately that it was his best work to date, an opinion that Thomas echoed in his review for *The Morning Post*:

* Persuading publishers to buy advertising-space by promising to review their books favourably in the critical columns.

It is not easy to define this poetry which appears to owe nothing to any directly literary influence since Wordsworth. It is simple in vocabulary and rhythm and thought, and it is without conscious art; and yet the forms, the occasional conceits, and certain turns of expression make it clear that it owes much to the Elizabethan, Jacobean, and Caroline lyric as well as to Wordsworth and Blake. The spirit which subdues those influences and combines them to a perfectly original result is that of a man who knows modern civilization only through the hideousness of its towns. It could probably be asserted without injustice that the only subject which Mr. Davies knows anything about is tramping. He has very little knowledge of facts, and what he knows he leaves out of his verse, and still less acquaintance with modern ideas. He loves animals, birds, and flowers, but he would probably have done so had he lived a thousand years ago. And withal he has no living equals except Mr. Charles M. Doughty and Mr. Yeats.[17]

Financial independence was finally secured for Davies in 1911. That year Thomas and Garnett circulated a petition among their literary associates in an endeavour to obtain him a Civil List Pension. It read:

The undersigned Petitioners respectfully represent to His Majesty's Government that William H. Davies, the author of *The Soul's Destroyer*, *New Poems*, *Nature Poems*, *A Farewell to Poesy*, etc. is eminently deserving of the grant of a Civil List Pension.

From the critical opinions set forth and signed below it will be recognized that W. H. Davies's *Poems* are of the class of rare spontaneous genius, and that he will come to rank in English Literature with the small group of isolated, self-taught poets in which are linked the names of Chatterton, Blake and Clare.

Though Mr. Davies's work has brought him fame and unquestioned rank in literary circles, the circulation of fine poetry is notoriously restricted, and the sale of Mr. Davies's books, including *The Autobiography of a Super-Tramp*, has not yielded him a sum, yearly, exceeding the wages of a day labourer. While Mr. Davies has no journalistic or other readily marketable gifts by which to increase his earnings, he is still in the prime of his creative productiveness, and may be expected to enrich further our imaginative literature.

Your Petitioners respectfully submit that the strain and anxiety of Mr. Davies's position—now continued for years—will reflect on the community at large should he be left alone to struggle.

Mr. Davies has risen from the ranks of the people and is now in the fortieth year of a life of hardship and privation. Your Petitioners respectfully submit that no more deserving case of genius than this poet's has been presented within their memory.[18]

In July Davies was granted his pension of £50 a year in the distinguished company of Conrad and Yeats. A year later his security and reputation were enhanced by his inclusion in *Georgian Poetry* I. Thomas's main effort on his behalf had now been accomplished, for which Davies was eternally grateful. Grief-stricken, he was to commemorate their friendship in 'Killed in Action', the simplest of all the poems written upon Thomas's death:

And we have known those days, when we
  Would wait to hear the cuckoo first;
When you and I, with thoughtful mind,
  Would help a bird to hide her nest,
For fear of other hands less kind.

But thou, my friend, art lying dead:
  War, with its hell-born childishness,
Has claimed thy life, with many more:
  The man that loved this England well,
And never left it once before.

2

Ironically, Thomas secured for Davies what he could never win for himself—an interval of calm to write solely as he wished. 'Oh for a little money to turn round for a year,' he sighed to Bottomley after his move in 1907, 'to make sure whether there is anything I should want to do if I had not to do reviewing.'[19] The same year he wrote to W. H. Hudson: 'Does "some months" seem a long time to you? I have done so little with my time . . . now and then comes a dreamlike, startled feeling that a year has gone by without my being conscious of it until that moment, but that passes, and then I merely wonder vaguely now and then what, and if anything, is going to happen. That comes no doubt largely of the nature of my work, which means nothing except food and drink for five or six people, and it does not occur to me to think that those things are much result. Journalism is as tedious and meaningless as clerk's work, and, unlike that, cannot be escaped from. It fills *my* normal days from 10 a.m. to 12 p.m., and haunts me all the other days.'[20]

They had moved to Berryfield Cottage at Ashford, near Petersfield, so that Mervyn, who was nearly seven, could attend Bedales School, one of the newer co-educational establishments. He had settled in well, and so had Helen. Before long her social life—attending parents' meetings and the Sunday services, calling on and being called on by the married members of staff, even addressing meetings on suffrage for women—revolved entirely around the school. When a vacancy occurred on the staff she was asked to fill it, which she did for three terms to defray her son's fees. Only Thomas remained aloof. 'Here I am surrounded by good men, masters at Bedales School,' he told Berridge, 'and so far I simply look at them with a "how I wonder what you are." '[21]

1907 slipped by in a welter of reviewing and in preparation for a critical biography of Richard Jefferies. It was commissioned in May and Thomas had been allowed a whole year in which to write it. With Helen he went for a brief holiday to Coate, where Jefferies was born, explored parish registers and interviewed anyone who had known his boyhood idol (including Mrs. Jefferies, to whom Garnett had managed to get him an introduction), then spent weeks at the British Museum, re-reading and taking endless notes. The result was a labour of love in the best sense, a book which Mrs. Q. D. Leavis has described as 'a classic in critical biography, to stand with Lockhart's Scott and Mrs. Gaskell's Brontë. . . . His is a model biography.'[22]

While he was still putting the finishing touches to it in July 1908, he accepted Dent's proposals to write another book called *The South Country* in three months. 'I do nothing but work nowadays,' he informed Berridge. 'Even when I take five days walking I fill notebooks all the time with observations and ideas. When I undertook all this work I thought it would be splendid getting so much out of myself: now I doubt the well is not a bottomless one. . . .'[23]

Much energy was being expended—and therefore lost—for the sake of the transitory pages of the newspapers. Some indication of how he might more profitably have been spending his time may be gained from his review of a book entitled *Highways and Byways in Hampshire* by D. H. Moutray Read. The surrounding Hampshire countryside (which now began at the Thomases' front door) furnished the inspiration for many of his poems, the promise of which is disclosed by the review whenever he expresses *himself* on the subject. The following paragraph, for example, provided the setting for 'The Combe':

> Perhaps the wooded combes are most characteristic of all. They are steep-sided bays running and narrowing far into and up the sides of the chalk hills, and especially of those hills with which the high flinty plateau breaks down to the greensand and the plain. These steep sides are clothed with beeches, thousands of beeches interrupted by darkest yews or, in the spring, by the green smoke of a few larches and the white flames of the beam-tree buds. Sometimes a stream rises at the head of the combe, and before its crystal is a yard wide and ankle deep over the crumbling flat bed of chalk it is full of trout; the sunny ripples are meshed like honeycomb.

Details of two other poems are closely foreshadowed in these passages:

> All the year round the watery combes, dripping, green and still, are magical cauldrons for the making and unmaking of mists. They breed whole families, perfect genealogical trees of echoes, which the child delights to call up; so, too, do fox and owl at night, and the cow on some calm evening; and as to the horn and the cry of hounds, the beechen hangers entangle and repeat them as if they would imprison them for ever, so that the phantom exceeds the true.

I read no more
Than in the storm smoking along the wind
Athwart the wood. Two witches' cauldrons roar.
From one the weather shall rise clear and gay;
Out of the other an England beautiful
And like her mother that died yesterday.
('No Case of Petty Right or Wrong')

> Never was ivy so luxuriant as under the beeches; nor moss so powerful as where it clothes them from crown to pedestal. The lichens, fine grey-green bushy lichens on the thorns, are as dense as if a tide full of them had swept through the combe. From the topmost branches hangs the cordage of ivy and honeysuckle and clematis.

Lichen, ivy, and moss
Keep evergreen the trees
That stand half-flayed and dying,
And the dead trees on their knees
In dog's-mercury and moss . . .
('The Hollow Wood')

His concluding section is worth quoting in its entirety:

The missel-thrush rolls out his clear song. The woodpecker laughs his loud, shaking laughter as he bounds in his flight; in April he laughs so much that he may be said to sing. The chiffchaff repeats his name in a small voice that reaches from the valley to the top of the highest hill. Among the golden green mistletoe in the poplars and old shaggy apple trees at the entrance of the combe the blackbird sings, composing phrases all the sweeter for being strangely like some in the songs that countrymen used to sing. Earth has no dearer voice than his when it is among chilly rain at the end of the day. All day perhaps there have been blue skies and white clouds, and no wind, with sudden invasions of violent wind and hail or rain, followed by perfected calm and warmer sun—sun which lures the earliest tortoiseshell butterflies to alight on the foot-worn flints in the path up the combe. At last the sky seems finally blue above the hangers, and a clear small star or two pricks through it. But, emerging from the combe, you see that the west has wonderfully ordered and dressed itself with pale sky and precipitous, dark, modelled clouds and vague woods, and above them a new moon. The blackbirds sing and the dim Downs proceed, and the last shower's drops shine on the black boughs and the palest primroses. Why should this ever change? It seems at the time that it never can change. A wide harmony of the brain and the earth and the sky seems to have begun, when suddenly the clouds are felt to have ascended out of the north-west, and to have covered the heavens. The beeches roar with rain. Moon and Downs are lost. The road bubbles and glows underfoot. A distant blackbird still sings in the bosom of the rain.[24]

The woodpecker reappeared in 'Ambition'—

With loud long laughter then a woodpecker
Ridiculed the sadness of the owl's last cry . . .

the 'golden green mistletoe' in 'Man and Dog'—

the mistletoe
That hung too high in the poplar's crest for plunder
Of any climber . . .

the 'earliest tortoiseshell butterfly' in 'The Brook'—

And down upon the dome
Of the stone the cart-horse kicks against so oft
A butterfly alighted. From aloft
He took the heat of the sun, and from below . . .

the 'precipitous, dark modelled clouds', the 'wide harmony of the brain and the earth and the sky' in 'The Other'—

dark impossible
Cloud-towers, one star, one lamp, one peace
Held on an everlasting lease:

And all was earth's, or all was sky's;
No difference endured between
The two . . .
I stood serene,
And with a solemn quiet mirth,
An old inhabitant of earth.

These illustrations are taken from one average review (1,000 words). And Thomas's reviews run into hundreds.

By August he was half-way through *The South Country* and considered it his worst book yet. Utter despair of ever making his way as a writer forced him to accept the post of assistant secretary to a Royal Commission on Welsh Monuments, for which his father had recommended him. For the first time in his life he had a regular income. But he hated living in London and working in an office. Even the travelling to Wales he had anticipated did not materialize—apart from one visit to Swansea. At Christmas, preferring to give his worst as a writer rather than his best as a clerk, he resigned.

At the beginning of 1909 he had 'six weeks of unusual energy' during which he wrote the score of tales and sketches published later as *Rest and Unrest* and *Light and Twilight*. Not for years had he contemplated anything that had not been previously commissioned, and now he strove too hard to give freely of his best. As one reviewer put it, 'in many the effort is obvious, however nice the accomplishment.'[25]

If he had not yet discovered himself, he continued to discover other poets. In June he reviewed Ezra Pound's *Personae* for *The English Review*:

> It is easier to enjoy than to praise Mr. Pound, easier to find fault with him, easiest to ridicule. His *Personae*, probably a first book, is strewn with signs of two battles not yet over, the battle with the world of a fresh soul who feels himself strong but alone, and the battle with words, the beautiful, the soiled, the rare, the antique words. It is not wonderful then that one coming up from the outside should be tempted for a moment to turn away from the battlefield with a promise to come back and see who and what is left. And yet such tumults are fascinating for themselves, especially if we know that sometimes when they are over, nothing, from the spectator's point of view, is left. In Mr. Pound's case we feel sure there will be a great soul left. Also, in the meantime, the book is well worth having for itself and regardless of its vague large promise....
>
> To say what this poet has not is not difficult; it will help to define him. He has no obvious grace, no sweetness, hardly any of the superficial good qualities of modern versifiers; not the smooth regularity of the Tennysonian tradition, nor the wavering, uncertain languor of the new, though there is more in his rhythms than is apparent at first through his carelessness of ordinary effects. He has not the current melancholy or resignation or unwillingness to live; nor the kind of feeling for nature that runs to minute description and decorative metaphor. He cannot be usefully compared with any living writers, though he has read Mr. Yeats. Browning and Whitman he respects, and he could easily burlesque Browning if he liked. He knows mediaeval poetry in the popular tongues, and Villon, and Ossian. He is equally fond of strict stanzas of many rhymes, of blank verse with many unfinished lines, of rhymeless or almost rhymeless lyrics, of Pindarics with or without rhyme. But these forms are not striking in themselves, since all are subdued to his spirit; in each he is true in his strength and weakness to himself, full of personality and with such power to express it that from the first to the last lines of most of his poems he holds us steadily in his own pure, grave, passionate world....
>
> The finest of his pieces are the love poems. In 'Scriptor Ignotus:

> Ferrara, 1715', he astonishes us by using again the poet's claim, Ronsard's and Shakespeare's, to give immortality to a mistress by words, by 'A new thing as hath not heretofore been writ'. But it is not a playing upon an old theme as, e.g., Locker-Lampson played on it. It is a piece of strong tender passion that happens to lean upon the old theme and to honour it. 'In Praise of Ysolt' is equally beautiful in an entirely different way, showing that the writer does not depend upon a single mood or experience. The beauty of it is the beauty of passion, sincerity and intensity, not of beautiful words and images and suggestions; on the contrary, the expression is as austere as Biblical prose. The thought dominates the words and is greater than they are. . . . In the 'Idyl for Glaucus' a woman hovers by the sea in search of Glaucus, who has tasted 'the grass that made him sea-fellow with the other gods'. Here the effect is full of human passion and natural magic, without any of the phrases which a reader of modern verse would expect in the treatment of such a subject.

After quoting 'And thus in Nineveh' and 'The White Stag' (a 'wonderful little thing that builds itself so abruptly, swiftly, clearly into the air'), Thomas concluded:

> In taking leave of this admirable poet we should like to mention other poems we have particularly enjoyed, 'La Fraisne', 'Famam Librosque Cano' (a prophetic sketch of the kind of reader he will one day have), 'Ballad for Gloom', 'For E. McC.' (these two last very brilliant and noble), 'Occidit', and 'Revolt against the Crepuscular Spirit in Modern Poetry'; and to apologise to him for our own shortcomings and to any other readers for that insecurity of modern criticism of which we feel ourselves at once a victim and a humble cause.[26]

Thomas's was the first favourable review that Pound had ever received. Edgar Jepson, a contemporary observer, recalled the stunned reaction of at least one literary coterie, the Square Club, whose critics had a damping effect on its other members:

> You could not be a poet in those days unless they discovered and made you.
>
> They would not allow it. . . .
>
> Then E.T. fairly tore it: in a review *he praised the verse of Ezra Pound!*

I shall never forget the meeting of the Square Club a few days after that monstrous action: the pale, shocked, contorted faces of the poet-makers, the men who discovered and made John Freeman; the nervous leaping into corners; the choked whispers; the jerky gestures; even between the courses the harsh sound of grinding teeth.

Poor Edward Thomas! He did look so hot and bothered. His protest that he had acted in good faith, that at the time of the writing of the review he had really fancied that he liked the verse of Ezra Pound, drew from his colleagues only horrid rumblings. How *could* he have liked the verse of a man whom none of them had discovered, much less made? Why, none of them even knew him! The thoughtlessness! The betrayal! The shattering blow to English Literature![27]

The remainder of 1909 passed less melodramatically. In December they moved into Wick Green, a house which had been specially built for them by Geoffrey Lupton, a master at Bedales and a disciple of William Morris. It was long and low, of heavy oak, overlooking a deep and densely-wooded combe from the edge of a plateau 400 feet above the sea. The land sloped so steeply away from the house towards the south that from the windows there was no foreground for the eye to rest on—only 'sixty miles of South Downs at one glance'. 'Often,' wrote Helen, 'a thick mist enveloped us, and the house seemed to be standing on the edge of the world, with an infinity of white rolling vapour below us.'[28] Thomas shared that sensation when he described the house in 'Wind and Mist':

> the eye watching from those windows saw,
> Many a day, day after day, mist—mist
> Like chaos surging back—and felt itself
> Alone in all the world, marooned alone.
> We lived in clouds, on a cliff's edge almost
> (You see), and if clouds went, the visible earth
> Lay too far off beneath and like a cloud . . .

The house was magnificent, but they never felt at home there.

Shortly after they moved Helen told him that she would soon have to give up her teaching as she was expecting their third child. Again the onus of school fees (for Bronwen now as well as Mervyn) fell entirely on Thomas's shoulders. Surprisingly, he still had very little work in hand. 'I seem to have reached a point where publishers will no longer pay me for books,' he reflected in a letter to Berridge. 'I shall either have to cease to produce [them] or to do only what is asked for and that seems likely to be less and less.'[29]

His misgiving was, however, unfounded; the calm merely that before the storm.

3

Between 1910 and 1912 he produced no less than twelve books, driving himself to the limits of his physical and mental endurance. Even before he began he was unwell and depressed. Harry Hooton, who visited the Thomases in January 1910, found Mervyn nervous of his father, though Bronwen was quite irrepressible. 'Edwy breaks out badly at times,' he confided to his wife, 'seems to lose all self-control, and frightens Hell Pell terribly. He repents awfully. But he is really much better, she says, than he used to be. . . . He is an artist, a sort of wild Shelleyan creature, and only he (if anybody) can possibly understand him.'[30]

In four weeks he finished *Windsor Castle* and followed it immediately with *The Isle of Wight*. He was then offered two much longer hack jobs, a book called *Feminine Influence on the Poets* and a study of Maurice Maeterlinck. He accepted both. The first—'an interesting book,' he wrote objectively, 'but shockingly put together'—took him until midsummer. The second was far less interesting and he began 'pushing it through anyhow so long as it is finished.'[31] Desperately tired, he dragged himself away to visit the Conrads in August (where news reached him of the birth of his second daughter, Helen Elizabeth Myfanwy), and then he walked with Haynes over the Sussex Downs to see Belloc. In September Brooke invited him for a weekend at Grantchester, eager for the professional glance of the older man over his verse. 'It would be splendid if you found the time and patience to come,' he wrote.[32] Doubtless Thomas saw some of the poems which appeared in Brooke's first volume the following year, of which he gave this friendly mention in *The Chronicle*: 'He is full of revolt, contempt, self-contempt, and yet of arrogance too. He reveals chiefly what he desires to be and to be thought. Now and then he gives himself away, as when, in three poems close together, he speaks of the scent of warm clover. Copies should be bought by everyone over forty who has never been under forty. It will be a revelation. Also, if they live yet a little longer, they may see Mr. Rupert Brooke a poet. He will not be a little one.'[33]

Maeterlinck was finally settled in January 1911. After only a few free days to 'wipe away some of the dirt', he committed himself to *four* more commissions: a critical study of Lafcadio Hearn, *Celtic Stories* and its successor *Norse Tales*, and a country book on the Icknield Way. 'If I live much longer,' he told David Uzzell, with whom he still kept in touch, 'and they put a list of my books on my tombstone I shall want one as big as one of the stones at Stonehenge.'[34]

His plight was scrutinized rather more seriously when he wrote to Harold Monro in May. The two men had corresponded briefly after Monro had sent him a copy of his *Chronicle of a Pilgrimage: Paris to Milan on Foot* in 1909. By 1911 Monro was preparing to return to England in order to establish himself on the literary scene. Writing from Locarno, he asked Thomas about possible openings in journalism for his friend Arundel del Re, who intended to accompany him. Thomas's reply was not enthusiastic: 'At present I am in a worse position than usual and am being threatened with the necessity of writing many more books and losing most of my reviewing. Low as reviewing is it is only for the day and can be shaken off, but continuous hack-writing of books seems to me worse, more damaging to freedom and reputation. This I mention because it may not be without bearing in your friend's case . . . I am dropping out, I believe . . . I have done hard work, it is true, and made a living, but I have never made my way . . . I hope you are not going to meddle much with journalism. I shall be glad to see your book [*Before Dawn*], tho I have so many to read and write now that it needs an effort to regard a book as anything but an enemy, though a helpless one. I have three books in hand, to be done before the year's end, have written two short ones already this year, and have just published one and am about to correct the proofs of another. Let me know your plans and if I can be of use in any particular way I will try. At present, as you can guess, I cannot subscribe to your belief that good things are bad for one, if it has the corollary that unpleasant things are good. And yet I am not so sure, because after all, unpleasant as things seem to one now I have always believed myself to be choosing what was pleasantest and least troublesome at the moment; and with such a motive I suppose it is inevitable that nothing should come up to one's standard of pleasantness.'[35]

Throughout August he slaved over *The Icknield Way*, ostensibly the record of a ten days' journey along it. When it was published two years later a reviewer for *The Athenaeum* characterized it mercilessly: 'The ordinary reader may gain the impression of a tired man struggling with blistered feet over hot, dusty roads, with so many miles a day to walk in order to write a book so many words in length, rather than of a writer fresh and eager, entering upon his task with zest. A tired author too soon fatigues his reader. . . . His absorption in his own views and sensations leads him to occupy much space that might have been devoted to matters more germane to the subject.'[36]

Probably those personal 'views and sensations' to which the reviewer took exception are the most interesting part of the book as far as a modern reader is concerned. For they express at length an anguished death-wish, an earnest desire to 'fade far away, dissolve, and quite forget'. A death-wish had appeared intermittently in many of Thomas's earlier books and letters. But never so powerfully as this.

4

'I am sorry to hear that Thomas has broken down again,' Hudson wrote to Garnett in November. 'Why will he work so incessantly and so furiously?'[37]

That autumn the predictable crisis had occurred. No one could have driven himself as harshly as Thomas and come through unscathed; a weaker man would have broken years before. Now Thomas stood on the brink. Helen grew to fear the 'terrible days when I did not know where he was; or, if he was at home, days of silence and brooding despair.'[38] In one such mood he rummaged in a drawer where he kept all sorts of tools and fishing tackle, and where there was also a revolver. This he pocketed and strode ashen-faced out of the house. Soon he was lost among the trees at the top of the hill. Hours later he summoned the strength to return.

At last Helen feared so greatly for his life and sanity that she wrote frantically to Haynes for help. He sent a cheque by return and soon arrived himself. Without more ado Thomas was packed off to Wales for a 'holiday'—though he insisted on taking with him materials for his latest commission, 80,000 words on George Borrow. After walking in Pembrokeshire and Carmarthenshire, he finally settled at Laugharne to write his book. Monro, who was rapidly fulfilling his literary plans after only a few months in London, offered to place his Locarno house at Thomas's disposal. Yet Thomas was always reluctant to consider foreign travel, especially then: 'If it were a question of resting in beautiful conditions your cottage would be the place,' he replied, 'but I can't give up work, and to go away and work beyond reach of *my* kind would be risky.'[39] He was at least feeling somewhat restored by Wales. Within a few weeks he could write to Helen in a lighter vein, telling her that she needed a prosperous husband, twelve children, and £2,000 a year. 'You are quite right about the twelve children and £2,000 a year,' his wife agreed. 'But I can't cotton on to the red-faced husband with an embryonic paunch. My idea of a husband is tall, thinnish, handsome (sometimes ever so handsome), fair, and tho not red, certainly not pale. But the best of him is his smile, and with twelve children and £2,000 a year he'd often be smiling. Oh I do love him when he smiles, it gets everything right, and if everything does not want getting to rights, it makes me then grow younger and more in love with him than ever.'[40] To Garnett, however, he was his rueful self: 'I told you I was doing a book on Borrow,' he wrote. 'What more is there to say? . . . Something will have to take place which cannot be brought about by any deliberate method, I think. . . .'[41]

The book (dedicated to Haynes) was complete when he returned home in December, and it provides one of the reasons why Thomas never gave up his writing career. In this exchange which he quotes, he believed that 'Borrow was both questioner and answerer'. It also implied a pertinent truth for himself:

> 'With respect to your present troubles and anxieties, would it not be wise, seeing that authorship causes you so much trouble and anxiety, to give it up altogether?'
>
> 'Were you an author yourself,' replied my host, 'you would not talk in this manner; once an author, ever an author—besides, what could I do? return to my former state of vegetation? No, much as I endure, I do not wish that.'[42]

With *Borrow* finished, Thomas did anything but vegetate. He agreed to write a critical study of Walter Pater by March 1912, and while *Pater* was only half-done he planned his next work, a similar study of Swinburne. Incredibly, both books contain some of the most poised and trenchant criticism he ever wrote. Later that year, being 'empty-handed', he wrote a long essay, published as *The Country*, and began his fictional autobiography called *The Happy-Go-Lucky Morgans.* At the same time he wrote to C. F. Casenove, his literary agent: 'Is a book on Dryden possible? Or on Evelyn the diarist? Or on England (I mean particularly the rural parts, but also the country as a whole) as seen in literature, both native and foreign? Or on Lord Jeffrey?' As a postscript he added: 'I should like Cowper better than any of the above. . . .'[43]

He was bloody, but not bowed.

4

ELECTED FRIENDS

1913–1915

softly circled round
From all division time or foe can bring
In a relation of elected friends.
ROBERT FROST: 'Iris by Night'

I

Harold Monro's Poetry Bookshop was officially opened on 8 January 1913. Thomas, reflecting on his name as a reviewer, had accepted Monro's invitation to attend on condition that he could 'guarantee me against assault by your friends the poets . . . and in any case won't introduce me to any of them or them to me.'[1] That afternoon about three hundred people were crammed into 35 Devonshire Street for the ceremony, which was performed by Henry Newbolt. Edward Marsh, as might be expected, was sitting with the guest of honour. Davies was there, and so was Brooke. Quite by accident the man who was to become the greatest friend of his life was there, sitting beside F. S. Flint on the staircase leading to the balcony. Presumably Thomas's wish was respected and they were not introduced.

Six days after the opening Thomas reviewed the Bookshop's first (and most phenomenally successful) enterprise, the anthology *Georgian Poetry 1911–1912*:

> 'The Poetry Bookshop' has, as a good beginning, given us an anthology of the poetry published under George V. The editor, 'E.M.'—Mr. Edward Marsh—introduces it with the remarks that 'English poetry is now once again putting on a new strength and beauty', and that this collection may help readers to see that 'we are at the beginning of another "Georgian period", which may take rank in due time with the several great poetic ages of the past.' The authors represented are Messrs. Abercrombie, Bottomley, Brooke, Chesterton, Davies, de la Mare, Drinkwater, Flecker, Gibson, D. H. Lawrence, Masefield, Monro, Sturge Moore, Ronald Ross, E. B.

3. Robert Frost in England, 1913

4. Edward Thomas, 1913

> Sargant, Stephens and R. C. Trevelyan. Not a few of these had developed their qualities under Victoria and Edward, and it cannot be said that any uncommon accession of power has very recently come to Messrs. Chesterton, Davies, de la Mare, Sturge Moore and Trevelyan, though it has to Messrs. Bottomley, Masefield and Gibson. . . . These three, together with Messrs. Abercrombie, Brooke, Lawrence, Sargant and Stephens, have most of the Georgian tone, and would alone give a scientific critic material for defining that tone. Messrs. Brooke, Lawrence and Sargant, are, as it were, the core of the group.
>
> . . . Room might have been made for several other writers whose work has lately appeared in books and magazines. There are writers more Georgian than half a dozen of these, and as worthy of inclusion. Then, to be precise, 'The Kingfisher' of Mr. W. H. Davies is Edwardian in date. But the volume is more representative and striking than if twice the number of poets had been drawn from. It shows much beauty, strength, and mystery, and some magic—much aspiration, less defiance, no revolt—and it brings out with great cleverness many sides of the modern love of the simple and primitive, as seen in children, peasants, savages, early men, animals, and Nature in general. Everyone, except Messrs. Davies and de la Mare, is represented either by narrative or by meditative verse, and by practically nothing else.[2]

Despite this rather curt review, Monro was anxious to involve Thomas in other current ventures of the Bookshop. In February he chose a panel of judges to select the best poem published in his *Poetry Review* during 1912.* Besides Monro and Thomas, Henry Newbolt, Ernest Rhys, Victor Plarr, Edward Marsh and T. E. Hulme were given the opportunity to vote. Thomas eventually chose 'The Stone' by W. W. Gibson. 'I *like* de la Mare's and Davies's best,' he informed

* Monro had issued his first number in January 1912, only four months after returning to England. He had then tried to get Thomas to contribute, but the latter had begged out of writing for nothing. Thomas also felt that the *Review* might become 'a sort of home for incurables—I mean that it would be too select and not reproductive.' A compromise was reached in 1913 for its successor, *Poetry and Drama*. Thomas agreed to review for nothing if he were paid for articles. His scrupulousness in honouring this agreement is shown by the fact that when Monro sent him a cheque for a long review of Hardy, Thomas returned it, insisting that it was a review and that he did not want Monro to feel he had lengthened it on purpose.

Monro. 'I *admire* Sturge Moore's effort. But Gibson's is the most *interesting*.'[3] The verdict of a 'decided majority', however, awarded the £30 prize to Rupert Brooke for his 'Old Vicarage, Grantchester'. The result was announced in the initial number of *Poetry and Drama*, in which Thomas also had a devastatingly satirical article on the poetry of Ella Wheeler Wilcox (whose vogue was then enormous). In the guise of praising her verse, he ruthlessly exposed its utter facility at every point. 'Her glory is the more bright,' he ended, 'that it has been attained with the help only of a metrical skill commonly possessed by minor poets, a light sympathy with all sorts of ideas, and without principle or sense of beauty.'[4] By the time the war brought the journal to a close, Thomas had contributed a wealth of discriminating criticism, becoming 'perhaps the most valuable of *Poetry and Drama*'s acquisitions.'[5]

During the remainder of February he walked in Wiltshire 'in a rather superannuated condition, having no work to do and not yet disposed to set myself to work at what nobody asks for.'[6] At the end of the month he went to Broughton Gifford and called on Clifford Bax, in whose cricket team he had been prevailed upon to play the previous summer. Also staying there with her mother was Eleanor Farjeon, a talented, versatile girl, the first of the 'elected friends' of his last four years. They had been brought together by her brother Bertie, another member of Bax's cricket eleven, and had recently begun to correspond. Their friendship, which Helen approved and encouraged, brought a new cheerfulness into his life and they often met when he was in London or when she was passing through their part of the country. 'He counted on me for friendship,' wrote Eleanor, 'and I loved him with all my heart. He was far too penetrating not to know this, but only by two words, in one of his last letters from France, did he allow himself to show me that he knew. Our four years were undemonstrative and unfailing.'[7] They were unfailing precisely because they were undemonstrative, for it is obvious that Thomas did not love her in the way that she loved him. A darting image from one of his earliest letters suggests and accepts her remoteness from his world. 'Try not to give any thought to this flat grey shore,' he told her, 'which surprises the tide by being inaccessible to it.'[8]

In April he bicycled from London to the Quantock Hills, collecting material for his next book, *In Pursuit of Spring*. 'The end of Ewell touched the beginning of Epsom,' he wrote, 'which had to be entered between high walls of advertisements—yards of pictures and large letters—asserting the virtues of clothes, food, drugs, etc., one sheet, e.g., showing that by eating or drinking something you gained health, appetite, vigour, and a fig-leaf. The exit was better.'[9] The book was dedicated to Dorothy and Vivian Locke Ellis, at whose house he had often stayed of late whenever his nervous irritability with his own family grew too much for him. However, he was back home in May, typing 4,000 words a day and preparing for yet another move in order to cut their expenses to a minimum. Brooke had promised to revisit their hill-top house before they left, but now he was preoccupied with a move of his own and could only send them a breathless note. 'I couldn't come down to your parts,' he apologised. 'London gripped me too firmly by the ankle. I have been inextricably tangled in the net of this existence—*Maya*, the Orientals call it, don't they?—often, not even escaping for weekends. I'm sorry. I wish I'd been able to come. Now, I'm off to America. I sail next Thursday. I shall stay—I don't know how long. Perhaps next March's primroses'll fetch me back. I'm rushing round buying things: and making farewells. Will you be in London any late evening at the beginning of next week? If so, you might charge me with some message for the continent of America and for Ella Wheeler. And I could leave the Muses of England in your keeping—I do that anyhow. Feed the brutes.'[10]

Yewtree Cottage, their last home together, was a cheap-semi-detached house, built for a workman in the village of Steep. After they moved in July Thomas grew more restless than ever, and he was frequently absent, as much for Helen's sake and that of the children as for his own. During August, while his wife went to Switzerland with friends, he and Mervyn joined Gertrude and Stacy Aumonier for a week on the Broads as guests of Eleanor Farjeon. Afterwards, in a happier frame of mind, he set off to visit the Guthries who were looking after the two girls for Helen. At Flansham he 'bathed to excess' with Guthrie's sons, being a powerful and passionate swimmer, playing with them near shore, then suddenly swimming far out to sea until his head was a speck in the distance. Guthrie himself, like several of Thomas's friends, had no suspicion of the self-torment that could overtake him. 'I have often wondered,' he declared after Thomas's death, 'how others could think of him as melancholy or unfriendly.'[11] But when Eleanor met him again within a few days, it was apparent to her that his mood had shifted from the relatively carefree one on the

Broads to 'a very grey one [which] weighed him down till the end of the year.'[12] When she left him, he intended to pay a visit to his latest doctor, Godwin Baynes, a specialist in nervous diseases and some time afterwards a friend of Jung.

He returned to Steep in September to find de la Mare's most recent volume of poetry, a book he relished even more than *Songs of Childhood* and *The Listeners.* 'How pleasant it would be only to review books when I like them—not when I think I see them from afar off that they are good, but when I really like them,' he wrote wistfully in his full-length review for *The Bookman.* 'Yet I am not sure, because the muscles of happy praise become stiff and I shrink for the other man's sake and my own, from giving a display of ungainliness. I feel this very much after reading *Peacock Pie.* . . . The book is worthy of its name. That is to say, in the first place, it is a pie. It is something to be eaten. Furthermore, it consists of pastry and of something else covered up by the crust. In the second place, that something else in the pie is discovered to be so much above the ordinary pigeon, steak and kidney, or veal and ham, that it must be called Peacock Pie. . . .'[13]

The other business awaiting him was not so pleasant. A statement had arrived, with a rejected MS and a refusal, telling him that two of his books had earned 5s in six months. He therefore had no option but to accept 'rotten terms to do a rotten little book on Keats'. 'I'm sick of talking and writing about books,' he told Eleanor, 'and I am trying to hit on a subject—an itinerary or a fiction—I can't yet do an autobiography—which will enable me to put my material in a continuous and united form instead of my usual patchwork. Can you help?'[14] He also tried to diagnose the cause of his 'grey mood' for her benefit: 'You see the central evil is self-consciousness carried as far beyond selfishness as selfishness is beyond self-denial (not [a] very scientific comparison), and now amounting to a disease and all I have got to fight it with is the knowledge that in truth I am not the isolated self-considering brain which I have come to seem—the *knowledge* that I am something more, but not the belief that I can reopen the connection between the brain and the rest.'[15]

An example from his work illustrates part of this 'disease' at the same time as it shows his need for a 'continuous and united form'. In 1913 he was writing the 'children's stories' that comprise *Four-and-Twenty Blackbirds*, in which he retold a series of familiar proverbs and expressions. In one, 'People who live in Glass Houses shouldn't throw

Stones', there occurs this passage which tends to stand apart from the rest of the tale:

> He dreamed that he was living in an enormous palace with rooms and halls too many for him to count. They were full of beautiful things, and all were his. Nevertheless Archie was not happy; for the walls, the floors, and the roof of his palace were made of glass. Nobody else was in the palace; yet he kept looking round, out of the glass walls, up out of the glass roof, and down through the glass floor; he was afraid to do anything lest he should be peeped at, and somebody should tell tales about him. He was afraid to eat. He did nothing but wander up and down the staircases and along the passages, from room to room, searching for a corner where there was no glass. His search was vain. Miserable and helpless, he looked out through the walls. The palace was surrounded by a yew hedge as high as the hills: he could not see over it, nor could anyone standing on the hill-top see into the enclosure. But though he could see nobody he had a feeling that he was being looked at through the hedge. It was more than he could endure. Downstairs he rushed, and out of the palace into the grounds. Without a pause he picked up a stone and hurled it at the walls. A crash, a hundred clashes, and a long clattering dissolved the palace to a heap like a pyramid, and Archie awoke, saying to himself the words of Will Reynolds, as if they were a line out of a copy-book: 'People who live in glass houses shouldn't throw stones.'[16]

The central evil here is self-consciousness; the impulse is to break out into a more wholesome existence. When the theme was realized more poignantly and personally, it was in the form of the poem 'I Built Myself a House of Glass'. For the moment, however, when Eleanor tried to help by asking 'Haven't you ever written poetry, Edward?' his reply was obdurate: 'Me? I couldn't write a poem to save my life.'[17]

This conviction was to be drastically revised before very long. Early in October he had arranged to meet Eleanor in town for tea, but at the last minute he had to put her off. 'Will you forgive me if I do not turn up tomorrow?' he asked. 'I have an appointment of uncertain time with an American....'[18]

2

On 5 October he went through a little side door of the St. George's, up two flights of brass-lined stairs, through a door with 'Smoking' on it, and into the chess-room. There Ralph Hodgson introduced the American he had come to meet as Robert Frost, a thirty-nine-year-old farmer, poet, and sometime teacher, whose first book of poetry *A Boy's Will* had been published that April. Their casual introduction was to ripen into an important friendship for both men, the significance of which was not lost on their first meeting. 'When . . . their almost identical light-blue eyes met,' writes Lawrance Thompson, 'each may have felt that he saw himself mirrored. Obviously they had more in common than a love of literature.'[19]

Obviously both men thought so, for in the remaining sixteen months of Frost's stay in England they sought each other out on every occasion. By February of the following year the possibility of Thomas's accompanying the Frosts back to America had already been broached. As usual Thomas was enthusiastically doubtful. 'I wish I knew that I should see that country,' he told Frost. 'But you know already how I waver and on what wavering things I depend.'[20] One instance of his wavering was still irksome in his mind. His first act in 1914 had been to try once more to get out of the rut of hack work by applying for a temporary lectureship at one of the L.C.C.'s Non-Vocational Institutes. Hudson and Garnett had supplied impeccable testimonials, but almost immediately Thomas withdrew his application. He explained himself to Garnett: 'The fact is that knowing I had to do something I had stupidly pretended to be brave, when really lecturing was as impossible to me as sailoring. Simply fear of standing up alone and looking at a hundred people and being looked at. I am very sorry indeed that I troubled you before I discovered what I was really going to do.'[21]

What he did in fact was to return home from the Locke Ellises, where he had spent the last few months, and become embroiled in *A Literary Pilgrim in England* ('omes and 'aunts he scornfully called it after the title originally proposed by the publishers—'Homes and Haunts of Writers'). This put a temporary stop to two fresh experiments he had been making to find a more satisfying medium, the first an unvarnished account of his early years (published as *The Childhood of Edward Thomas*), the second another attempt to write fiction in a popular vein.[22] Now his daily routine of writing and typing was broken in March only by a last visit to the Frosts at Beaconsfield before they moved to a new house called Little Iddens on the Gloucester–Herefordshire border. He was also their first visitor in April after the move. 'Rob and I think everything of him,' wrote Elinor Frost to her sister. 'He is quite the most admirable and lovable man we have ever known.'[23]

The publication of *North of Boston* coincided with his April visit, and Frost was promised ample reviews for his second book. Thomas kept that promise in some of his finest 'notices', for *The Daily News*,* *The New Weekly*, and *The English Review*:

> This is an original book which will raise the thrilling question, What is poetry? and will be read and re-read for pleasure as well as curiosity, even by those who decide that, at any rate, it is not poetry. At first sight, some will pronounce simply that anyone can write this kind of blank verse, with all its tame common words, straightforward constructions, and innumerable perfectly normal lines. Few that read it through will have been as much astonished by any American since Whitman. Mr. Frost owes nothing to Whitman, though had Whitman not helped to sanctify plain labour and ordinary men, Mr. Frost might have been different. The colloquialisms, the predominance of conversation (though not one out of fifteen pieces has been printed in dramatic style), and the phrase 'by your leave' (which is an excrescence), may hint at Browning. But I have not met a living poet with a less obvious or more complicated ancestry. Nor is there any brag or challenge about this.
>
> Mr. Frost has, in fact, gone back, as Whitman and as Wordsworth went back, through the paraphernalia of poetry into poetry again. With a confidence like genius, he has trusted his conviction that a man will not easily write better than he speaks when some matter has touched him deeply, and he has turned it over until he has no doubt what it means to him, when he has no purpose to serve beyond expressing it, when he has no audience to be bullied or flattered, when he is free, and speech takes one form and no other. Whatever discipline further was necessary, he has got from the use of the good old English medium of blank verse. . . .
>
> The effect of each poem is one and indivisible. You can hardly pick out a single line more than a single word. There are no show words or lines. The concentration has been upon the whole, not the

* See pages 146–7.

parts. Decoration has been forgotten, perhaps for lack of the right kind of vanity and obsession. . . . Naturally, then, when his writing crystallizes, it is often in a terse, plain phrase, such as the proverb, 'Good fences make good neighbours', or . . . 'Pressed into service means pressed out of shape'. But even this kind of characteristic detail is very much less important than the main result, which is a richly homely thing beyond the grasp of any power except poetry. It is a beautiful achievement, and I think a unique one, as perfectly Mr. Frost's own as his vocabulary, the ordinary English speech of a man accustomed to poetry and philosophy, more colloquial and idiomatic than the ordinary man dares to use even in a letter, almost entirely lacking the emphatic hackneyed forms of journalists and other rhetoricians, and possessing a kind of healthy, natural delicacy like Wordsworth's, or at least Shelley's, rather than that of Keats.[24]

This is a collection of dramatic narratives in verse. Some are almost entirely written in dialogue: in only three is the poet a chief character, telling a story, for the most part, in his own words. Thus he has got free from the habit of personal lyric as was, perhaps, foretold by his first book, *A Boy's Will*. Already there he had refused the 'glory of words' which is the modern poet's embarrassing heritage, yet succeeded in being plain though not mean, in reminding us of poetry without being 'poetical'. The new volume marks more than the beginning of an experiment like Wordsworth's, but with this difference, that Mr. Frost knows the life of which he writes rather as Dorothy Wordsworth did. That is to say, he sympathizes where Wordsworth contemplates. The result is a unique type of eclogue, homely, racy, and touched by a spirit that might, under other circumstances, have made pure lyric on the one hand or drama on the other. Within the space of a hundred lines or so of blank verse it would be hard to compress more rural character and relevant scenery; impossible, perhaps, to do so with less sense of compression and more lightness, unity, and breadth. The language ranges from a never vulgar colloquialism to brief moments of heightened and intense simplicity. There are moments when the plain language and lack of violence make the unaffected verses look like prose, except that the sentences, if spoken aloud, are most felicitously true in rhythm to the emotion. Only at the end of the best pieces, such as 'The Death of the Hired Man', 'Home Burial', 'The Black Cottage', and 'The Wood-pile' do we realize that they are masterpieces of deep and mysterious tenderness.[25]

Such reviews, coming after years of neglect in his own country and after the mixed reception of *A Boy's Will* in England, were extremely gratifying for Frost. In later life he was not slow in acknowledging his debt to Thomas which he felt he could 'never repay'.[26]

Yet he did repay it in part, for his presence began to stimulate creative impulses which had lain dormant in the hack writer for years. Shyly, Thomas approached him on the subject in a roundabout letter in May:

'Today I was out from 12 till sunset bicycling to the pine forest by Ascot and back. But it all fleets and we cannot lock up at evening the cake one ate during the day. There must be a world where that is done. I hope you and I will meet in it. I hardly expect it of New Hampshire more than of old. . . . You really should start doing a book on speech and literature, or you will find me mistaking your ideas for mine and doing it myself. You can't prevent me from making use of them: I do so daily and want to begin over again with them and wring all the necks of my rhetoric—the geese. However, my *Pater* would show you I had got on to the scent already. . . .

I wonder whether you can imagine me taking to verse. If you can I might get over the feeling that it is impossible—which at once obliges your good nature to say "I can". In any case I must have my "writer's melancholy" though I can quite agree with you that I might spare some of it to the deficient. On the other hand even with registered post, telegraph or all modern conveniences I doubt if I could transmit it.'[27]

Frost was encouraging, but still Thomas did not begin. The reason, apart from his natural diffidence, is perhaps found in his next letter in which he speaks of being 'so plagued with work, burning my candle at three ends'. He had already dropped the fiction and exasperated himself by adding up his earnings. 'Something has got to happen,' he told Frost. 'I keep saying, why worry about a process that may terminate a kind of life which couldn't be worse?'[28]

After a Midsummer visit to Little Iddens, chiefly to complete arrangements for a lengthy stay that autumn, he returned to a commission for a flower anthology which was wanted in three weeks, to finish *A Literary Pilgrim*, continue reviewing and writing his autobiography, think about a book on Shelley, and offer a book on modern poets to Harold Monro. He was still 'a writing animal', and his list of prospective work seemed endless. Throughout July he mechanically covered twenty sheets a day of 'omes and 'aunts, taking only a weekend off when Frost called at Steep. 'His wanting me is some encouragement,' he wrote to Eleanor Farjeon. 'I am beginning to think of New Hampshire as the only possibility though really not thinking of it as quite possible either.'[29]

A Literary Pilgrim was despatched at the beginning of August with a few days to spare before the awaited holiday. 'Who will want the thing now?' he asked Eleanor on the second, referring to the spread of war rumours. 'I may as well write poetry. Did anyone ever begin at thirty-six in the shade?'[30] Next day he threw all cares to the wind and set off with Mervyn to bicycle to Gloucester via Basingstoke and Kingsclere. Helen and the girls were to follow by train on the fourth.

3

Frost's first reaction to the outbreak of war was the feeling that he must provide for the duration. He went straight into Ledbury to lay in stocks, and returned with a tin of mixed biscuits and a box of fancy soap. While he was there his intonation aroused the suspicion that he was a German spy, and though the villagers were soon undeceived, it was not before the windows of Little Iddens had been stoned. This act, and the war in general, quickened the homesickness felt by every member of the Frost household.

Thomas's first reaction to the war was also personal as he foresaw how his precarious literary existence would be severely curtailed. Yet, as he had assured Frost, he saw no reason to worry over the termination of a way of life that 'couldn't be worse'. Even now *A Literary Pilgrim* had come back to haunt him with a demand from the publishers for a further 10,000 words to complete his quota.

Undeterred by the news of war, Helen and the children had started out on what was to be a trying journey to Ledbury. Everywhere the platforms were thronged with anxious families returning home from their holidays and reservists being called up. Trains were late and disorganized, and the one they caught stopped at Oxford where everyone was ordered out. After waiting hours they got on another which took them only as far as Malvern. The rest of their journey through the silent, unfamiliar countryside was finished by car under a huge harvest moon, and it was early morning before they saw Thomas waiting at the gate of Chandlers' farm where they had hired rooms.

Even in the depths of the country the war could not be avoided and it was only ten days old when their host, Mr. Chandler, a forty-four-year-old farmer who had seen twenty-one years' service, was sent for by the Hereford barracks.[31] Nevertheless, Thomas and Frost were determined not to allow their fears to encroach too much on their holiday. The Chandlers' farm was only 'three meadows away' from the small cottage of black timber and whitened brick that the Frosts were renting, and every day the two families intermingled. Unlike their husbands, Elinor Frost and Helen Thomas were complete opposites. Elinor, silent, fragile and weariable, avoided all housework as much as possible and there were few regular meals to interrupt the activities of poet or child. Helen was astonished to see her often take a bucket of potatoes into the field and sit on the grass peeling them—without water—as the only visible preparation for a meal. Eleanor Farjeon, who joined them on the twentieth to meet the Frosts, perfectly distinguished the two wives: 'Elinor . . . was not the naturally joyful housewife that Helen was, the home-maker who bustled from job to job on a breath of laughter, whose hearth glowed from her own warm centre; the centre of the Frosts was out-of-doors, and household standards mattered very little.'[32]

Both women were pleased, however, by their husbands' close friendship, and Helen was quick to see its psychological origin. In *World Without End*, she wrote: 'He [Robert] believed in [Edward] and loved him, understanding, as no other man had ever understood, his strange complex temperament.'[33] Frost understood that temperament so well because he felt it was analogous to his own. During their early conversations concerning *A Boy's Will*, it became clear to him that this Englishman saw more deeply than anyone else the theme of attempted escape and necessary return in the arrangement of the lyrics. As Frost filled in the background to the poems, each man must have been struck by the resemblance of their stories. Frost had repeatedly tried to run away from himself and from Elinor. Throughout his life he had fought off major fears and depressions which had sometimes expressed themselves in suicidal tendencies. Once he had flourished a revolver in his wife's presence and threatened to kill himself—or her. Even now he could not be sure that he would always be able to save himself. There was the recurring feeling that he was a failure—as father, husband, man, and poet.[34] Several passages in Lawrance Thompson's *Robert Frost: The Early Years 1874–1915* remarkably suggest this likeness. The following extract, for example, describes some of Frost's darkest moods on his Derry Farm:

> Whenever the storms of his 'inner weather' grew too violent, he was almost lost to his recurrent wish that he might run away—steal away, stay away—and never come back. It was a mood against which he had to fight or a mood he could slake at times merely by getting out of the house and off the farm—particularly if he and Elinor had built up too much abrasive tension between them. Often he would plunge into the woods behind his farm and walk until he was exhausted. Then he would come back, repentant.[35]

World Without End offers any number of similar passages, describing how Thomas would fling off into the night, sometimes for days at a time—and once with a revolver—to return haggard and repentant. Out of the quarrel with himself Frost had produced two exceptional books of poetry; Thomas had not even this to show, and his self-contempt, self-distrust, were more insistent, more difficult to shake off.

Every day that August they were together, sitting in the shade of an orchard or strolling through the countryside in the perfect weather, talking, in addition to their main theme, of 'flowers, childhood, Shakespeare, women, England, the war':

> The sun used to shine while we two walked
> Slowly together, paused and started
> Again, and sometimes mused, sometimes talked
> As either pleased, and cheerfully parted
>
> Each night. We never disagreed
> Which gate to rest on. The to be
> And the late past we gave small heed.
> We turned from men or poetry
>
> To rumours of the war remote
> Only till both stood disinclined
> For aught but the yellow flavorous coat
> Of an apple wasps had undermined;
>
> Or a sentry of dark betonies . . .

However much they tried to avoid it, the war preyed on their minds. Frost was bent on returning home as soon as it was reasonably safe, and his open invitation remained a tempting proposition. Probably an escape to America came as close as it ever would to being a reality during those long summer days. It was decided in any event that Mervyn, then fourteen, should sail with the Frosts and stay with friends in New Hampshire.

Thomas knew the region like the back of his hand, and he escorted Frost through mysterious by-lanes and meadows that had swarmed with daffodils at the time of his spring visit to show him the panoramic view from the top of May Hill. 'What he gave to a friend in his company,' wrote de la Mare, 'was not only himself, but that friend's self made infinitely less clumsy and shallow than usual, and at ease. To be with him in the country was to be in one's own native place'.[36] Frost was well aware of this delightful side of his friend, as was John W. Haines, a Gloucester barrister and botanist who used to join them on their walks. 'He seemed to be able to use all his senses more acutely than most people use a single one,' he recalled.[37] He found Frost 'almost as lovable' as Thomas and, interestingly, 'almost as melancholy . . . on occasion' though at other times he could be 'riotous with good spirits'. Sometimes they all walked to Lascelles Abercrombie's house, The Gallows, to the south-east of Dymock; more often they dropped in on their other neighbour, W. W. Gibson, at the Old Nailshop, an ancient thatched cottage at Greenway. (It was at their joint suggestion that Frost had gone to live in Gloucestershire.) A second issue of *New Numbers*, devoted exclusively to the poetry of Gibson, Drinkwater, Brooke and Abercrombie, was then in preparation, and Brooke, again in England, had been staying briefly at the Nailshop to help pack and mail the magazine. One evening the whole covey of poets nestled in Gibson's cream-washed living-room, an event he commemorated in his poem 'The Golden Room':

we all talked and laughed—
Our neighbours from The Gallows, Catherine
And Lascelles Abercrombie; Rupert Brooke;
Elinor and Robert Frost, living awhile
At Little Iddens, who'd brought over with them
Helen and Edward Thomas. In the lamplight
We talked and laughed; but, for the most part, listened

While Robert Frost kept on and on and on,
In his slow New England fashion, for our delight,
Holding us with shrewd turns and racy quips,
And the rare twinkle of his grave blue eyes . . .

Now, a quick flash from Abercrombie; now,
A murmured dry half-heard aside from Thomas;
Now, a clear laughing word from Brooke; and then
Again Frost's rich and ripe philosophy,
That had the body and tang of good draught cider
And poured as clear a stream . . .

Several other first-hand descriptions of the main figures are worth noticing. First Frost as seen by Helen Thomas: 'Robert was a thickset man, not as tall as Edward, with a shock of grey hair. His face was tanned and weatherbeaten and his features powerful. His eyes, shaded by bushy grey eyebrows, were blue and clear. It was a striking and pleasing face, rugged and lined. I remember his loose, earth-stained trousers, his brown arms and chest, his gnarled hands, his slight American accent.'[38] On the evidence of 'The Golden Room' he even managed to steal the thunder from that 'golden young Apollo' Rupert Brooke. The latter is described thus by Thomas: 'He stretched himself out, drew his fingers through his waved, fair hair, laughed, talked indolently, and admired as much as he was admired. No one that knew him could easily separate him from his poetry: not that they were the same, but that the two inextricably mingled and helped one another. He was tall, broad, and easy in his movements. Either he stooped, or he thrust his head forward unusually much to look at you with his steady, blue eyes. His clear, rosy skin helped to give him the look of a great girl.'[39] Finally, there was Thomas himself. Withdrawn in the most intimate company, he was never insignificant. 'Like still waters there was nothing shallow about him,' testified Frost.[40] And Catherine Abercrombie declared: 'I think Edward was the most beautiful person I have ever seen. It was quite a shock on first meeting him unless one had been warned. He suffered very much from recurring melancholy, which stamped itself on his face but only made his beauty more apparent.'[41]

Brooke had been the first to depart, leaving no doubt about his intentions. 'If Armageddon is *on*,' he said, 'I suppose one should be there.'[42]

4

While his family returned to Steep, Thomas set off by train to gather impressions for three commissioned essays about the war, 'Tipperary', 'It's a Long, Long Way' and 'England'.[43] He was not sorry to leave. 'I felt as if I were rather the grub in the apple,' he confessed to Eleanor Farjeon.[44] From 29 August to 10 September he travelled as far afield as Newcastle-on-Tyne, talking to people who had 'as little to do with the pen as with the sword'. 'I shall write down, as nearly as possible,' he stated, 'what I saw and heard, hoping not to offend too much those who had ready-made notions as to how an Imperial people should or would behave in time of war, of such a war, and while the uncertainty was very dark.'[45]

Near the coast the fear of invasion was uppermost in people's minds, and at Brecon he had to reassure his lodging-keeper that the Germans would not cut off her hands if they invaded. Farther inland, where people caught few 'newspaper phrases of the grand style to stand between them and the facts', feelings were on the whole more charitable. When a cottage woman in a Hampshire hop-garden learned that the Germans had lost several thousands the day before, she said: 'Well, what I say is, God bless every mother's son of them.' Another, more sophisticated, hearing of Germans slaughtered by the bayonet, went so far as to suppose that they also have 'human feelings as we have.'[46]

In the towns opinion was more hostile and more savagely expressed. Two workmen at Coventry held a strong, simple idea of a perfidious, barbaric Germany. ' "They're savages, killing children and old men," exclaimed one. "I'd like to get at the Kaiser. I wouldn't kill him. I'd just turn him loose. . . ." "I wouldn't," retorted the other. "If I could get at him, I'd . . . and choke him with them." '[47]

Everywhere men were enlisting, though not all in conformity with any ready-made notions as to how an Imperial people should behave. 'Some of these recruits had enlisted for "hunger", some for fun, not all to serve their country. So said the landlord, an old soldier. "I wouldn't enlist for anything," said a man with his cheese waiting on his knife-tip, "not unless I was made. I would if it was a fair war. But it's not, it's murder. . . ." "That's right," said the postman. "A man's only got seventy years to live, and ninety per cent don't get beyond fifty. I reckon we want a little peace. Twentieth century too." '[48]

Most able-bodied men were being left with no choice but to enlist. Only the boot-manufacturers at Leicester, the harness-makers at Walsall, or the explosive factories at Elswick (all profiting handsomely from the war) were expanding. Elsewhere he was told the same story: 'Wherever I went I was told that employers—"the best firms"—were dismissing men, the younger unmarried men, in order to drive them to enlist. "Not exactly to drive them," said one, "but to encourage." Nobody complained. They suggested that the "Government" had put the employers up to it, or that "It don't seem hardly fair," or "It comes near conscription, and only those that don't care will give up good wages and leave their wives to charity." One old man at Sheffield remarked that it used to be, "Oh, you're too old" for a job; now it's "You're too young." '[49]

Nevertheless, all sorts of people claimed it was 'the greatest war of all time', and anyone questioning this in public was likely to be branded a Socialist. 'For instance, near the statue of James Watt at Birmingham a man had got into an argument about the provision for soldiers' wives. Moistening dry lips with dry tongue, he declared that the working-class made fifty times the sacrifice of the upper class. He met nothing but opposition. . . . At length a vigorous elderly man in a grey suit stepped in with fists clenched, said he was a working-man himself, and laid it down that everyone's business was to fight, to sink class, and to avoid quarrelling. His wife, smiling behind him, told the heretic that he ought to be ashamed. Someone chipped in, saying that as a matter-of-fact many wives were better off with their one-and-twopence than when the men were working. "God help them before!" ejaculated the solitary man. Then another said he was going himself, and would go if his wife were penniless. "Hear, hear!" said several; and others muttered, "These here Socialists." '[50]

The war also had its more light-hearted moments. 'Publicans were flourishing though still ambitious; one public house at Manchester had these "Imperial Ballads" printed on a placard:

> What plucks your courage up each day;
> What washes all your cares away?
> What word do you most often say?
> Why, Imperial!

the reference being to a drink of that name. A photographer at Manchester had to resort to this advertisement:

Gone to the front!
A beautiful enlargement of any photo of our
brave comrades may be had at a discount of
25 per cent.'[51]

Already the division between the 'two Englands' (the Nation at Home and the Nation Overseas) was being created. Three years later it was necessary for Wilfred Owen to carry around his own set of photographs.

5

'The obvious thing is to join the Territorials,' he wrote to Berridge upon his return to Steep in September, 'but I can't have other people to keep my family till I know I can't do it myself . . . I am slowly growing into a conscious Englishman.'[52] Brooke had already enlisted, and so had Hulme. Thomas continued to fret and waver. Twice he called on Frost, who was then staying with Abercrombie at The Gallows, to help make up his mind. Again he inclined more towards America, and arrangements were settled for his son's departure. When he last saw Frost he would not say goodbye, promising to bring Mervyn over himself on a final visit that never took place.

He was, in fact, as undecided as ever. In November he wrote to Hudson: 'I have no news of myself. As you will have supposed, I have not enlisted, though I should have done if I had been in company that had encouraged me. At least I think so. Not that I pretend to be warlike or to think, except with blank misgiving, of any sort of life different from my past. . . . It is just a little too late to jump at so very complete a release from the mess of journalism. The only pleasure I have had lately has been in reading the best of Wilfred Blunt's poems. I thought Hardy's poem in *The Times*

Ere the barn-cocks say
Night is growing gray,

the only good one connected with the war. . . . Rupert Brooke was in the trenches at Antwerp, which is the most I've heard of a poet so far. There are so many we could have sacrificed, too.'[53]

A week later he wrote again: 'I have now got the form to fill in or not, and hesitated because I would sooner enlist in London with a friend (if possible) than be pitchforked anywhere suddenly. It is an insoluble problem till one has some really strong impulse one way, and one doesn't get that by thinking about it.'[54]

Every day, though he was now very short of work, he still walked to his study at the top of the hill, within a stone's throw of his old house. Half of it was used as an apiary while he wrote in the other. 'The bees seemed a natural part of his equipment on a hot day,' remarked Ernest Rhys, 'and you could smell the honey in his own hive.'[55] Here, on 3 December 1914, when he was finishing one or two outstanding reviews, there came that 'really strong impulse' which transformed him not into a soldier but a poet.

On successive days, from 3 to 7 December, he wrote 'Up in the Wind', 'November', 'March', 'Old Man' and 'The Sign-Post'—poems of a quality rare not only in his generation. At least five more poems were written in the same month, and from then on he often wrote every day, sometimes twice a day, sometimes three times a day. 'I am in it and no mistake,' he announced to Frost. 'I have an idea I am full enough but that my bad habits and customs and duties of writing will make it rather easy to write when I've no business to. At the same time I find myself engrossed and conscious of a possible perfection as I never was in prose. . . . Still, I won't begin thanking you just yet, tho if you like I will put it down now that you are the only begetter right enough.'[56] Frost was full of admiration and later picked out 'Old Man' as 'the flower of the lot'.[57]

Others received them less kindly. On the same day as he sent copies to Frost, he addressed Monro: 'I enclose some poems which I should like you to look at. If you think anything of them the writer, who wishes to be very strictly anonymous, would like to see a small book of these and others. I deliver myself into your hands.'[58] Monro, though he published such *avant garde* volumes as *Des Imagistes*,[59] was wary of anything he considered too 'modern', and only that summer he had rejected 'The Love Song of J. Alfred Prufrock' as 'absolutely inane'. It was more difficult for him to reject Thomas because of his knowledge of the poet's circumstances and his obligation to him for his contributions to *Poetry and Drama*. None the less, he returned the selection in four days.* Thomas was crestfallen. 'Thanks for saying it,' he replied.

* Monro's tragedy as a publisher was 'not that he liked what was bad, but that he failed to respond sufficiently quickly to what was good. In this way the

'I am sorry because I feel utterly sure they are me.'[60] He consoled himself in a letter to Eleanor Farjeon with the thought that Monro had probably been unable to 'get anyone to help him to an opinion.'[61] Rather less hopefully, he sent poems anonymously to a number of magazines. All were returned, though one editor said he might like to see them again in a few weeks 'when the present trouble was over'.

He would almost certainly have enlisted early in 1915 but for a serious accident. On New Year's Day he was running home from his study when he slipped and sprained his ankle so severely that he was in bed a week, in the house for the rest of January, and uneasy on his feet for nearly three months. It postponed all thought of enlisting and left him with absolutely nothing to do but write as he wished. From 7 to 9 January alone he wrote 'A Private', 'Snow', 'Adlestrop', 'Tears' and 'Over the Hills'; in the month as a whole he nearly doubled his previous output. 'Just look at all these verses,' he exclaimed to Eleanor, 'mostly written since my ankle went wrong three weeks ago. This will prejudice you against them. A man can't do all that and be any good. I haven't thrown away anything.'[62]

Meanwhile, if he could not serve his country as a soldier, he was determined to do so as a writer. During his inactive months he compiled a patriotic collection called *This England: An Anthology from her Writers*. It was to be 'as simple and rich as a plum pudding', redolent of all that people meant by the name of England. In it he slipped two of his own poems under the pseudonym of Edward Eastaway.[63] No one noticed except Abercrombie.

Frost had borrowed enough money to see him home and had booked passages aboard the *St. Paul*, sailing from Liverpool. Because of his father's ankle, Mervyn finally had to join them alone. 'I am sorrier than I would tell them that they are going,' Thomas confided to Eleanor Farjeon, 'because although I very much want to, I know how many things more likely than not will prevent my going out to them. But I don't think I ever pretended to be more certain than I was.'[64]

chance of publishing Thomas and Eliot was lost.' Joy Grant, *Harold Monro and the Poetry Bookshop* (London, 1967), p. 267.

Monro rejected a second selection of his poems in April 1915, and it was not until after Thomas's death that he revised his opinion of them. Then he wrote to Helen Thomas acknowledging his mistake and offering to bring out an edition. In an undated reply, she informed him that the poems were already in the hands of another publisher.

On the night of 13 February 1915, as their ship took its place in the heavily-guarded convoy, Frost must have thought with misgiving of his absent friend. For them both it seemed the end of a chapter, though an unforgettable one. He later paid this simple tribute to his memory: 'Edward Thomas was the only brother I ever had. I fail to see how we can have been so much to each other, he an Englishman and I an American and our first meeting put off till we were both in middle life. . . . We were together to the exclusion of every other person and interest all through 1914—1914 was our year. I never had, I never shall have another such year of friendship.'[65]

5

LIGHTS OUT

1915–1917

Only an avenue, dark, nameless, without end.

'Old Man'

I

Brooke died suddenly on 23 April. 'All the papers are full of his "beauty" ', Thomas wrote to Frost, 'and an eloquent last sonnet beginning "If I should die". He was eloquent. Men never spoke ill of him. . . . I should like another April week in Gloucestershire with you like the one last year. You are the only person I can be idle with. That's natural history, not eloquence.'[1] He also teased Frost on the belated recognition of his work in his own country (where *North of Boston* was already going into a third edition). 'Has fame swallowed the farm,' he asked, 'or are you waiting to know how big a one you can take now? . . . I hope people aren't going to crowd to see you milking and find out whether your private life also is like a page from Theocritus. It will spoil the milk.'[2]

He was then labouring at what was to be his last hack book, a life of the Duke of Marlborough. It was 'a filthy job' he began in March with strenuous note-taking at the British Museum and finished early in June after twenty-six days' solid writing. It was 75,000 words long. Frost, knowing his friend's scrupulous habit of visiting the places he was to describe, mischievously inquired: 'Will you have to visit the battlefields of Oudenarde, Blenheim and Malplaquet?'[3]

The book had evidently been commissioned by the publishers in the hope that it would have some topical interest. When it appeared the dust-jacket read: 'The achievements of the First Duke of Marlborough acquire particular interest at the present time, when Britain is once more fighting on the fields of Flanders for the freedom of the world.' Thomas, as he wrote, kept an eye on the current situation, though not in the way the publishers might have expected. Throughout the book his tone was 'coolly and consistently disenchanted':[4]

> They fought in armour by lantern and candle in galleries thirty or forty feet underground at Tournay; they mined and counter-mined, and blew men into the air or were blown up, by hundreds at a time; they were suffocated by smoke, buried alive by falling earth, drowned by inundations; meeting unexpectedly sometimes these moles fought by mistake with friends. What with cannon, bombs, grenades, small shot, boiling pitch, tar, oil, brimstone and scalding water, the English Grenadiers had scarce six sound men in the company after the siege of Lille.[5]

> Then, as now, the soldier on active service and the soldier at home appeared to be two men, not one. Another early writer (*A Short Narrative of the Life and Actions of the Duke of Marlborough*, 1711) speaks of how the officers came home from Flanders with 'a good air and genteel mien', and bringing the newest fashions with them, and people who never saw their hardships fancied them designed only for pleasure and ease. Such people hear of fights, sieges and many deaths. But they see nothing; the talk leaves a slight and transient impression. They ought, says he, to see the dead horses in the intolerable marshes of a rainy season; they should smell 'the stinks of mortality'.[6]

> It became a tedious game, suited particularly to Kings and elderly generals. It was very bloody work, especially for the besiegers, but could be watched in safety by kings, ladies, and children. A battle was an accidental incivility in the course of a game. The genius of Marlborough was shown as much in the number of battles he brought about as the number he won. . . . Sir Thomas Morgan is the man to remember. . . . He and his men fought all over the sands and the dyked lands where the English lie now (1915). What was once a battlefield was likely to be so again. . . . Continually in Marlborough's letters he names the places everybody knows today. He posts 1600 men to Armentières . . . La Bassée was important as a central point in the long defensive French lines which were named after it. Mons was besieged again and again.[7]

Such extracts show how Thomas's poetry might have developed had he lived through the real thing. The first passage, for instance, might have led to the horror of Arthur Graeme West's 'Night Patrol (March 1916)':

Next was a bunch of half a dozen men
All blown to bits, an archipelago
Of corrupt fragments . . .

The second passage touches on the already-mentioned idea of the 'two Englands', a recurring theme in the work of later trench poets, as in Owen's 'Dulce et Decorum Est' and 'Smile, Smile, Smile'. Finally, the attitude behind his reference to 'Kings and elderly generals' in the third passage is potentially the same as that of Sassoon in 'The General' or 'Base Details'. Anyone who approached Thomas's *Marlborough* in the hope of finding a glamorous history would have been left not only disappointed but uncomfortable.

Under the stress of writing it his own poetic stream dried up almost completely, and for the first time he began to send out some of his earlier pieces to his friends. (Previously such an action had seemed 'too much like begging for compliments'.)[8] Until then, apart from Helen, not one had seen them except Frost (for criticism), Eleanor Farjeon (for typing), and Monro (for publication). Strangely, some of the very people who had been advocating poetry to him for years were thrown as much off balance as the magazine editors when it eventually materialized. 'I fancy they are sufficiently new in their way to be unacceptable,' Thomas wrote to Berridge, 'if the reader gets caught up by their way and doesn't get any effect before he begins to consider and see their "unfinish".'[9] Berridge tried very hard to like them, but without conviction. Hudson disliked them and said so. Davies thought they were the work of Frost. Locke Ellis was 'very elderly and masterly' on the subject, not finding one he liked but seeing the 'elements of poetry'. Bottomley liked 'Lob' but was rather non-committal about the rest, feeling that Thomas was still bound too much by prose methods of statement. Garnett wanted him to 'chisel' 'Lob' and alter 'Tears' to make it marketable, yet though Thomas had often changed his prose at Garnett's suggestion, he now steadfastly refused to alter his poetry. The rest of Garnett's letter was, however, especially welcome. 'I am glad to find you preferring certain things—like 'Old Man' and 'The Cuckoo' and 'Good-Night',' Thomas replied, 'and sorry to find you preferring them to certain others like 'The Sign-Post'. But the great satisfaction is you obviously find them *like me*. I had fears lest I had got up in the air in this untried medium.'[10] Guthrie liked them without reservation. He included 'House and Man' and 'Interval' in his quarterly

Root and Branch in 1915, and arranged for 'Lob' and 'Words' to appear in *Form* the following year. He also published *Six Poems** by Edward Eastaway at his own Pear Tree Press. These, along with the two that Thomas had included himself in his *This England* anthology, were the only poems that he ever saw in print.

With *Marlborough* out of the way, there was nothing to prevent him from scrutinizing his position closer than ever. 'America is still unsettled,' he informed Eleanor Farjeon, 'but looks nearer as I go on.'[11] Yet shortly afterwards when he wrote to Frost, he was not so certain. 'These last few days,' he told him, 'I have been looking at two alternatives, trying to enlist or coming over to America. Helen points out that I could try America and then enlist if it failed, but not the other way round. Is it asking you to prophesy if I ask you to say what you think I might do in New York and Boston? You see I must not think of coming over to see you and cut down trees if I can't persuade myself there are definite chances of coming back with a connection or getting connections that would make it worth while staying for good or returning soon. Tell me what strikes you.'[12]

There were three main reasons why he was holding back. The first was the expense involved. If he stayed away four months, he told Frost, his savings would be exhausted. Secondly there was his crippling self-consciousness, his belief that he could make contact with no one who did not meet him at least half-way. He exchanged several letters with Garnett on the subject, and reported his advice to Eleanor Farjeon in a tone of hopelessness: 'He advises me to go to America and change my nature and become warm and approachable, and give lectures, and like Americans. So the outlook is difficult.'[13] His third, and possibly his strongest, reason was the feeling that he could not leave England while the war was on—unless it was to take part. Again his 'dejected shyness' made him as reluctant to enlist as it made him unwilling to sail for America. The problem seemed insoluble.

His wavering took the usual form of examining every possible alternative. He applied for a job at the historical section of the War Office, but only had his name put down on a very long list. He thought of taking up some kind of Civil National Service, and then of joining the cyclist corps. He even asked Garnett if there were a chance that he might qualify for something from the Civil List. Late in June he

* 'Sedge-Warblers', 'This is No Case of Petty Right or Wrong', 'Aspens', 'A Private', 'Cock-Crow' and 'Beauty'.

bicycled to Coventry to interview the Headmaster of Bablake School, where the post of English master was vacant. It appealed to him no more than lecturing for the L.C.C. He returned home convinced that America was the only solution. Then, on 11 July, he wrote to tell Frost that he had reached his decision: 'Last week I had screwed myself up to the point of believing I should come out to America and lecture if anyone wanted me to. But I have altered my mind. I am going to enlist on Wednesday if the doctor will pass me. . . . If I am rejected, then I shall still perhaps come out in September.'[14] He did not want anyone else to know lest he should be refused. He feared that his age, his bad ankle, and the general condition of his health were against him.

But on 13 July he was accepted.

2

His first two months in the Artists' Rifles were spent in London, drilling, cleaning rifles, and washing out lavatories. 'So far,' he informed Frost, 'it is very dull defending one's wives and mothers and sisters and daughters from the Germans.'[15] He was billeted with his parents at Balham, where his father (whom he had nicknamed 'The Public Man') was so rampant in his cheery patriotism that Thomas became pro-German every night. The old antagonism remained to the end. His father's real feeling towards him, he resolved, was one of contempt, which made him ashamed to be alive. His bitterness was made worse by the reminder that he had probably made Helen feel exactly the same. His sense of isolation had not improved either, of which he was more conscious than ever when he considered the youth of his companions. So far he felt 'an undigested lump in the battalion'. He hoped that close quarters in camp would help.

It didn't. 'I have made one or two acquaintances,' he wrote to Frost from High Beech, his first camp in Epping Forest, 'but it is still solitude. Nobody seeks me out and I am too something to seek out those I want.'[16] On 11 October his basic training was enhanced by a lecture from the Colonel on 'Discipline, Duty, etc.'—'such a lot of ordinary brutal morality masquerading as something very unGerman and gentlemanly'[17]—followed by bayonet fighting and a night operation. Thomas would not agree with Frost that the war might soon be over. At the camp rumour had it that any push by the Allies would take them all to Flanders. 'Apparently any man who will stand up and get shot is useful however hurried his training.'[18]

In November he was 'exalted' to the rank of lance corporal and moved to Hare Hall Camp, Gidea Park, Essex,[19] where he became a map-reading instructor for 3d a day extra. (His letters still reveal a minute preoccupation with his finances—he was aghast that he had cleared only £40 by his *Marlborough*.) Usually he took a squad of men out to Hampstead Heath in order to show them how to sketch a map with the help of a prismatic compass and a little maths. Already an expert, he found himself entirely suited to what he called 'the gentlest of military arts'. His course of instruction also gave him his first practice in giving orders, and gradually he was getting 'less confidential' in tone.

However, in the long run the job palled as it was bound to. He had been asked to remain indefinitely and could probably have spent the rest of the war there. But instructing was too safe, too comfortable, too 'schoolmasterish', and trivial events began to wear him down. For a start he had written practically nothing during his initial months of training, and now, just as he was producing some of his best ever poems —'October', 'Liberty', 'Rain'—he could get none of the peace or secrecy he desired. 'I never have any time to myself,' he complained to Eleanor Farjeon, 'and have continually to be putting my paper away.'[20] In January a rule against going more than two miles out of camp added to the congestion and confinement. In the same month he reported a man present in his hut who had not turned up after leave. Some hours later when he had still not arrived, Thomas had to report him absent, for which 'offence' his second stripe was delayed. In March an epidemic of measles raged through the camp, turning it into a prison with all leave cancelled.

It is absurd to write of him at this time, as does R. P. Eckert, that 'with regular Army life . . . his melancholy and dark agonies disappeared for ever . . . he seemed to regain the radiant smile of his boyhood, and his eyes lost their haunted look.'[21] Equally sentimental is John Moore's declaration that he had 'shaken hands with the past and shut his eyes to the future, so that he was troubled neither with regrets nor apprehensions.'[22] The poems themselves tell quite a different story. Certainly the novelty of discipline and the regularity of army life held his melancholy in check; certainly he was in some respects a 'new man', having gained 'incredibly in health and stature and confidence' as Nevinson thought when they met briefly during the war.[23] But underneath the same doubts, apprehensions, and regrets remained. 'Does one really get rid of things at all by steadily inhibiting them for a long time on end?' he demanded of Frost. 'Is peace going to awaken me as it will so many from a drugged sleep? Am I indulging in the pleasure of being someone else?'[24]

In April he received his second stripe and started thinking about taking a commission. He also made a few friends among a number of new instructors who had just arrived, one of whom knew Bottomley well. 'He is wonderful at finding birds' nests,' he told Frost, mentioning the name of the 'young artist' for the first time—Paul Nash. 'I am really lucky to have such a crowd of people always round and these two or three nearer. You might guess from ' "Home" '* how much nearer.'[25]

'Thomas . . . always seems to have been oppressed by some load of sadness and pessimism,' Nash later wrote to Bottomley. 'I believe I saw one of the happiest bits of his life while we were in the Artists—he was always humorous, interesting and entirely lovable but others who knew him speak of him as the most depressed man they ever met.'[26] Together, on 19 May, they went to see Bottomley's 'King Lear's Wife' performed at a 'Georgian Matinee' at His Majesty's Theatre, with Brooke's one-act play 'Lithuania' and Gibson's 'Hoops'. Thomas's objections to Bottomley's play were directed at what was becoming a characteristically 'Georgian' convention—deliberate nastiness for its own sake. He felt that the play dwelt too much on thought-out cruelty, worse by far, he considered, than cruelty itself with passion behind it. Brooke he liked better, though 'he was only painting with Russian paints.'* As they were leaving, Thomas passed within a yard of Sturge Moore, R. C. Trevelyan and Edward Marsh without being recognized, so much had his closely-cropped hair changed his appearance. He did not stop, sparing what might have been an embarrassing moment for the latter and himself.

* *Collected Poems* (1965 edn.), pp. 85–6.

* During his correspondence with Frost, the American insisted on knowing his true opinion of Brooke. Earlier when he had been writing a short memoir for *The English Review*, Thomas had told him that he had not dared say that 'those sonnets about him enlisting are probably not very personal but a nervous attempt to connect with himself the very widespread idea that self-sacrifice is the highest self-indulgence. You know. And I don't dispute it. Only I doubt if he knew it or would he have troubled to drag in the fact that enlisting cleared

Marsh had invited Thomas to his residence at No. 5 Raymond Buildings, Gray's Inn, only once, in March 1913, a meeting that seemed to go wrong from the first.[27] Thereafter the two men met only accidentally, Thomas becoming one of Marsh's blind spots, as a man and as a poet. When *Georgian Poetry* II came out in November 1915, Thomas had assessed it for Frost's benefit, beginning with a trace of disappointment. 'I had a faint chance of getting in,' he wrote. 'At least Bottomley wanted to show some of my things to Marsh. But they have kept in Monro. The only things I really much like are de la Mare's and perhaps Davies's. Bottomley may be all right. The new man Ledwidge isn't any good, is he? . . . I couldn't really spend much time on the volume after looking to see if there was anything new in it and except Ledwidge there wasn't.'[28]

He was destined never to be included in any of the anthologies, despite strong representations made on his behalf when *Georgian Poetry* III was being compiled shortly after his death (Sassoon, Rosenberg and Graves were other new names in this volume). Christopher Hassall, in his biography of Marsh, gave this rather inadequate reason for his omission:

> Turner, Freeman and de la Mare recommended Edward Thomas. De la Mare even offered to stand down so as to make room for him. On de la Mare's initiative Marsh had secured a maintenance grant for Thomas in the previous June, but he was largely ignorant of him as a poet, and never appreciated his quality until it was too late. So many hundreds of bereaved parents had begged Marsh to include unacceptable poems in memory of their sons that he made a strict rule never to represent any writer for the first time posthumously. . . . Had he made this fine poet an exception he would have been embarrassed with protests. . . . In two years' time the same exclusive principle was to contribute decisively to the growing conviction among critical readers that Georgian Poetry was a thing of the past.[29]

him of "All the little emptiness of love"?' Now he added: 'I think he succeeded in being youthful and yet intelligible and interesting (not only pathologically) more than most poets since Shelley. But thought gave him (and me) indigestion. He couldn't mix his thought or the result of it with his feeling. He could only think about his feeling. Radically, I think he lacked power of expression. He was a rhetorician, dressing things up better than they needed. And I suspect he knew too well both what he was after and what he achieved.' (ET to RF, 13 June 1915, 19 Oct. 1916, *DCL*.)

Of course, as Thomas's earlier letter shows, Marsh had every opportunity to publish his work *while he was alive*. And his 'strict rule' for *Georgian Poetry* III was coolly received by John Freeman, as the implications in his reply to Marsh suggest. 'Perhaps it's unfortunate that fine work should be permanently excluded from representation,' he wrote. 'I've had the privilege of seeing probably the whole of his verse . . . and I only made the suggestion because as far as my own opinion might stretch or be worth anything, it would be splendid if the next Georgian book included any other new poetry of comparable individuality and power.'[30] Marsh remained unmoved.

On 25 August 1916 Thomas was posted as a cadet to the Royal Artillery School in Handel Street, London. 'Why Artillery?' asked Bottomley, thinking it too dangerous. 'To get a better pension for my wife,' came the answer.[31] In September he was transferred to Trowbridge Barracks to learn gun-drill and the duties of an observation officer. He was still out of sorts after a series of vaccinations and found himself less apt at the work than the engineers, surveyors and teachers who were also on the course. 'I am not enjoying this half-and-half cadet stage a bit,' he confessed to Berridge.[32]

Mervyn, having returned from America, was apprenticed to the London United motor works at Walthamstow. Helen wished to be nearer him and her husband, and in October she moved to High Beech, a cottage deep in Epping Forest. On his week-end leaves Thomas studied diligently to reclaim a sufficient working knowledge of mathematics to see him through his final examinations in November. When Eleanor Farjeon paid them a visit and they went walking in the country, she asked him: 'Do you know what you are fighting for?' He stopped, and picked up a pinch of earth. 'Literally, for this,' he said, crumbling it between finger and thumb before letting it fall.[33] His action typifies that mixture of idealism and earthy common sense which is found in the poems. It was to this that Frost was referring when he wrote: 'His concern to the last was what it had always been, to touch earthly things and come as near them in words as words would come.'[34]

He scraped through his exams, and on 20 November he was commissioned Second Lieutenant with Number 244 Siege Battery, stationed at Lydd in Kent. There he discovered that he was three years older than the commanding officer and twice as old as the youngest member. Nevertheless, on 7 December he volunteered to go to France with the next draft.

From then on, in the intervals from continual shooting practice, he started to pay as many farewell calls as possible. In late November he had stayed with Bottomley at Carnforth, where he confirmed the choice of eighteen of his poems for *An Annual of New Poetry*.* Afterwards he went to the Guthries in Sussex, to Berridge at his new parish in Brentwood, to Conrad living only twelve miles away from his camp. Some of his friends could not be reached. De la Mare was off to America; Monro, also gazetted in the Royal Artillery, was in command of an anti-aircraft station near Manchester; Hulme had returned to the trenches after being slightly wounded (he survived Thomas by only a few months). Those he managed to see sensed that this was his *final* visit, an impression which Conrad's wife gained most forcefully: 'There was something in his quiet resignation to his fate, that fate which seemed to both Conrad and myself to be sealed in some strange fashion, that impressed us all. Three of the men who sat that night in my husband's study have crossed over, but not one of them seemed at the time to have that tragic air of fate and finality, as the man whose very gentleness seemed the strongest protest against the senseless taking of life. One felt his uncomplaining acceptance of the inevitable, and yet by mutual consent no word of the war was uttered, even though our own boy was on the French front.'[35]

The worst parting was yet to come. After his Christmas leave, which Helen has described incomparably in *World Without End*, he saw her only once more for a few brief days early in January 1917. On the sixth Eleanor Farjeon stayed over-night with them. The Christmas decorations were still about, the children were eager to show off their presents, and, as usual, while Helen made supper, Thomas bathed Myfanwy in front of the wood fire, singing her favourite Welsh songs as he dried her. Next morning he walked part of the way to the station with Eleanor, and they parted as undemonstratively as they had met, by shaking hands. They turned once to wave to each other. On the eleventh came the parting with his wife—'so terrible,' wrote Helen, 'that I did not know one could live through such agony'. A letter transcending that agony, written three years later to her closest friend, leaves nothing unsaid: 'Three years ago today Edward went away from

* A collection planned by Lascelles Abercrombie and R. C. Trevelyan which was published on 13 March 1917. It contained the following poems by Thomas: 'Old Man', 'Snow', 'The Cuckoo', 'The New House', 'Wind and Mist', 'The Unknown', 'The Word', 'After Rain', 'Aspens', 'A Private', 'Sedge-Warblers', 'For These', 'Roads', 'The Source', 'Lovers', 'Beauty', 'The Brook' and 'Song'.

me. The snow was deep on the ground and he soon disappeared in a thick fog, and we cooied to each other until we could not hear any more. I was left alone knowing I would never see him, never hear him, never hold him in my arms again. Tonight I think of all our life together, and I think of my life during these three years. Our life together was a restless sea, tide in, tide out, calm and glorious despair and ecstasy; never still, never easy, but always vivid and moving, wave upon wave, a wild deep glorious sea. Our life was terrible and glorious but always life. And I think of my life these three years. And again it has been like a sea, calm and cruel, happy and despairing, just the same as always but without a harbour, without an anchorage, and I have been tired to death of its tossing to and fro on to this beach and that, on to this rock and that. For life to me cannot be otherwise until that new life comes to me and I am gathered into my anchorage and him and get a calm.'[36]

He was mobilized at Codford late in January. As he passed through London he saw Davies and Roger Ingpen, the latter a brother-in-law of de la Mare who had undertaken to publish sixty-four of his poems.* 'I beg you,' Thomas wrote to him in his last letter, 'not to make use of my situation, as a publisher might be tempted to, now or in the event of any kind of accident to me, to advertise the book.'[37] He impressed upon him, however, that the poems should be dedicated 'To Robert Frost'.

On 22 January he stayed with John Haines at Hucclecote, who saw him off on the train with a fresh wad of manuscript paper and Frost's new book, *Mountain Interval*. 'Very good,' was Thomas's comment, 'though never better or different from *North of Boston*.'[38] His last night in England, the twenty-eighth, was spent at Arthur Ransome's at Tisbury, where Ivy Ransome was looking after Myfanwy for Helen. Thomas, being so near, was able to pass the evening with the youngest of his family. She sat on his knee by the fire and told him how she had been singing folk-songs for Ivy's mother, a rather conventional lady. Thomas asked her what she had sung, and to his amusement she told him 'Gorblimey O'Riley you are looking well'—a song he often used to sing for his children. Then she prayed for his safety in crossing the sea. For Myfanwy it seemed the only possible danger.

* *Poems* (1917) contained the first sixty-four poems as they stand in the *Collected Poems*.

3

He reached Arras, where the build-up for the Easter offensive was in progress, on the afternoon of 9 February. The remaining two months of his life, with the exception of a fortnight as 'a glorified lackey to an old Indian Colonel perplexed in the extreme',[39] were spent mostly in the front line, directing the fire of his battery from exposed observation posts. In his determination to prove himself he had taken on one of the most dangerous jobs of all. 'My nerves are excellent so far,' he assured John Freeman after several shoots, 'but the battle is still ahead.'[40]

In March, a few days after his thirty-ninth birthday, Frost wrote to tell him that 'Old Man', 'The Word' and 'The Unknown' had been accepted by Harriet Monroe's *Poetry*. 'I should like to be a poet, just as I should like to live,' Thomas acknowledged, 'but I know as much about my chances in either case.'[41] A veteran now of over a month, he warned Frost: 'I already know enough to confirm my old opinion that the papers tell no truth at all about what war is and what soldiers are.'[42] On the same day he rebuked a playful remark by Eleanor Farjeon with uncharacteristic sharpness: 'You mustn't joke about leave. There is no leave for anyone in this army, neither for men who have been out nine months nor for men whose wives are dying.'[43]

Throughout March the massive build-up went on, hampered by the changing weather conditions. After the snow, days of driving rain turned the ground into a quagmire. On the eighteenth the Germans retired from Arras, and the battery moved up into a new position, a disused quarry pit close to the village of Achicourt. A few hundred yards across the plain in front of the quarry lay a sunken road, which ran parallel to the enemy front. This road had to be crossed on the way to the O.P. At the end of February there were two field batteries there. By the middle of March it was lined with guns and howitzers standing wheel to wheel as far as the eye could reach. Roads and tracks, trenches and battery positions, were soon churned up into thick mud by the increased traffic. 'You have often heard of the mud out here, haven't you?' he asked Eleanor. 'Well, I have been in it. It is what you have heard. You nearly pull your leg off, and often your boot off, at each step in the worst places. . . . The telephone wires are deep in this and have to be repaired in the dark. Imagine it.'[44] Everyone feared that the battle would have to be postponed, though 'we long to be into it, I suppose because then it will be nearer over.'

On the thirtieth the rain stopped. That evening it was still and quiet, and a host of blackbirds sang. The next day brought only showers, and then April came in fine and sunny. On the second he wrote to Frost for the last time:

'My dear Robert, hearing that the mails have been lost several times lately at sea I thought I had better make another shot at you. This is another penultimate letter. Things are closely impending now and will have happened before you get this and you will know all about them, so I will not try to tell you what they are, especially as I could not get them past the censor.

I have seen some new things since I wrote last and had mud and worse things to endure which do not become less terrible in anticipation but are less terrible once I am in the midst of them. Jagged gables at dawn when you are cold and tired out look a thousand times worse from their connection with a certain kind of enemy shell that has made them look like that, so that every time I see them I half hear the moan of the approaching and hovering shell and the black grisly flap that it seems to make as it bursts. I see and hear more than I did because changed conditions compel me to go up to the very front among the infantry to do an observation and we spend nights without shells in the mud chiefly in waiting for morning and the arrival of the relief. It is a twenty-four-hour job and takes more to recover from. But it is far as yet from being unendurable. . . . I think I get surer of some primitive things that one has got to get sure of about oneself and other people, and I think this is not due simply to being older. In short, I am glad I came out and I think less about return than I thought I should—partly no doubt I inhibit the idea of return. I only think by flashes of the things at home that I used to enjoy and should again . . . I doubt if anybody here thinks less of home than I do and yet I doubt if anybody loves it more.

. . . We expect soon to have to live in damp dug-outs for safety. There are some random shots but as a rule we know where to expect trouble and you can feel quite safe close to a place that is deadly dangerous. We work or make others work practically all day with no rest or holidays, but often we have a quiet evening and can talk or write letters or listen to the gramophone playing "John Peel" and worse things far. People are mostly friendly and warm, however uncongenial. I am more than ten years older than four of the other five officers. They are nineteen, twenty, twenty-five, twenty-six and thirty-three years old. Those of twenty-five and twenty-six regard me as very old. I don't know if the two boys do—I get on better with them: in a sort of way we are fond of one another—I like to see them come in of a night back from some job and I believe they like to see me. What more should anyone want? I revert for ten minutes every night by reading Shakespeare's Tragedies in bed with a pipe before I blow the candle out. Otherwise I do nothing that I used to do except eat and sleep: I mean when I am not alone. Funny world. What a thing it is. And I hear nothing of you. Yet you are no more like an American in a book than you were two-and-a-half years ago. You are among the unchanged things that I can not or dare not think of except in flashes. I don't have memories except such as are involved in my impressions as I see or hear things about me. But if I went on writing like this I should make you think I was as damnably introspective as ever and practised the art too. Good-night to you and Elinor and all. Remember I am in 244 Siege Battery, B.E.F. France, and am and shall remain 2nd Lieut. Edward Thomas, Yours ever.'[45]

An Annual of New Poetry had appeared in March, and Bottomley hastened to send him a copy, followed by its earliest reviews. The book never reached him, but on 4 April Thomas was pleased to see that Edward Eastaway had been impartially and reasonably well received by a reviewer for *The Times Literary Supplement*. The latter half of the review was devoted solely to Thomas's contributions:

> There remains Mr. Eastaway, whose name will be new to most readers of the volume. He is a real poet, with the truth in him. At present, like most of his contemporaries, he has too little control over his eyes. They are too strong for him; and, roving at their will, seeing everything with equal clearness, moving too fast for much growth of thought or love, they make the world for him too like a chaos of scattered and disconnected impressions. What he and others like him seem to need is more concentration of vision, more selection of material, more decision of will as to what the world is to mean for him and what as a poet he is to try to do with it. . . . But he has real imagination. We feel the touch at once in his first poem, 'Old Man'. . . . A finer thing still is 'Roads'. All walkers will rejoice in seeing set down in verse what they have vaguely felt of the majesty of a great road.

The reviewer then recognized, and was alarmed by, the 'outsider' quality of Thomas's verse, its solitariness, its austere comfortlessness. After quoting 'The Source', he went on to compare it with Wordsworth's 'On the Death of Fox':

> Mr. Eastaway makes his poem wholly out of the natural fact. Wordsworth passes from it at once to human things. Before he began to write much verse he had escaped from the stage of his development in which Nature was or could be 'all in all'. Great experiences, as he himself tells us, had 'humanized' his soul—and so the voice of Nature is always afterwards a human voice, or at least a voice that has a human message, whether of endurance and consolation, as here, or often of faith and love. Is that to be the difference between Wordsworth's age and ours? Or is the new method an unconscious survival of a materialism and naturalism which the tremendous life of the last three years has made an absurdity? If spirit is more, much more, than it was three years ago, how can Nature be kept outside the charm of its compelling unity? How, above all, can poetry, always the very voice of spirit and prophet of unity, think of Man and Nature except as two aspects of One Life, two children of One Mind?[46]

Thomas read the review with approval. 'I don't mind now being called inhuman,' he informed Bottomley, 'and being told by a reviewer now that April's here—in England now—that I am blind to the 'tremendous life of these three years'.[47]

Next morning the full-scale bombardment prior to the attack began. For three days the sky was bright with gunfire, winking all night with broad flashes as the firing 'flapped and flapped like great sails in the heavy misty air'. On the sixth, in a letter to his wife, he gave a clear exposition of the nature of his mental state: 'My dear, you must not ask me to say much. I know that you must say much because you feel much. But I, you see, must not feel anything. I am just, as it were, tunnelling underground and something sensible in my subconsciousness directs me not to think of the sun, at the end of the tunnel there is the sun. Honestly this is not the result of thinking; it is just an explanation of my state of mind which is really so entirely preoccupied with getting through the tunnel that you might say I had forgotten there was a sun at either end, before or after this business. . . . If I could respond as you would like me to to your feelings I should be unable to go on with this job in ignorance whether it is to last weeks or months or years. I never even think will it be weeks or months or years. . . .'[48] The sun set as he wrote, but the sky would never go dark. Behind him a bright brassy glare marked the spot where waste cartridges were being burnt.

On the eighth, Easter Sunday, he was on duty with his battery when it came under heavy fire. 'The quarry was about thirty yards wide by a hundred long,' wrote Franklin Lushington, the battery commander. 'In order to enable them to clear the lip of the forward bank, the guns were placed with their trails against the backward slope where they were quite exposed, without gun pits or shelter of any kind. Shells were raining into the position when the time for firing . . . arrived, but by one of those inexplicable turns of fortune, no casualties were sustained. A 5.9 plunged into the ground a foot from [Thomas], and failed to explode though the wind of its passing knocked him down. That night in the mess somebody said, "[Edward], you were evidently born to live through this war," and they all drank his health.'[49] Lushington then asked whose turn it was for the O.P. next morning, the day of the attack. Thomas said it was his. There was more leg-pulling about his charmed life.

Easter Monday dawned cold and wintry. In the packed trenches long lines of men, bayonets fixed, waited. In the gun positions, shells were being fused and final preparations made. Two minutes before seven Lushington looked at his watch. '[Thomas] should be at the O.P. by now,' he thought. 'He had started late. That 9.2 battery behind were ramming their shells home badly. Why was the fool firing at all? Nobody else was. . . . Why didn't [Thomas] ring up? CRASH! The air was rent with a swelling thunder of sound, stunning, ear-splitting, deafening. The Battle of Arras had begun.'[50]

A few minutes later a telephone message from the O.P. told them that Thomas was dead. He had been killed instantly by the blast of a shell.[51]

Part 2

CRITICAL

6

THE ROAD NOT TAKEN

The Prose

Oh, I kept the first for another day!

ROBERT FROST: 'The Road Not Taken

I

Edward Thomas's first book, *The Woodland Life* (1897), has been passed over as juvenilia and never been critically examined. It is best approached through a retrospective essay entitled 'How I Began', which was first published in January 1913. The essay reviews his early development as a writer from the standpoint he had reached in 1913, when he was writing very much as he spoke. More important, it looks directly forward to the poetry which would occupy the last two years of his life.

'How I Began' also gives several clues as to why that poetry was so late in appearing. At the root of his trouble, he felt, was the fact that he had been taught to read before he could write: 'I can only remark here that the result of teaching a child to read before it can write is that it begins and usually ends by writing like a book, not like a human being.'[1] It was his own experience:

> From the age of one, I could express by words and inflections of the voice all that ever sought expression within me, from feelings of heat, cold, hunger, repletion, indigestion, etc., to subtle preferences of persons and things. But when I came to write the slowness of that unnatural act decimated and disconcerted my natural faculties. I laboriously covered a square foot of notepaper, communicating nothing much beyond the fact that I had begun to hold a pen, and to master English grammar.[2]

He enlarged on what was to be the first major difference between his prose and poetry a few lines later:

> The slowness made it practically impossible to say what I was

> thinking, even if I had tried. I did not try hard. I do not believe that it was by any means my sole or chief aim to write what I was thinking, or what I should have spoken had my correspondent been in the same room with me. I felt it to be highly important that I should use terms such as I had met in books, seldom if ever in speech. Nor do I remember hearing it said that I could, or should, write as I thought or as I spoke.[3]

His own thought, feeling and expression were secondary in his conscious efforts to impress, to be adult, to be above all *literary*:

> I virtually neglected in my writing the feelings that belonged to my own nature and my own times of life—an irreparable loss, whether great or not. If I wrote about what really pleased or concerned me, like a walk all day or all night in Wiltshire, I had in view not the truth but the eyes of elders, and those elders clothed in the excess and circumstances of elderliness regularly assumed in the presence of children. I was considered to excel in this form of rhetoric.[4]

Not until he had stripped away all affectation and the least nuance of pretended emotion could he make some amends for that 'irreparable loss'. His poetry is concerned not with rhetoric, but with an uncompromising honesty:

I should prefer the truth
Or nothing.

('The Chalk-Pit')

To repent that day will be
Impossible
For you and vain for me
The truth to tell.

('P.H.T.')

It is significant that his prose grew more directly personal as it became less and less elaborate. Both his autobiographical works, *The Happy-Go-Lucky Morgans* and *The Childhood of Edward Thomas*, were written in 1913 before he kept an 'intimate poetic journal'[5] of his last days. And certainly neither *The Childhood* (first published in 1938) nor 'P.H.T.' (first published in 1949) was written for 'the eyes of elders'.

At seventeen, with acceptances by well-known periodicals, success confirmed the habit:

> So seriously, too, did I take myself in it, that from the time I was sixteen I found myself hardly letting a week pass without writing one or two descriptions—of a man, or a place, or a walk—in a manner largely founded on Jefferies' *Amateur Poacher*, Kingsley's *Prose Idylls*, and Mr. Francis A. Knight's weekly contributions to the *Daily News*, but doubtless with tones supplied also by Shelley and Keats, and later on by Ruskin, De Quincey, Pater, and Sir Thomas Browne. I had quite a number of temptations to print, and at the age of fifteen easily gave way. At seventeen, some of these descriptions were printed in the *Speaker* and the *New Age*, and soon afterwards took the form of a book.[6]

That book was *The Woodland Life*. At eighteen he was a formed writer with disastrous results:

> . . . in papers intended for print, I ravaged the language (to the best of my ability) at least as much for ostentation as for use, though I should not like to have to separate the two. This must always happen where a man has collected all the colours of the rainbow, 'of earthquake and eclipse', on his palette, and has a cottage or a gasometer to paint. A continual negotiation was going on between thought, speech and writing, thought having as a rule the worst of it. Speech was humble and creeping, but wanted too many fine shades and could never come to a satisfactory end. Writing was lordly and regardless. Thought went on in the twilight, and wished the other two might come to terms for ever. But maybe they did not and never will, and perhaps, they never do. In my own case, at any rate, I cannot pronounce, though I have by this time provided an abundance of material for a judgment.[7]

Several more fundamental distinctions emerge from this passage. The exuberance of the adolescent resulted in an overwriting which was 'as much for ostentation as for use'. The poems are frugal—'bare as a bone'[8]—and instead of 'all the colours of the rainbow' they are often sketched in black and white. Finally, his determination to '*ravage*' the language in no way points to the economy of the poems; neither does it suggest the humility and tenderness of the poet. The change in attitude was from oppressor to supplicant:

> Will you . . .
> Choose me,

You English words?
('Words')

His first book exemplifies most of these precocious tendencies. *The Woodland Life*, 'with its eleven slight essays and its rather boyish chronicle of a year's trivial happenings in field and hedgerow'[9] (as one biographer describes it), is important for a proper understanding of Thomas's development. The diary (from 1 April 1895 to 30 March 1896) consists of shorthand impressions recorded on his travels through 'English fields and woods'. It was meant to provide a foundation for the eleven essays and originally was not intended for publication. He eventually included it as a supplement to the main section at the suggestion of James Ashcroft Noble. 'These notes,' he wrote in 'How I Began', 'aimed at brevity: they were above syntax and indifferent to dignity'[10]—that is, they were written not to impress but to guide him in the later process of 'writing up'. They are, however, by far the better part of the book, remarkable for the economy and observation which are associated with his poetry. Extracts may be quoted just as they stand. The following are taken from the 1895 section, written when Thomas was seventeen:

True May forget-me-nots in the wet
hollows, and densely among the water-
side rushes: some flowers, pure white
with the blue trembling through as in
the lining of a shell.
(27 May)

Sparrows flocking in the unmown fields:
as they rise their combined wings sound
like a horse shaking himself in the meads.
(5 July)

Rain glistens on the walls at night
like the path of many snails.
(1 December)

At this point it is worth recalling F. R. Leavis's description of Thomas's poems:

A characteristic poem of his has the air of being a random jotting down of chance impressions and sensations, the record of a moment

> of relaxed and undirected consciousness. The diction and movement are those of quiet, ruminative speech. But the unobtrusive signs accumulate, and finally one is aware that the outward scene is accessory to an inner theatre.[11]

Not unnaturally, some of the random impressions entered in the diary were to reappear in those poems. The entry for his seventeenth birthday recorded simply

The first violet
(3 March 1896)

which was to constitute one of the conditions in letting 'Codham, Cockridden, and Childerditch' to his elder daughter in 'If I Should Ever by Chance':

The rent I shall ask of her will be only
Each year's first violets, white and lonely . . .
(6 April 1916)

The entry for 2 November 1895 mentioned

'Old man's beard' of the wild clematis
flecking the hedges; like the tail-
feathers of a bird of paradise.

A prose poem written on 17 November 1914 was called 'Old Man's Beard', which was shortened to 'Old Man' a few weeks later when it found its true form as a poem. An earlier entry reads

Grass of the rising aftermath or 'lattermath'
beautifully green after a quickening rain,
while the thistled pastures are grey.
(30 June 1895)

It is perhaps the memory of this scene which is recalled 'after the interval / Of a score years' in his poem 'It Was Upon':

It was upon a July evening.
At a stile I stood, looking along a path
Over the country by a second Spring
Drenched perfect green again. 'The lattermath
Will be a fine one.' So the stranger said,

A wandering man. Albeit I stood at rest,
Flushed with desire I was. The earth outspread,
Like meadows of the future, I possessed.

And as an unaccomplished prophecy
The stranger's words, after the interval
Of a score years, when those fields are by me
Never to be recrossed, now I recall,
This July eve, and question, wondering,
What of the lattermath to this hoar Spring?
(21 June 1916)

The repetition of 'lattermath' fuses together the past moment of happiness ('beautifully green' / 'perfect green') with the present moment of uncertainty and foreboding ('hoar'). The memory of the outward scene is now used to express the poet's inward mood.

The similarity, and yet essential difference, between the diary notes and the poetry may be pin-pointed in a second example. Compare this note with an extract from 'Bright Clouds':

Wind breaks up the sheets of scum
upon the ponds, so that it appears
to sink, but collects again in calm.
(8 August 1895)

The light wind frets
And drifts the scum
Of may-blossom.
(4 June 1916)

In the note Thomas is intent on recording the outward scene; in the poem 'frets' is one of Leavis's 'unobtrusive signs' which make one aware that 'the outward scene is accessory to an inner theatre.' It suggests not only the agitation of the blossom caused by the wind, but also the mental agitation of the poet watching the scene. 'Bright Clouds' (like 'It Was Upon') was one of those poems written a year after he had enlisted, when he was experiencing what Alun Lewis described as 'the rootless life of soldiers having no enemy and always, somehow, under a shadow . . . death in battle, death on a large scale, and all the attendant finalities and terrors—these are outside.'[12] Though they are 'outside' they are never forgotten, and John Freeman remembered how Thomas 'visibly *fretted* at the long training which withheld him from a scene where, as he wrote, he had yet to prove whether he could do anything at all.'[13] There is this chafing edge to the poem. Indeed it is possible to indicate 'the precise instant when a thing outward and objective transforms itself, or darts into a thing inward and subjective':[14]

Bright clouds of may
Shade half the pond.
Beyond,
All but one bay
Of emerald
Tall reeds
Like criss-cross bayonets
Where a bird once called,
Lies bright as the sun.

Momentarily, as the tall reeds flash upon the inward eye, the surface calm is broken. Like the scene in the poem, the poet's mind embraces both sunlight and shade.

However, two thirds of *The Woodland Life* are made up of eleven essays in which some of the daily shorthand notes are elaborated. It is an astonishing performance for a boy of nineteen, and that is just what is wrong with it. For it is a performance which deliberately sets out to astonish those 'eyes of elders' rather than satisfy his own nature. The contrast with the diary is marked and may be established with the help of a further description by Leavis. Here he is comparing the poetry of Thomas with that of Blunden:

> His art offers an extreme contrast with Mr. Blunden's. Mr. Blunden's poems are frankly 'composed', but Edward Thomas's seem to happen.[15]

If this distinction is related to *The Woodland Life*, it could be said that the diary notes 'seem to happen' while the essays are frankly 'composed'. Consider a four-day extract from the diary, written when Thomas was eighteen:

March 1896

25 Marsh-marigolds flowering.

26 Elms in leaf.

Flowers of wood-sorrel.
Blackthorn bloom.

27 An early cuckoo-flower.
Water-crickets stirring.
Purple periwinkle in flower.

28 Orchard trees lit with blossom.
Chestnuts coming into leaf.

The freshness of such glimpses was to be recaptured only in his poetry. The essays are quite different. In 'The Sweet o' the Year', the entry for 28 March

Orchard trees lit with blossom

is given a full literary treatment:

> Like the snow-incrusted boughs of winter, the pear-tree branches of the orchard seem almost to bow beneath the weight and wealth of hoary blossom, sunlit and flashing from the dew beads that rim the faint petals. In the wind, warm and caressing from the bright sun, the crisp blossomed boughs bend and rise with a languid dreamy motion, for the odour and beauty of the million petals seem inconsistent with brisk movement. The orchard, one heaving mass of bloom, looks from afar like the foam-line that seethes and scatters spray along the sea-shore, though the wind in its frolics does not yet fling showers of petal-flakes to rise and drop twirling to the sward below among the daffodils.[16]

Such writing is frankly 'composed'. It compulsively aims to impress—and it does impress—though only at the expense of the finer qualities of the diary. The immediacy of the note has been lost. Moreover, 'sunlit and flashing' is a poor substitute for the original perception of the blossom 'lighting' the trees. Lastly, as he confessed in 'How I Began', thought as a rule has the worst of it. After describing the 'languid dreamy motion' of the blossom as 'inconsistent with brisk movement', his very next simile—'like the foam-line that seethes and scatters spray'—introduces that inconsistency.

The working of the adolescent mind as opposed to that of the mature artist may be further revealed if a sequence from an essay is considered in relation to a poem. The following passage from 'In Autumn Woods' (it has been dated as early as 1894)[17] strikes a characteristic note in Thomas of the fall of autumn leaf:

> The leaves are falling from the poplars steadily one by one, and occasionally in little showers. The frosty night has done its work, and what were erstwhile glowing green leaves are now fast spreading the sward with a sombrely yet sumptuously coloured carpet.[18]

There is a hint in these lines of the conflict expressed in 'How I Began': 'If I wrote about what really pleased or concerned me . . . I had in view not the truth but the eyes of elders'. That the scene really did concern him is proved by the fact that he was to return to it, as though he felt he had not fully succeeded in exploring its significance. In this first attempt the simplicity of the opening is already being displaced by terms he had met in books ('erstwhile', 'sward', 'carpet'), seldom if ever in speech. The promise of exact observation in 'steadily one by one' is not fulfilled—not, that is, until he wrote his poem 'October' in 1915:

> The green elm with the one great bough of gold
> Lets leaves into the grass slip, one by one,—
> The short hill grass, the mushrooms small, milk-white,
> Harebell and scabious and tormentil,
> That blackberry and gorse, in dew and sun,
> Bow down to . . .

The voice is the quiet, meditative one of soliloquy and there is a complete absence of any strong gesture or rhetoric. In their place is the 'exquisite particularity'[19] which distinguishes it so utterly from Georgian nature poetry.

The essay proceeds directly:

> There is no wind, and the pearly haze hangs oppressively over the tree-tops, thereby obscuring the true outline of the branches. It is this dead stillness and gloom that makes the fall of the leaves so arresting; no flutter of wind drifts them through the air, no subtle rays of sunlight play upon their glossy surfaces to make ephemeral fairy glintings as they wave; not even the robin sings to them as they glide through the stirless space from branch to earth: their disappearance from the picture is marked by nothing but the solemn rustle as each leaf touches and settles upon the growing heap.[20]

This sense of 'sheltered stillness' is also created in the poem:

> . . . and the wind travels too light
> To shake the fallen birch leaves from the fern;
> The gossamers wander at their own will.
> At heavier steps than birds' the squirrels scold.

A few lines later, the prose continues:

> Even as we gaze on this wondrous scene of colour, the mist disperses and the sunbeams pour down, further to enliven what was already gay. As far as eye can see through the maze of trunks, the earth is strewn with gorgeous hues lit up anew. As the light varies the shadows shift, and now the orange, now the gold, is all aflame.[21]

Once more there are several points of contact with the poem:

> The rich scene has grown fresh again and new
> As Spring and to the touch is not more cool
> Than it is warm to the gaze; and now I might
> As happy be as earth is beautiful,
> Were I some other or with earth could turn
> In alternation of violet and rose,
> Harebell and snowdrop, at their season due,
> And gorse that has no time not to be gay . . .

The 'wondrous scene' of *The Woodland Life* has become the 'rich scene' of the poem. 'Gaze', a verb of acclaim, has been replaced by the noun from that verb. '*We* gaze' (i.e. Thomas and 'the eyes of elders') is suitable for the visual aspects of the prose; in 'and to the touch is not more cool/Than it is warm to the gaze' there is the quiet, thoughtful tone of the first person singular, of someone responding with more than one of his senses but making no attempt to impress them on anyone else. Indeed, there is no awareness of anyone else—it is as if the reader were eavesdropping on the poet's thought-track. This accounts for the absence in the poem of the oppressive (pictorial) quality of the essay—'pour down', 'further to enliven', 'as far as eye can see', 'strewn with gorgeous hues', 'all aflame'. The keynote of 'October' is 'grown *fresh* again', an idea which is implicit in 'milk-white', 'dew', 'cool' and 'snowdrop' to prevent any sense of cloying. The final difference between the two pieces has already been indicated in the analysis of 'Bright Clouds'. Thomas's interest in the prose is in exhibition; in the poem it is in exploration. 'The end of the poem is not description; Edward Thomas's concern with the outer scene is akin to Mrs. Woolf's: unobtrusively the focus shifts and we become aware of the inner life which the sensory impressions are notation for.'[22] The essay does not develop from the outward scene to any statement of his inner life; in 'October' the monologue grows out of, and develops in terms of, the detail of the described scene. 'Gay' in the prose ('what was already gay') is a neutral touch; in the poem ('And gorse that has no time not to be gay') it is an integral part in the examination of his own mood.

In conclusion, it is fair to say that the poet in embryo is revealed by the 'rather boyish chronicle' of *The Woodland Life*; the essays look forward to the stylist and hack. And before long those 'eyes of elders' whom he desired so much to impress would become the eyes of publishers, and the poet in him would remain unfulfilled for nearly twenty years.

2

Horae Solitariae (1902), *Oxford* (1903) and *Rose Acre Papers* (1904)* help to fill in the brief outline of his development in 'How I Began'. His first serious writing—'of a man, or a place, or a walk'—was in the manner of Jefferies, Kingsley, and naturalist contributors to the newspapers. 'A Man of the Woods' is just such a sketch:

> This tenderness stays with him now; he remembers the caged dormouse clicking for food over him, even in his nightly armchair. Keepering and poaching rank together in his education. Both gave him intricacies of knowledge in woodcraft that are impossible otherwise. Had he been a worse keeper, he would never have made so good a poacher, a worse poacher, and he were a useless keeper.[23]
>
> (1897)

In the same year as this sketch he published *The Woodland Life* in which the influence of the poets ('with tones supplied also by Shelley and Keats') vied with that of the naturalists:

* *Rose Acre Papers* (1904) contained four essays. A volume of the same title was published in 1910 in which two essays were reprinted from the 1904 edition and twelve from *Horae Solitariae*. Several sketches which appeared in the posthumous collection *Cloud Castle* (1922) were also written during this period and ought to be included here. They are: 'A Man of the Woods' (1897), 'Felix' (1899), 'A Colloquy in a Library' (1900), 'Seven Tramps' (1902) and 'Bronwen' (1903).

> Flaring lights of gold and purple fade in the eye of day, and barred clouds drive slowly over from the west.[24]
>
> (1897)

These poetic 'tones' are supplied by Keats's 'Ode to Autumn':

> While barred clouds bloom the soft-dying day,
> And touch the stubble-plains with rosy hue . . .

By the time of *Horae Solitariae*, these 'tones' involved imitation in cold blood. In this passage he is again describing a sunset:

> Great clouds began to troop toward the west, sombre, stealthy, noiseless; hastening and yet steadfast, as if some fate marshalled their jetty columns—hushing all that lay beneath—all moving in one path, yet never jostling, like hooded priests. To what weird banquet, to what mysterious shrine, were they advancing—to what shrine among the firs of an unseen horizon, with the crow and the bat?[25]
>
> (1902)

'Priests' is the touchstone that has taken him to the 'Ode on a Grecian Urn':

> Who are these coming to the sacrifice?
> To what green altar, O mysterious priest,
> Lead'st thou that heifer lowing at the skies . . . ?

He was also turning to more pervasive sources ('tones supplied . . . later on by Ruskin, De Quincey, Pater, and Sir Thomas Browne'). In *Oxford*, he introduced an undergraduate on his first night craving a book 'more megalophonous than De Quincey, more perfect than Pater, more fantastic than Browne, more sweet than Newman'.[26] His own essays satisfied part of that need. Here is a third and final sunset from *Rose Acre Papers:*

> Everywhere, the languid perfumes of corruption. Brown leaves laid their fingers on the cheek as they fell. . . . On that day, burning like an angry flame until noon, and afterwards sinking peacefully into the soundless deeps of vesperal tranquillity as the light grew old, life seemed in retrospect like the well-told story of a rounded melodious existence, such as one could wish for one's self. . . . For a little while, troubled tenderly by autumnal maladies of soul, it was sweet and suitable to follow the path towards our place of rest—a grey immemorial house with innumerable windows.[27]
>
> (1904)

As the 'poetic' had replaced the influence of the naturalists, so the 'decadent' replaced the poetic, and all his university reading was ravaged for linguistic spoils:

> In pursuit of words, which soon enthrall him, he goes far rather than deep. Wherever the word has been cherished for its own sake, in all 'decadent' literature, he makes his mind a home. He begins to write, but in a style which, along with his ornate penmanship, would occupy a lifetime, and result in one brochure or half a dozen sonnets. It is a kind of higher philately. . . . He can talk with ease and point about the 'strange beauty of grey'.[28]

Thomas was literally describing himself. He went through his own 'grey' period in 'February in England' from *Horae Solitariae:*

> Over the grey water rose and fell continually the grey wings of gulls; others screamed with a melancholy 'dying fall' in the grey spaces of heaven, soaring doubtless into silence beyond the mist, in the enjoyment of we knew not what amenities of light and warmth.
>
> *Solemque suum, sua sidera norunt.*
>
> Grey roofs, grey ships; indeed, only one immobile ruddy sail of a barge, drifting up, coloured the Quakerish raiment of the day. By dipping my pen into the grey Thames ripple I am fain to make grey the reader's mind as it did mine. But words are frail; even the word 'grey', which of all chromatic epithets is most charged with mental and sentimental meaning, has boundaries. The grey changed somewhat; it was night.[29]

In the poems the 'unobtrusive signs' accumulate to make one aware of the intimate relation between observation and feeling. In 'February in England' the intrusive signs accumulate ('grey' is repeated nine times) in an effort to force that relation. Yet finally, Thomas can make only a languid declaration of failure ('But words are frail . . .').

Despite this emphasis on grey, he did not forsake his addiction to the 'palette'. In 'Colloquy in a Library', he imagined Malory at work:

> The watchful lamp shining for miles over the sleepy land; the quill (a rhabdomancer's wand); the library overhead and around; the white paper on which the mind was casting lines of shadow; and he writing alone in the hushed midnight with 'earthquake and eclipse' for ink. . . .[30]

The image is more suitable for one of Thomas at work, pointing to compositions that smell of the lamp and library. The most significant phrase is the one quoted from Shelley's *Revolt of Islam*:

> With hue like that when some great painter dips
> His pencil in the gloom of earthquake and eclipse.

When it came to be restated thirteen years later in 'How I Began', it was no longer in a spirit of admiration ('all the colours of the rainbow, "of earthquake and eclipse" . . . and has a cottage or a gasometer to paint'). The length of time it took him to check what his critics called the 'over-excitation of his colour sense'[31] is shown by the following extracts, the first a description of oast-houses on the Kentish Weald from *Horae Solitariae*, the second a rural scene from *Light and Twilight*:

> They are of many hues—dull red, yellow, and the colour of pomegranate rind; they may be seen of the tint of good toast. Something of the ruddiness of earth, as it is found in ripe wheat, in October leaves, and in the lotus flower, has penetrated the brick, and expresses the lust of the earth for a gaudier flora. The oasthouse is indeed among the Lares on the vast hearth of the sun, and on gloomiest days it has its divinity.[32]
>
> (1902)

> A low, level country . . . pierced by straight yellow roads and once or twice interrupted by orange gravel pits. Here and there the roof of a solitary house glowed with tiles of olive and ochre and orange amid rough tussocky grass at the edges of the forest.[33]
>
> (1911)

The colours are superinduced from without and come from his own decorative instinct. In 'The Manor Farm' there is a scene similar to the one described in the last passage, though, as in so many poems, colour has been subdued or excluded altogether:

> The steep farm roof,
> With tiles duskily glowing, entertained
> The mid-day sun; and up and down the roof
> White pigeons nestled.
>
> (1914)

The result of cherishing words and colours for their own sake was an overwriting which, he admitted, was 'at least as much for ostentation as for use'. When it *is* used, it succeeds; when Thomas merely indulges in it, he fails completely. In *Horae Solitariae*, his portrait of a 'superb' labourer is engaging since it is humorous rather than strenuous:

> Like all good men, he is an assiduous smoker; his pipe is to him a temple of Vesta, and he is a goodly stoker; out of his nostrils goeth smoke, and his wife calls him Leviathan.[34]

He has in mind not so much the labourer as the work of Dyer and Cowper. In *Oxford*, the exalted strain occasionally scores off the pretension of university life:

> Here was a pale seraph, his eyes commercing with the sky. He has taken every possible prize. Nobody but his friends can think that he is uninteresting.[35]

The fault of both books is that the reader is often expected to take such affectation seriously. Only a page after the 'Leviathan' passage, Thomas can write:

> They seem exotic, out of place—Heliades, daughters of the Sun indeed, condemned to weep amber tears—horribly slender, unprotected, naked to the world.[36]

He is describing a group of poplars in an area which has been built up. Similarly, he writes of the first light of an Oxford dawn:

> It was beautiful as the Grail with many angels about it—awful as the woman of stern aspect and burning eyes that visited the dream of Boethius. It was worthy to have ushered visions yet more august. Ah! the awful purity of the dawn![37]

The intrusive exclamation, the deadening references, the repetition ('awful' is an example of his 'philately', collected from Milton by way of *Hyperion*) are typical of his writing of this period. He himself realized that it was too literary, too self-conscious, and he knew perfectly well what it should be: 'modest, restrained, colourful, and truthful'.[38] He had succeeded only in making it 'colourful', a quality he was later to reject. *Horae Solitariae*, *Oxford* and *Rose Acre Papers* tell us little more about Thomas than what he was reading. He would never again be so far from his poetry.

3

His first poem appeared in *Beautiful Wales* (1905). More than any other of his commissioned works the book relies on massive quotation, forced irrelevance, and sheer expediency to cover the required space. A host of minor characters are introduced who are usually no more than fragments of Thomas himself. One of them, Llewelyn the Bard, is a frustrated poet destined for oblivion* who praises above all the quality of 'clear-eyed simplicity' and 'mournfulness direct as the cry of a child' in other men's verse. Thomas proceeds to quote one of his 'imitative songs, reduced to its lowest terms by a translator':

She is dead, Eluned,
Whom the young men and the old men
And the old women and even the young women
Came to the gates in the village
To see, because she walked as beautifully as a heifer.

She is dead, Eluned,
Who sang the new songs
And the old; and made the new
Seem old, and the old
As if they were just born and she had christened them.

She is dead, Eluned,
Whom I admired and loved,
When she was gathering red apples,
When she was making cakes and bread,
When she was smiling to herself alone and not thinking of me.

She is dead, Eluned,
Who was part of Spring,
And of blue Summer and red Autumn,
And made the Winter beloved:
She is dead, and these things come not again.[39]

When Bottomley asked him about the 'original', Thomas was forced to admit that there was no original, that it was in fact one of his own

* A recurring figure in Thomas's work. See, e.g., *The Heart of England*, p. 120; *The Last Sheaf*, p. 52; *The Happy-Go-Lucky Morgans, passim.*

early poems.[40] It is interesting in so far as it shows how different his early verse was from his highly-mannered prose. For if *Horae Solitariae* and *Rose Acre Papers* are a logical extension of the essays of *The Woodland Life*, 'Eluned' is in many ways a successor to the diary. His description of both is similar: the poem is 'reduced to its lowest terms' while the diary notes 'aimed at brevity' and were 'indifferent to dignity'. Both are 'modest, restrained . . . and truthful', and only the last stanza of the poem betrays the more colourful pursuits of the prose artist. 'Eluned' was the first poem that Thomas ever published and the last for ten years. It might almost have been addressed to his adolescent Muse: it is her premature burial, and for ages and ages hence these things came not again.

Yet it was not for want of trying. H. Coombes has declared that he is 'not aware that [Thomas] ever complained of lack of time for writing poetry'.[41] In fact Thomas's complaints show him obsessed with the problem of time and the inhibition of his best work. 'Now if I have any *time*—' he wrote to Bottomley in 1913, 'No, I will not say what I might—but should not—do if I had time, which is impossible. However, when I have exhausted the books which publishers and I can seem to agree on—and that will not be very far hence—I may find myself with time.'[42] That such complaints were not confined to his later years may be determined from his early letters. His hack work did little to help him discover his true voice and everything to prevent it:

> You [Berridge] are right in saying I am 'busy enough' but wrong in saying I am 'paid for my imaginings'. My imaginings [are] all in a cupboard and only my lies are in print.[43]
>
> (1902)

> What makes me desperate is the little leisure (from reviewing and much thinking about money) left me to write my best in. . . . Moreover, when for a time I am free from all business, tho my tendency then is to write, I am not always willing to. For I must have some time in which to be non-literary, free to think or better still not to think at all, but to let the wind and the sun do my thinking for me.[44]
>
> (1903)

> Think of yourself [Bottomley] publishing the first drafts of the poems in 'The Gate of Smaragdus'—the very first: think of me writing often 1,000 words a day and then with practically no cor-

rection copying them out . . . I have just done a wintry white and lonely mountain. It took two hours and is just a series of notes; but I must copy it out in haste and either leave much out or not amend it at all. If I had succeeded the result would have been as much like a poem of yours as verse can be like prose. . . . But know, that only a revolution or a catastrophe or an improbable development can ever make calm or happiness possible for me.[45]

(1905)

The pressures of such work stunted his growth and, as Helen Thomas perceived, 'dammed up' his own creative impulse. Norman Douglas reached the same conclusion in a discerning analysis of his friend's predicament:

Thomas was . . . too much of a hack writer. He talked and wrote of books, and of books about books,* till the lyrical core of his mind was submerged, imprisoned, encysted in an impenetrable capsule . . . he was always in need of supporting a family; always yearning for a moment's rest, and never getting it. His genius was rendered sapless by these daily harassments, and drained of all its freshness. Cost what it might, he should have lain fallow for a while and allowed himself time to recuperate.[46]

Thomas's complaints point in this direction. In the first he states that his 'imaginings' have had to be shelved indefinitely in his 'cupboard'. Presumably, since he was so busy, he is implying a *mental* cupboard, a place akin to Henry James's 'deep well of . . . cerebration'.[47] (It is perhaps no coincidence that he refers to an 'unwilling hoard of song' in one of his first poems.)[48] The second complaint indicates the beginning of that process of 'imprisonment' witnessed by Norman Douglas. The lyrical core of his mind is already stiff and unresponsive ('tho my tendency then is to write, I am not always willing to'), and he is left yearning for time to lie fallow, for time to rediscover that lyrical spontaneity in which he was finally to write his best, when the wind ('The Wind's Song') and the sun ('There's Nothing Like the Sun') helped to do his thinking for him.

His third complaint tells of the inevitable compromise to which he was reduced—the attempt to find some measure of fulfilment in the

* Cf. Thomas's dedication to *The Icknield Way*: 'This book for you [Harry Hooton] was to have been a country book, but I see that it has turned out to be another of those books made out of books founded on other books.'

hack books themselves. His 'wintry white and lonely mountain', which was to have been 'as much like a poem . . . as verse can be like prose', refers to a passage in *Beautiful Wales*:

> All day I wandered over an immense, bare, snowy mountain which had looked as round as a white summer cloud, but was truly so pitted and scarred and shattered by beds of streams and valleys full of rotten oak trees, that my course wound like a river's or like a mouse's in a dense hedge. The streams were small, and, partly frozen, partly covered up by snow, they made no noise. Nothing made any noise. There was a chimney-stack clearly visible ten miles away, and I wished that I could hear the factory hiss and groan. No wind stirred among the trees. Once a kite flew over among the clouds of the colour of young swan's plumage, but silently, silently. I passed the remains of twelve ancient oaks, like the litter of some uncouth, vast monster pasturing, but without a sound.
>
> The ruins of a farm lay at the edge of one valley: snow choked the chimney and protected the hearth, which was black with flames long dead, and as cold as a cinerary urn of the bronze age. I stumbled over something snowy near by, and exposed the brown fragments of a plough, and farther on, a heavy wheel standing askew on its crumbling axle.
>
> The trees below were naked on one side of their boles, but above was the snow, like a stiff upright mane on every branch, which seemed to have forced them into their wild and painful curves. All the fallen rotten wood broke under my foot without a sound, and the green things disclosed were as some stupid, cheerful thing in a house of tremendous woe.
>
> It was impossible to think of the inn to which I was going, and hardly of the one which I had left. How could their fires have survived the all-pervading silent snow? When one is comfortable, near a fire or within reach of one, and in company, winter is thought of as a time of activity, of glowing faces, of elements despised, and even a poetry book brings back the spring: one will run, or eat chestnuts, or read a book, or look at a picture tomorrow, and so the winter flies. But on the mountain there was no activity; it was impertinent: there was the snow. . . .[49]

The over-literary quality of his former work has been largely purged though never quite eliminated ('house of tremendous woe'), and for the first time several characteristic features of the poems are present. There is the promise of a 'timeless moment' ('No wind stirred . . . without a sound') so familiar to the poetry:

> There was no sound but one . . .
> ('The Manor Farm')

> It rains, and nothing stirs within the fence
> Anywhere . . .
> ('It Rains')

In the prose it reinforces his feeling of intense loneliness—'born into this solitude'[50]—so that he even wishes he could hear the unlovely 'hiss and groan' of a distant factory. The hearth of the ruined farm (an image of man's domestic life) is barren and cheerless; the fires of the inn to which he is going (images of man's social life) are difficult to believe in. In the poetry the 'forest' became the dominant symbol to suggest that area of isolation and uncertainty here represented by the winter landscape, but it was still the inn which offered the viable alternative:

> Here was both road and inn, the sum
> Of what's not forest.
> ('The Other')

Fire and inn are also pertinent to 'The Watchers', while the dichotomy of solitude and cold, warmth and comfort, in the final paragraph closely foreshadows 'The Owl':

> Then at the inn I had food, fire, and rest,
> Knowing how hungry, cold, and tired was I.

Thomas was at last concentrating on themes and images which were of considerable importance to him. He fails ultimately because he has found neither the occasion nor the medium to express them properly.

The same might be said of another excerpt from *Beautiful Wales*. The cloudiness of some of the following episode is not wholly due to the fact that he is describing a twilight area of consciousness:

> As sleep came, out of this darkness peered the early timorous warble of a blackbird, and gradually all the birds in orchard, hedge, and wood made a thick mist or curtain of innumerable and indistinguishable notes through which still crept the bolder note of that same nearest blackbird. As the night lost its heaviness, though not its

stillness, the continuous mist of songs grew thicker and seemed to produce or to be one with the faint darkness which so soon was to be light. It seemed also to be making the landscape which I saw being made, when I looked out. There, was the side of the hill; there the larches, the dark hedges, and the lingering snow and the orchard: there were what I had seen before, but changed and increased; and very subtle, plaintive, menacing, vast, was the work, though when the light had fully come, once more the larches, the hedges, and the orchard were as if they had never been sung to a new order of beauty by the mist of songs, and yet were not the same, any more than a full coffin is the same as the lips and eyes and hands and hair, of which it contains all that we did not love.[51]

(1905)

Although he never returned to his 'wintry white and lonely mountain', he did rework one of the effects he was trying to create in this passage. One day, mysteriously halted at an empty rural station, he felt the countryside 'sung to a new order of beauty by the mist of songs', and realized the impression in a climax as simple as it was effective:

And for that minute a blackbird sang
Close by, and round him, mistier,
Farther and farther, all the birds
Of Oxfordshire and Gloucestershire.

(1915)

Ten years separate those two extracts during which he wrote twenty-two books of prose and more than a million words in articles and reviews.

4

'Victor Hugo,' wrote Thomas in *Horae Solitariae*, 'has called reverie a poison of the brain, but he forgot that reverie is the substitute of meditation in the minds of children, i.e. of three quarters of the adult population of the world.'[52] This rather dubious explanation was an attempt to justify a habit that lingered on through much of his work—the habit of lapsing into a dream world of his own making. These 'imaginings', which were committed to paper instead of to his 'cupboard', make for some of the best, and worst, parts of his prose books. They seem to answer a need for an ideal perfection,[53] a freedom from responsibility,[54] and a compensation for a tawdry present.[55] At the same time his acceptance of the dream world is accompanied by a sufficient awareness of the dangers of over-indulging in such a world. In *Beautiful Wales* both lovers of poetry, Llewelyn and Morgan Rhys,* come to a bad end. For Morgan Rhys social life became too difficult: 'he began to shrink not only from all men but from all outward experience, and to live, as only too easily he could, upon his own fantasy.'[56] Likewise, Llewelyn was 'for ever building castles in the air and filling them with splendid creatures, whom he calls men . . . I think that he likes men truly because they remind him of something he has read or dreamed, or because they make him dream . . . the most unreal and unliving of all the persons of literature please him most.'[57] The source of Thomas's dream world and his own 'splendid creatures' is threefold: he reverts to the Golden Age of the pastoral, the medieval, or the classical. Only the pastoral is relevant to the poetry and it finds its fullest expression in *The Heart of England* (1906).

At first we expect the worst, for Thomas's preliminary introduction to the rural scene reminds us of the workings of Llewelyn's fantasies:

> The mower, the man hoeing his onion-bed . . . these the very loneliness of the road has prepared us for turning into creatures of dream. . . . They are no more real than the men and women of pastoral. . . . The most credible inhabitants are Mertilla, Florimel, Corin, Amaryllis, Dorilus, Doron, Daphnis, Silvia and Aminta, and shepherds singing to their flocks—
>
> 'Lays of sweet love and youth's delightful heart'.[58]

And yet they are more real. For Thomas had himself witnessed the stabilizing vision of the England of traditions and crafts, of Jefferies and Cobbett, of Sturt's *Wheelwright's Shop*. He had experienced perhaps the final phase of that England. Consequently, unlike his insipid dreams of knights and nymphs, his 'symbols of peace, security and everlastingness' in the English grain are alive with a new energy of detail:

> The house, half a mile off, seems to have been restored by this fair and early light and the cooing of doves to the seeming happy age in which it was built. The long tearing crow of the cock, the clink

* Another of Thomas's 'selves'. The name Morgan turns up throughout his prose until it appears in the title of his autobiographical fiction *The Happy-Go-Lucky Morgans.*

of dairy pans, the palpitating, groaning shout of the shepherd, Ho! ho! ho! ho! ho! now and then, even the whirr of the mowing machines, sounds as if the distance that sweetens them were the distance of time and not only of space. They set a tune on this fair morning to 'What a dainty life the milkmaid leads'.[59]

The old man's tools in the kitchen are noble—the heavy wrought-iron, two-toothed hoe, that falls pleasantly upon the hard clay and splits it without effort and without jarring the hand, its ash handle worn thin where his hand has glided at work, a hand that nothing will wear smooth; the glittering, yellow-handled spades and forks; the disused shovel with which he boasts regretfully that he could dig his garden when he lived on deep loam in a richer country than this; and still the useless 'hop-idgit' of six tynes—the Sussex 'shim'—which he retains to remind others, and perhaps himself, that he was a farmer once.[60]

Yonder the road curves languidly between hedges and broad fringes of green, and along it an old man guides the cattle in to afternoon milking. They linger to crop the wayside grass and he waits, but suddenly resumes his walk and they obey, now hastening with tight udders and looking from side to side. They turn under the archway of a ruined abbey, and low as if they enjoy the reverberation, and disappear. I never see them again; but the ease, the remoteness, the colour of the red cattle in the green road, the slowness of the old cowman, the timelessness of that gradual movement under the fourteenth-century arch, never vanish.[61]

These idealized pictures of 'the heart of England' always give a strong impression of an actual and observed basis (as in '*tight* udders'). It was the England that shaped such later poems as 'The Manor Farm', 'The Huxter', 'Head and Bottle' and 'The Barn'. The 'palpitating, groaning shout of the shepherd' from the first extract rang out again in 'The Cuckoo':

> Ten times with an angry voice he shouted
> 'Ho! Ho!' but not in anger, for that was his way...

The 'long tearing crow of the cock', the 'clink of dairy pans' can also be heard in 'Cock-Crow':

> Out of the night, two cocks together crow,
> Cleaving the darkness with a silver blow...
> The milkers lace their boots up at the farms.

Last but not least, the 'implements' of the second passage, the 'timelessness' of the third, are brought together in the visionary close of 'Haymaking':

> The tosser lay forsook
> Out in the sun; and the long waggon stood
> Without its team: it seemed it never would
> Move from the shadow of that single yew . . .
> The men leaned on their rakes, about to begin,
> But still. And all were silent. All was old,
> This morning time, with a great age untold,
> Older than Clare and Cobbett, Morland and Crome . . .
> The men, the beasts, the trees, the implements . . .
> Immortal in a picture of an old grange.

However, though Thomas experienced the final phase of that England he was not of it, for he also inherited a modern scepticism. This led him to question the validity of that pastoral vision (as in his gently probing '*seeming* happy age' above) at the same time as he lamented its passing in a modern age. Occasionally, vision and scepticism vie in the same paragraph:

> Over all is the stillness of after harvest. Long ago the gleaners went home under the frosty moon, and the last wain left its memorial wisps in the elms. The rain possesses all, and a strange, funereal evocation calls up the bronzed corn again, and the heavy waggon and the grim, knitted chests of the bowing horses as they reach the bright-fruited walnut tree. The children laugh and run—who remember it in the workhouse now—and in a corner of the field the reaper slashes hatefully at the last standing rows. . . .[62]
>
> (1906)

The vision is splendidly evoked—'*grim, knitted chests*'—but it is forced to concede to the actual and distressing. In his later books, as he saw an industrial revolution in miniature break down the rhythms of a life he had once known, the vision recedes even further:

> Backwards and forwards went the workers to and fro from their work, swift, thin men, gossiping young women, children saluting those who were lately their school-fellows. Cattle passed through and sometimes lost their way among the planks and bricks of half-built houses or the refuse of the factories.[63]
>
> (1910)

In this 'brand-new hurrying world' the little thatched cottages were allowed to remain only for postcards, the animals for their commercial value:

> The flocks no longer feed much on the hills, and, except when folded in squares of turnips or mustard, are seldom seen there. They have become more and more a kind of living machinery for turning vegetables into mutton, and only in their lambhood or motherhood are they obviously of a different tribe from sausage-machines, etc.[64]
>
> (1913)

The dream has been replaced by nightmare. Even the countryman was disappearing, a subject on which Thomas vented an unusual bitterness:

> The countryman is dying out, and when we hear his voice, as in George Bourne's *Bettesworth Book*, it is more foreign than French. He had long been in a decline, and now he sinks before the *Daily Mail* like a savage before pox or whisky. Before it is too late, I hope that the Zoological Society will receive a few pairs at their Gardens. With them . . . should be some Gypsies. They are at least as interesting, though often not as beautiful, as anything at the Zoo. At the price of a first-rate cigar one of them could be fed for a week, or a family for a bottle of wine; they will eat almost anything. They give endless quiet amusement to civilized men who behold what they have risen from, and what some would like to return to again.[65]
>
> (1913)

More often, he resigned himself to a note of wistful regret:

> There is nothing left for us to rest upon, nothing great, venerable, or mysterious, which can take us out of ourselves, and give us that more than human tranquillity now to be seen in a few old faces of a disappearing generation. To be a citizen of infinity is no compensation for the loss of that tranquillity. When we grow old what will grant any of us that look? Certainly not statistics and the knowledge that we have lived through a time of progress unparalleled in history.[66]
>
> (1913)

Although that generation was disappearing in 1913, Thomas had already stocked his books with many portraits taken from life. Two in particular are worth noticing, not only for their own sakes, but also to determine by contrast his own nature. The first, a description of a poacher from *Beautiful Wales*, reveals that reverence for the 'great, venerable, or mysterious'; the second, a farmer from *The Heart of England*, portrays a 'more than human tranquillity':

> He would give twelve hours a day at least to the open air, as a scholar to his books. . . . His belief in the earth as a living thing was almost a superstition. I shall not forget how he took me to a hilltop one autumn day, when the quiet gave birth to sound after sound as we listened and let our silence grow. By a process of elimination he set aside the wind, the birds, the falling leaves, the water, and tried to capture for my sake the low hum which was the earth making music to itself. And what I heard I can no more describe than the magic of an excellent voice when once it is silent. . . . None ever chattered less about past happiness and future pain. He seemed to owe a duty to the present moment of which he partook as if he were eating ripe fruit.[67]

> Though nearly seventy, he is staunch and straight, and spending most of his day on horseback, with his calm, large-featured, sandstone face, filling easily and handsomely with clear-souled anger and delight, he suggests the thought of a Centaur, an impossible, noble dream of horse and man created by a god dissatisfied with man and beast. Thirty centuries ago such a man, so marvellously in harmony with the earth, would have gone down in men's memories as a demi-god or the best-loved of the fauns. His voice rings over the meadows or across the table at the inn as strong as a cow's, as deep and humming and sweet as a bee's in a chimney. When he passes by men look at him, I think, as if he cast no shadow, so compact of light is he. He has known sorrow, he has known pains that threaten to crack the brain, but never melancholy. There is a kind of gaiety in his sorrow even as in his joy; for sorrow changes him only as a shadow changes a merry brook. He breathes of a day when men had not so far outstripped the lark and nightingale in heaviness as we have done. His jesting bathes the room or the lane in the light of a Golden Age and the freshness of all the May days we can never recover. Nor do I know anything human more pleasant than his grave smiling as he stands in the newly-reaped cornfields under the last light and sees the large purple land and takes it all unto himself, and then turns without a sigh and, drawing a long draught of his own cider in the cool granary, drinks deep. He rises early and yet is as cheerful when he goes first afield as when he goes to bed.[68]

Thomas responds strongly to his 'impossible, noble dream', but aligns himself throughout with the moderns ('a Golden Age . . . *we* can never recover'). His poems complete the contrast. In 'The Glory' he cannot accept the sunrise with the same self-assurance as the farmer who took the whole land unto himself at sunset:

> The glory invites me, yet it leaves me scorning
> All I can ever do, all I can be . . .

Neither is the present moment as palatable for him as it was for the poacher who partook of it 'as if he were eating ripe fruit'. The sensibility revealed in the poem is never less than modern:

> . . . shall I perhaps know
> That I was happy oft and oft before,
> Awhile forgetting how I am fast pent,
> How dreary-swift, with naught to travel to,
> Is Time? I cannot bite the day to the core.

The last line creates a sense of the physical appetite attributed to the poacher—in a negative statement! There is, moreover, a concern with 'past happiness and future pain' which the poacher ignored. In Thomas's poetry it is generally described in terms of that 'melancholy' which was so foreign to both his countrymen:

> What I desired I knew not, but whate'er my choice
> Vain it must be, I knew . . .
>
> ('Melancholy')

> Once the name I gave to hours
> Like this was melancholy, when
> It was not happiness . . .
>
> ('The Other')

The farmer has had his share of misfortune, yet 'sorrow changes him only as a shadow changes a merry brook'. When Thomas used a similar image to describe himself, he saw his existence as one of total shade:

> I am like a river
> At fall of evening while it seems that never
> Has the sun lighted it or warmed it, while
> Cross breezes cut the surface to a file . . .
>
> ('Beauty')

However, in 'Beauty' his own lack of integration is apparent in the swift transition of mood, from tired despair to an uneasy peace. He is in harmony neither with the earth nor with himself, and he pays the harsh penalty of frustration and restlessness. One last juxtaposition summarizes and concludes these attitudes. The farmer is of more than human stature and the old-world image of the Centaur suggests his mastery, speed and strength. Thomas typifies his own way of life by choosing what was to become in the poetry of T. S. Eliot and Allen Tate a powerful and peculiarly 'modern' symbol of anguish—that of the crab:

> this my right hand
> Crawling crab-like over the clean white page,
> Resting awhile each morning on the pillow,
> Then once more starting to crawl on towards age.
> ('The Long Small Room')

5

The South Country (1909), *Rest and Unrest* (1910) and *Light and Twilight* (1911) have received an inordinate amount of praise. Both of Thomas's biographers single out the last volume of essays for special acclaim:

> Unquestionably, Thomas's finest prose is to be found in this book; it is the work of the poet 'in essence and in outlook'. . . . It is unfortunate that the critic has continued to view all of Thomas's prose works as pot-boilers. The discerning reader will find this book and Thomas's other essays worthy additions to the literature of the English-speaking world. They were written, not for bread and butter, potatoes and shoes, but to express the creative impulse of a poet.[69]

> The essays which Edward wrote at this time did very nearly say what he wanted to say; only because the essay was not the ideal medium for him did they fail to say it completely. They were the attempt, falling just short of perfection, at that which in his poems he perfectly achieved.[70]

Both find that the essays are fundamentally the work of the poet 'in essence and in outlook' and that it was a short creative step to the actual poetry. As a generalization this is entirely misleading. *Rest and Unrest* and *Light and Twilight* were the first books that Thomas had written voluntarily since *Horae Solitariae* and *Rose Acre Papers*, and they fully reveal the consequences of having to write too much, too often, and too quickly. Indeed, whenever the poetry approaches the 'essence and outlook' of these books, it generally fails. Compare the style of the following extract from *Light and Twilight* with that of an unsatisfactory section from his poem 'March':

> Day after day the sun poured out a great light and heat and joy over the earth and the delicately clouded sky. . . . So mighty was the sun that the miles of pale new foliage shimmered mistily like snow. . . .[71]

> The sun filled earth and heaven with a great light
> And a tenderness, almost warmth, where the hail dripped,
> As if the mighty sun wept tears of joy.

These essays show Thomas striving desperately hard to write his 'best' out of an area of his mind that had never been allowed to lie fallow. As a result their quality is thin and forced. In the course of their composition, several were sent to Garnett who condemned them as 'romantic' and 'intolerably affected'. Thomas wrote to defend himself, but succeeded only in stating the apparent hopelessness of his position: 'You are unjust in your view of what you call literary "phrases" that "smell of the lamp". Such phrases however bad came to me without thinking or seeking. It is your "simple and direct" phrases that I have to seek for.'[72] The lyrical core of his mind had finally been 'submerged, imprisoned, encysted in an impenetrable capsule'.

Certainly it is those elusive 'simple and direct' phrases which come closest to the poetry. The kernel of observation in passages such as these from *The South Country* and *Light and Twilight* naturally took its place there:

> Down each side of every white road runs a stream that sings and glitters in ripples like innumerable crystal flowers. Water drips and trickles and leaps and gushes and oozes everywhere, and extracts the fragrance of earth and green and flowers under the heat that hastens to undo the work of the snow.[73]

> The rock-like mud unfroze a little and rills
> Ran and sparkled down each side of the road
> Under the catkins wagging in the hedge.
> But earth would have her sleep out, spite of the sun . . .
> ('The Manor Farm')

Another day, a wide and windy day, is the jackdaw's, and he goes straight and swift and high like a joyous rider crying aloud on an endless savannah, and, underneath, the rippled pond is as bright as a peacock, and millions of beech leaves drive across the open glades of the woods, rushing to their Acheron.[74]

Jackdaws began to shout and float and soar
Already, and one was racing straight and high
Alone, shouting like a black warrior
Challenges and menaces to the wide sky.
('Ambition')

They [his eyes] delighted, as if they had been but ephemeral creatures and not instruments of an immortal soul, in the silkiness and darkness of the long grass, in the towering of one tree, the forking of another, and the inexplicable ramifications of hundreds; in the flight of the swift which was as if the arrow and bow had flown away together.[75]

The swift with wings and tail as sharp and narrow
As if the bow had flown off with the arrow.
('Haymaking')

More often the 'literary phrases' predominate, and the poetry is essentially a break with this kind of idiom. Three descriptions of spring indicate just how far 'short of perfection' these books may fall. The first is from *The South Country* (hack work), the second from *Rest and Unrest* ('best' work), the third from his poem 'But These Things Also':

Out of the rain and mist Spring has now risen full-grown, tender and lusty, fragrant, many-coloured, many-voiced, fair to see, so that it is beyond a lover's power to make even an inventory of her lovely ways. She is tall, she is fresh and bold, sweet in her motion and in her tranquillity; and there is a soft down upon her lips as there is a silken edge to the young leaves of the beeches.[76]
(1909)

The lusty buxom spring, a pretty and merry slut, with her sleeves and skirts tucked up and her hair down over her eyes and shoulders, had fallen asleep in the midst of her toil and nothing could waken her but a thunderstorm in the night. The next day she was simply at play with showers and sunlight, sunlight and showers, at play with sky and earth as if they were but coloured silks and now she fluttered the white and blue and green together and then, wearying of that, held up the grey and the grey-white and the green, and lastly mingled all together inextricably.[77]

(1910)

But these things also are Spring's—
On banks by the roadside the grass
Long-dead that is greyer now
Than all the Winter it was;

The shell of a little snail bleached
In the grass; chip of flint, and mite
Of chalk; and the small birds' dung
In splashes of purest white.

(1915)

The prose is anaemic and there is little to distinguish his hack from his 'best' work. The poem—its very title is a warning—has discarded the showy artifice for an inventory of 'lesser things' ('little', 'chip', 'mite', 'small'), and 'purest white', which would once have graced one of his shadowy heroines, now graces 'the small birds' dung'.

One of those heroines ('Her whiteness . . . called to my mind the beauty of white on an October morning') appears in 'The Fountain' from *Rest and Unrest*. Her description is typical of the many imaginary or literary maidens who are met with in Thomas's work:

> If a brook might attain in a human form the embodiment of its purity, coldness, light, and desire to be ever moving, of its mysterious transformations in clouds of heaven and caves under the rocks, it would be in such a form as hers. The gravity, the dark simplicity, above all the exquisite combination of wildness and meekness in the girl would be worthy of the most sacred fountain, whether emerging among moss and crags and the shadows of crags or among sunlit grass. Surely, I thought, a lymph of crystal ran in her veins. It was the darkness of a hidden spring that chilled her pellucid brow. The radiance of her eyes, her face, her whole form, was of the dawn, which I dreamed that she was one of the few left to worship—Yes! She had listened to the nightingales when the dew and the hawthorn flower and the young grass were yet dark; and the thrill of their songs had entered her eyes and lips without one passionate or confusing thought.[78]

(1910)

Unlike his pastoral vision, this self-induced reverie is without substance or conviction. His love poems, in contrast, are deliberately anti-romantic and sting with the truth of their emotion. Only in 'Sedge-Warblers' does a nymph-like creature seduce his attention:

> This beauty made me dream there was a time
> Long past and irrecoverable, a clime
> Where any brook so radiant racing clear
> Through buttercup and kingcup bright as brass
> But gentle, nourishing the meadow grass
> That leans and scurries in the wind, would bear
> Another beauty, divine and feminine,
> Child to the sun, a nymph whose soul unstained
> Could love all day, and never hate or tire,
> A lover of mortal or immortal kin.
>
> (1915)

There is firm control here ('Long past and irrecoverable') and more interest in the actual scene ('bright as brass', 'leans and scurries') than in the imaginary nymph. The poem continues:

> And yet, rid of this dream, ere I had drained
> Its poison . . .

Thomas shakes off the romantic indulgence of 'The Fountain' and acclaims instead the vigorous song—'Quick, shrill, or grating'—of the unpoetic sedge-warblers:

> Their song that lacks all words, all melody,
> All sweetness almost, was dearer then to me
> Than sweetest voice that sings in tune sweet words.

The false nostalgia of the opening has been exploited, and when Thomas positively rejects it he does so in those adult terms (Hugo's 'poison') which had once seemed so irrelevant.

These radical changes may be underlined if further representative sections of the prose are considered together. 'Unfathomable' was one of Thomas's favourite epithets, usually in combination with 'sea' or 'deep'. It had been ravaged from Shelley[79] during his adolescent search for poetic 'tones', but it was first used in his own work when the 'decadent' was already ousting the 'poetic'. The following is a description of the interior of 'an autumn house' from *Rose Acre Papers*:

> In the upper rooms, the beds (and especially that one which owned the falcon's eye of an oriel)—the beds, with their rounded balmy pillows, and *unfathomable eiderdown* that cost much curious architecture to shape into a trap for weary limbs, were famous. All the opiate influence of the forest was there. Perhaps the pillow was daily filled with blossoms that whisper softliest of sleep.[80]
>
> (1904)

Shelley's adjective has been fused with a *fin de siècle* languor of the most stilted kind. In *Beautiful Wales* and *The Heart of England*, it serves to indicate Thomas's frequent absorption in a dream world:

> A cuckoo had been singing, but now I heard it not; no longer did the yellow-hammer insist, the thrush gossip, the blackbird muse; the sounds of the house were dead: and I saw a hundred cows, some lying down, some moving so lazily—like sailing ships on a wide sea—that I could not see the changing of their pattern on the grass, and I was entangled in the *unfathomable dream* of the unending hills and the unending valleys.[81]
>
> (1905)

> The solitary, dying ash-tree at the edge of the pond seems by day . . . to be but the skeleton of an old victim; or, in winter, the sad and twisted nymph of the water. But every night, like any dreaming child or musing lover . . . is it let into a varied, strange, exalted paradise. I have approached it on some moonlit midnights, when the sky was so deep that the tall oaks were as weeds at the bottom of an *unfathomed sea*, and it has stood up erect and puissant, as if it were the dreamer at one with all he sees, in a world of blind men with open eyes.[82]
>
> (1906)

In his later work this sense of 'at oneness' is given eloquent expression. His rapture in *The South Country* is inspired by the sight of a young girl:

> She is at one with the world, and a deep music grows between her and the stars. Her smile is one of those magical things, great and small and all divine, that have the power to wield universal harmonies. At sight or sound of them the infinite variety of appearances in the world is made fairer than before, because it is shown to be a many-coloured raiment of the one. The raiment trembles, and under leaf and cloud and air a window is thrown open upon the *unfathomable*

> *deep*, and at the window we are sitting, watching the flight of our souls away, away to where they must be gathered into the music that is being built. Often upon the vast and silent twilight, as now, is the soul poured out as a rivulet into the sea and lost. . . . For we stand ever at the edge of Eternity and fall in many times before we die.[83]
>
> (1909)

In 'Winter Music' from *Light and Twilight*, Thomas again stood 'at the edge of Eternity' upon such a 'vast and silent twilight':

> All sound had disappeared and was replaced by a beautiful soft silence, omnipotent and omnipresent. This was the perfect state. This was that great silence, the first of things and the last, on which life has intruded for a little while, that great silence which is all above us, and over the edge of it we may step anywhere and at any time, perhaps never to return. Its empire is eternity. Therefore it is very patient, very gentle, very grave, so that the bird or the trumpet knows not the *unfathomable ocean* into which the sound of its love or its insolence has fallen. As a rule, when we are aware of it, the frontier of it is elusive and moves with us: now it is yonder, across the river, and again it is beyond that lift in the twilight road. But this evening it swept on majestically.[84]
>
> (1911)

All the above extracts illustrate recurring themes and moods in Thomas's work, and all are stylized to a greater or lesser degree. The objection to such writing has already been made: it lacks conviction. There is little to separate the description of the 'unfathomable eider-down' from the 'unfathomable ocean' in the last passage—the cosiness is practically the same ('softliest of sleep', 'beautiful soft silence'). 'Lights Out' is a vastly different proposition:

> I have come to the borders of sleep,
> The *unfathomable deep*
> *Forest* where all must lose
> Their way, however straight,
> Or winding, soon or late;
> They cannot choose.

Many a road and track
That, since the dawn's first crack,
Up to the forest brink,
Deceived the travellers,
Suddenly now blurs,
And in they sink.

(1916)

The unfathomable 'eiderdown', 'dream', 'sea', 'deep' and 'ocean' have been modified and concentrated in the 'unfathomable deep/Forest'. Momentarily, as the rhyme pauses on 'deep', the word is read as a noun before the realization of an even more sinister darkness as it proceeds to qualify the personal symbol of the forest (very different from the decadent forest of *Rose Acre Papers*). The uneasy shift provides the faltering movement of someone actually losing his way, a feeling which is continued in the short parentheses. The whole mood has changed from that expressed in the prose extracts, particularly from the last. The mystical 'frontier' has become 'the borders of sleep' (death);* the 'edge' of the infinite is more precarious in 'forest brink'; the calm acceptance of *stepping* over it has been replaced by a feeling of *sinking* helplessly. Finally, the silence in the last stanza of the poem

Its silence I hear and obey
That I may lose my way
And myself

is not the 'beautiful soft silence' of eternity.

* Sleep is, of course, 'the death of each day's life' (*Macbeth*, II, ii. 38). Thomas used the above phrase more explicitly in *The South Country*, p. 27: 'We wish to prolong what we can see and touch and talk of . . . knowing that clothes and flesh and other perishing things may not pass over *the borders of death* with us.'

7

CRITIC AS ARTIST
The Criticism

For last year's words belong to last year's language
And next year's words await another voice.
T. S. Eliot: *Little Gidding*

I

'Say his poetry has the quality of bread, or tweed, or a ploughed field; strength, simplicity and a natural delicacy that together can express the most complex and mysterious moods—what he called "melancholy"—and at the same time convey a tremendous reality, both of place and time and mind.'[1] Those 'simple and direct' qualities which Alun Lewis extolled in a review of Thomas's poems were becoming conspicuous by their absence at the end of his first phase of prose (1897–1911). Yet overlapping was the most intense and fertile period of his hack work. From 1908 to 1913 he completed eight books of criticism, and the ideas he explored in them were to bear fruit in his self-critical essay 'How I Began' (1913), in a final phase of prose writing (1913–15), and in his poetry (1914–16).

Several of the major themes of these eight books lead directly into the poetry and none is more important than his treatment of the nature of words. The following passages, from *Horae Solitariae*, *The South Country* and his poem 'Words', illustrate the extremes of that subject:

> By dipping my pen into the grey Thames ripple I am fain to make grey the reader's mind as it did mine. But words are frail. . . .[2]
>
> (1902)

> Words are no longer symbols, and to say 'hill' or 'beech' is not to call up images of a hill or a beech tree, since we have so long been in the habit of using the words for beautiful and mighty and noble things very much as a book-keeper uses figures without seeing gold and power.[3]
>
> (1909)

I know you:
You are light as dreams,
Tough as oak,
Precious as gold,
As poppies and corn,
Or an old cloak . . .
(1915)

By 1909 the Oxford dilettante had been replaced by the sad spectacle of the aging hack. After years of having to give 'everything that can be turned into words at short notice',[4] he saw himself as a sedentary book-keeper of meaningless 'figures'. The poem's echo ('gold') marks the radical change in attitude. In 1915 the poet could rejoice in the strength ('Tough as oak'), simplicity ('an old cloak') and natural delicacy ('Light as dreams') of his words. In the interim, all his criticism was written.

The theme was introduced in his first book, *Richard Jefferies* (1909), and its prime importance accepted:

> Akin to, and part of, his gift of love was his power of using words. Nothing is more mysterious than this power, along with the kindred powers of artist and musician. It is the supreme proof, above beauty, physical strength, intelligence, that a man or woman lives. Lighter than gossamer, words can entangle and hold fast all that is loveliest, and strongest, and fleetest, and most enduring, in heaven and earth.[5]

With 'lighter than gossamer', Thomas began to dwell on the properties of words that were essential to his poetry. He went further in his next book, *Feminine Influence on the Poets* (1910), by restoring their separate, natural life:

> He [John Clare] reminds us that words are alive, and not only alive but still half-wild and imperfectly domesticated. They are quiet and gentle in their ways, but are like cats—to whom night overthrows our civilization and servitude—who seem to love us but will starve in the house which we have left, and thought to have emptied of all worth. Words never consent to correspond exactly to any object unless, like scientific terms, they are first killed. Hence the curious life of words in the hands of those who love all life so well that they do not kill even the slender words but let them play on; and such are poets. The magic of words is due to their living freely among

> things, and no man knows how they came together in just that order when a beautiful thing is made like 'Full fathom five' . . . grown men with dictionaries are as murderous of words as entomologists of butterflies.[6]

No one was more qualified than Thomas to speak on the wholesale slaughter of words, whether as adolescent spoiler ('a kind of higher philately') or as mercenary hack ('as a book-keeper uses figures'). Yet budding as a poet, he learned to recognize and respect their seeming 'half-wild nature':

> Sweet as our birds
> To the ear,
> As the burnet rose
> In the heat
> Of Midsummer . . .

Consequently, when he wishes to stand

> Fixed and free
> In a rhyme,
> As poets do

the 'fixed' is not the philatelist's, entomologist's or book-keeper's 'fixed', but the poet's, which is not incompatible with 'free'.

In his discussion of *Serres Chaudes* in *Maurice Maeterlinck* (1911), he found that Maeterlinck's words were merely 'fixed':

> The piece is hardly more than a catalogue of symbols that have no more literary value than words in a dictionary. It ignores the fact that no word, outside works of information, has any value beyond its surface value except what it receives from its neighbours and its position among them. Each man makes his own language in the main unconsciously and inexplicably, unless he is still at an age when he is an admiring but purely aesthetic collector of words; certain words—he knows not why—he will never use; and there are a hundred peculiarities in his rhythms and groupings to be discovered. In the mainly instinctive use of his language the words will all support one another, and, if the writing is good, the result of this support is that each word is living its intensest life.[7]

Two more 'admiring but purely aesthetic collectors of words' were dealt with in his *Algernon Charles Swinburne* (1912) and *Walter Pater* (1913). Their work was frankly 'composed':

He [Swinburne] can astonish and melt but seldom thrill, and when he does it is not by any felicity of as it were God-given inevitable words. . . . Since the adjective is most ready when words are wanted he used a great number, yet without equally great variety. He kept as it were a harem of words, to which he was constant and absolutely faithful. Some he favoured more than others, but he neglected none.[8]

The most and the greatest of men's powers are as yet little known to him, and are scarcely more under his control than the weather. . . . It appears to have been Pater's chief fault, or the cause of his faults, that he trusted those powers too little. The alternative supposition is that he did not carry his self-conscious labours far enough. On almost every page of his writing words are to be seen sticking out, like the raisins that will get burnt on an ill-made cake. It is clear that they have been carefully chosen as the right and effective words, but they stick out because the labour of composition has become so self-conscious and mechanical that cohesion and perfect consistency are impossible. The words have only an isolated value; they are labels; they are shorthand; they are anything but living and social words.[9]

Thomas's reaction to Pater was complete. He seized on one such word in the following lines:

Pater found several matters which he could not handle in print. . . . Unlike Ruskin he had to write *sordes* instead of 'dung', even when the animal was a sheep.[10]

As we saw in 'But These Things Also', Thomas finally had no such scruples himself:

—the small birds' dung
In splashes of purest white.

His own insistence on facing an unvarnished reality culminates in 'Gone, Gone Again':

And now again,
In the harvest rain,
The Blenheim oranges
Fall grubby from the trees

As when I was young—
And when the lost one was here—
And when the war began
To turn young men to dung.

The nostalgic vibrations of 'when I was young', 'when the lost one was here', are never allowed to dominate the tone. The 'Blenheim oranges' (a name that gains additional significance from its context) are 'grubby', a word which combines the sense of 'dirty' and 'eaten by grubs'. These darker implications are clinched by the rhyme (both end rhyme and internal) of 'young' with 'dung' (compare Brooke's 'richer dust'). As Thomas had written in his *Maeterlinck*, 'in the mainly instinctive use of language the words will all support one another, and, if the writing is good, the result of this support is that each word is living *its intensest life*.'

Pater disregarded or nullified those powers which were 'scarcely more under his control than the weather' out of choice; Thomas had been forced against the grain. As early as 1903 he had yearned for time in which to be 'non-literary, free to think or better still not to think at all, but to let the wind and the sun do my thinking for me.' In 'Words' the prayer was still the same, but this time it was answered:

Out of us all
That make rhymes,
Will you choose
Sometimes—
As the winds use
A crack in a wall
Or a drain,
Their joy or their pain
To whistle through—
Choose me,
You English words?

The 'relaxed and undirected consciousness' implicit in this image relates directly to the Romantic-Victorian ideal that the poet was divinely inspired; indeed, it reads as if it were a plain man's version of Shelley's theory of inspiration:

> A man cannot say, 'I will compose poetry'. The greatest poet even cannot say it; for the mind in creation is as a fading coal, which

> some invisible influence, like an inconstant wind, awakens to transitory brightness; this power arises from within, like the colour of a flower which fades and changes as it is developed, and the conscious portions of our nature are unprophetic either of its approach or its departure.[11]

Both poets believed that 'inspiration' (what Thomas called an 'impulse') was necessary to poetry. In his *Pater*, he wrote:

> Certainly deliberateness and patience alone can hardly make any writing perfect. . . . There must be an impulse before deliberate effort and patience are called in, and if that impulse has not been powerful and enduring the work of its subordinates will be too apparent.[12]

Yet he was never as extreme as Shelley. The latter's insistence on spontaneity was unqualified:

> When composition begins, inspiration is already on the decline, and the most glorious poetry that has ever been communicated to the world is probably a feeble shadow of the original conceptions of the poet.

Thomas's inspiration, on the other hand, was something to be clarified, defined and developed in composition. He was not against the 'active powers of the mind' except when they were used in excess. In *Lafcadio Hearn* (1912), he wrote:

> He had long kept note-books for 'every sensation or idea', every 'new and strong impression', and classified them. Yet he knew well that 'our best work is out of the unconscious'. For some writers the unconscious is strong and full in the first and only form of a book or chapter; for others, doubtless, only in the third or tenth revision. There is, however, a danger to those who are overmuch impressed by Flaubert's sweating and grunting at literature, that they may think the seventeenth revision in any case better than the sixteenth. It is certain that much of Hearn's elaboration ended in rhetoric which leaves us cold and even without admiration.[13]

For Thomas the 'unconscious' was generally strongest in the earlier forms of a poem, though it would also be true to say that several subsequent revisions were 'inspired'. His poem 'March', for example, is extant only in its original MS draft and a typescript of that draft. The MS, though heavily corrected in parts, is substantially the same as the printed version. Only the closing lines, describing the afterglow of the thrushes' song, are noticeably weaker. The typescript reads:

> Not till night had half its stars
> And never a cloud was I aware of silence
> Rich with all that riot of songs, a silence
> Saying that Spring returns, perhaps tomorrow.[14]

'A silence/Rich with all that riot of songs' is a revision of his extremely weak first attempt in which the silence had been 'sweeter for those screams and songs'. Neither was entirely satisfactory. Thomas needed a word sufficiently equivocal to concentrate the tumult of the birds' song ('riot') without deprecation. It also had to be a word which would allow the song to be absorbed by the silence ('Rich with') and not dispossessed by it. When the poem reached print, the word had been found, the lines perfected:

> Not till night had half its stars
> And never a cloud, was I aware of silence
> *Stained* with all that hour's songs, a silence
> Saying that Spring returns, perhaps tomorrow.

'Stain', as H. Coombes points out, 'may beautify or mar or beautify while it mars.'[15] Once more Thomas demands and obtains the intensest life of which a word is capable.

In the extract from *Maeterlinck*, he also stated that 'no word . . . has any value beyond its surface value except what it receives from its neighbours and its position among them.' A word may, however, sometimes have a submerged value that comes from its wealth of association. Thomas made good the omission in his comments on Swinburne and Pater. Swinburne's 'harem' of words was 'self-contained';[16] they were free from all traces of former experience. Likewise, Pater's work consisted of 'sterilized words in a vacuum':[17]

> The words in it [*Atlanta in Calydon*] have no rich inheritance from old usage of speech or poetry, even when they are poetic or archaic or Biblical.[18]

Pater was, in fact, forced against his judgment to use words as bricks, as tin soldiers, instead of flesh and blood and genius. Inability to

> survey the whole history of every word must force the perfectly self-conscious writer into this position. Only when a word has become necessary to him can a man use it safely; if he try to impress words by force on a sudden occasion, they will either perish of his violence or betray him. No man can decree the value of one word, unless it is his own invention; the value which it will have in his hands has been decreed by his own past, by the past of his race. It is, of course, impossible to study words too deeply, though all men are not born for this study: but Pater's influence has tended to encourage meticulosity in detail and single words, rather than a regard for form in its largest sense. His words and still less his disciples' have not been lived with sufficiently. Unless a man writes with his whole nature concentrated upon his subject he is unlikely to take hold of another man. For that man will read, not as a scholar, a philologist, a word-fancier, but as a man with all his race, age, class, and personal experience brought to bear on the matter.[19]

This inheritance, 'decreed by his . . . past, by the past of his race', is an essential attribute of his own 'Words':

> Strange as the races
> Of dead and unborn:
> Strange and sweet
> Equally,
> And familiar,
> To the eye,
> As the dearest faces
> That a man knows,
> And as lost homes are . . .

Words have been fully revitalized as 'flesh and blood and genius'. If their 'curious life' is thus respected, if they are allowed to remain equally 'Fixed and free', 'Strange . . ./And familiar', their value will be endlessly refreshed and made current:

> But though older far
> Than oldest yew,—
> As our hills are, old,—
> Worn new
> Again and again:
> Young as our streams
> After rain . . .

'Words exist in the mouth,' wrote Frost, 'not in books. You can't fix them and you don't want to fix them. You want them to adapt their sounds to persons and places and times. You want them to change and be different.'[20] T. S. Eliot expressed a similar point of view in an essay entitled 'The Music of Poetry'. He neatly summarizes the main points that Thomas has been making:

> The music of a word is, so to speak, at a point of intersection: it arises from its relation first to the words immediately preceding and following it, and indefinitely to the rest of its context; and from another relation, that of its immediate meaning in that context to all the other meanings which it has had in other contexts, to its greater or less wealth of association. Not all words, obviously, are equally rich and well-connected: it is part of the business of the poet to dispose the richer among the poorer, at the right points, and we cannot afford to load a poem too heavily with the former—for it is only at certain moments that a word can be made to insinuate the whole history of a language and civilization. This is an 'allusiveness' which is not the fashion or eccentricity of a peculiar type of poetry; but an allusiveness which is in the nature of words, and which is equally the concern of every kind of poet.[21]

It should equally be the concern of every kind of writer, and Thomas indicts those above not only for the poor quality of their work but also for their immaturity as artists (Pater's 'tin soldiers'). It is this maturity, this wholeness of the writer that is necessary if he is to take hold of another man. Pater, the scholar, philologist and word-fancier, was found wanting, but ultimately Jefferies was successful: 'he has found himself, and now it is no longer the naturalist . . . or the colourist, or the mystic that speaks, but a man who has played these parts and been worn and shaped by them, by work and pain.'[22] Thomas had played the parts of naturalist, scholar, word-fancier, colourist and mystic, all of which were made subordinate to his final major role—that of a man speaking to men.

2

In his article 'The Music of Poetry', Eliot had also written: 'Every revolution in poetry is apt to be, and sometimes to announce itself as, a return to common speech. That is the revolution which Wordsworth announced in his prefaces and he was right: but the same revolution had been carried out a century before by Oldham, Waller, Denham, and Dryden; and the same revolution was due over again something over a century later.'[23] In his finest review of *North of Boston*, Thomas announced that revolution:

> This is one of the most revolutionary books of modern times, but one of the quietest and least aggressive. It speaks, and it is poetry. It consists of fifteen poems, from fifty to three hundred lines long, depicting scenes from life, chiefly in the country, in New Hampshire. Two neighbour farmers go along the opposite sides of their boundary wall, mending it and speaking of walls and of boundaries. A husband and wife discuss an old vagabond farm servant who has come home to them, as it falls out, to die. Two travellers sit outside a deserted cottage, talking of those who once lived in it, talking until bees in the wall boards drive them away. A man who has lost his feet in a saw-mill talks with a friend, a child, and the lawyer comes from Boston about compensation. The poet himself describes the dreams of his eyes after a long day on a ladder picking apples, and the impression left on him by a neglected wood-pile in the snow on an evening walk. All but these last two are dialogue mainly; nearly all are in blank verse.
>
> These poems are revolutionary because they lack the exaggeration of rhetoric, and even at first sight appear to lack the poetic intensity of which rhetoric is an imitation. Their language is free from the poetical words and forms that are the chief material of secondary poets. The metre avoids not only the old-fashioned pomp and sweetness, but the later fashion also of discord and fuss. In fact, the medium is common speech and common decasyllables, and Mr. Frost is at no pains to exclude blank verse lines resembling those employed, I think, by Andrew Lang in a leading article printed as prose. Yet almost all these poems are beautiful. They depend not at all on objects commonly admitted to be beautiful; neither have they merely a homely beauty, but are often grand, sometimes magical. Many, if not most, of the separate lines and separate sentences are plain and, in themselves, nothing. But they are bound together and made elements of beauty by a calm eagerness of emotion. . . .
>
> The book is not without failures. Mystery falls into obscurity. In some lines I cannot hit upon the required accents. But his successes,

> like 'The Death of the Hired Man', put Mr. Frost above all other writers of verse in America. He will be accused of keeping monotonously at a low level, because his characters are quiet people, and he has chosen the unresisting medium of blank verse. I will only remark that he would lose far less than most modern writers by being printed as prose. If his work were so printed, it would have little in common with the kind of prose that runs to blank verse: in fact, it would turn out to be closer knit and more intimate than the finest prose is except in its finest passages. It is poetry because it is better than prose.[24]

Several phrases immediately call to mind Wordsworth's *Preface*. 'They depend not at all on objects commonly admitted to be beautiful' is reminiscent of 'poems so materially different from those upon which general approbation is at present bestowed'; the concern with language —'free from poetical words and forms'—may be paralleled by Wordsworth's declaration that 'there will be found in these volumes little of what is usually called poetic diction'; subject matter, too, and its treatment—'depicting scenes from life . . . the medium is common speech and common decasyllables'—relates to Wordsworth's wish for 'incidents and situations from common life . . . in a selection of language really used by men.' Almost as surely as if he knew it at the time, Thomas was writing his own poetic manifesto.

Despite the fact that he twice stresses the revolutionary nature of *North of Boston*, these poems came to him not so much as a revelation as a confirmation of everything towards which he had been working in his criticism. It is important to realize that the two poets *shared* certain basic convictions and that Thomas did not simply 'borrow' his poetic beliefs from the American. In the letter in which he tentatively approached the possibility of his taking to poetry, he remarked to Frost: 'And you really should start doing a book on speech and literature, or you will find me mistaking your ideas for mine and doing it myself. You can't prevent me from making use of them: I do so daily and want to begin over again with them and wring all the necks of my rhetoric—the geese. However, my *Pater* would show you I had got on to the scent already.'[25] Speech rhythms and a selection of language really used by men were the logical outcome of his wish for 'living and social words'. Moreover, his intention to 'wring all the necks of my rhetoric' was foreshadowed by the manner in which he dealt with 'the periphrastic study in a worn-out poetical fashion' in the writers under discussion. He ruthlessly uncovered any sign of 'rotten Victorianism' in Borrow, of 'exuberant picturesqueness' in Hearn, of 'superhuman longwindedness' in Swinburne. 'To strip some [writers] of all such ceremonious phrases,' he wrote, 'would leave them in rags, if not insufficiently covered for decency.'[26] Pater and Swinburne in particular bore the brunt of his exposure:

> When he [Pater] has to say that Leonardo was illegitimate, he uses eight words: 'The dishonour of illegitimacy hangs over his birth.' He at once makes the 'dishonour' a distinction with some grandeur: he almost makes it a visible ornament.[27]

> Not only is Pater commentating on things which his words alone cannot summon to the mind, but he is more or less plainly to be seen at times making efforts towards his desired, if unconscious, effect. . . . A remarkable instance of the use of words is where he describes the communicants receiving morsels of 'the great, white wheaten cake'. Pater is so bent on making it impressive that I see that fact and not the cake at all.[28]

> Instead of saying 'the nightingale' he [Swinburne] says 'the singing bird whose song calls night by name'; a thing 'eight hundred years old' is one 'that has seen decline eight hundred waxing and waning years'. Speaking of himself and others who read Tennyson in their teens, he says that it was 'ere time in the rounding rhyme of choral seasons had hailed us men', which is more than mere periphrasis.[29]

> A simple love of balance and inflation compelled Swinburne to translate into the Swinburnian as it did Johnson into the Johnsonian. . . . He would say, after mentioning George Eliot's Totty, Eppie and Lillo, that 'the fiery-hearted Vestal of Haworth had no room reserved in the palace of her passionate and high-minded imagination as a nursery for inmates of such divine and delicious quality'; he forgot that 'passionate and high-minded', 'divine and delicious', retard the sentence without giving it depth, and that 'divine' was in any case a vain vulgarism.[30]

> Rhyme certainly acted upon Swinburne as a pill to purge ordinary responsibilities. . . . In the next stanza of the same poem, 'The Commonweal', the rhyme 'deathless' leads him to speak of 'the breathless bright watchword of the sea'. This is extraordinary near nonsense, almost a bull's-eye.[31]

In his pursuit of absolute naturalness and transparency, Thomas also began to formulate his own ideas on 'speech and literature'. That he was more than 'on the scent'—and not only in his *Pater*—is apparent from the following comments:

> There can be no doubt that he [Pater] had taken great pains with the expression; no doubt at all that he did not write as he spoke. . . . Ordinary mortal speech, meaning so much more than it says, is better than this inhuman and yet imperfect refinement. . . . His very words are to be seen, not read aloud; for if read aloud they betray their artificiality by a lack of natural expressive rhythm. His closely packed sentences, pausing again and again to take up a fresh burden of parenthesis, could not possibly have a natural rhythm.[32]

> His [Hearn's] writing, then, was likely to be founded entirely on books, and he would revolt as far as possible from the influence of the colloquial language to which he was used. . . . In most of his letters . . . he was free from any such influence, but used only the words and phrases which were likely to come readily to his pen and made a style which was practically written speech, and slangy speech.[33]

> His [Cobbett's] style, with all its open-air virility, is yet lean and hard and undecorated, in accordance with his shrewd puritanism. . . . It is like watching a man, a confident, free-speaking man, with a fine head, a thick neck, and a voice and gestures peculiarly his own, standing up in a crowd, a head taller than the rest, talking democracy despotically. He comes to us offering, as only a few other men do, the pleasure of watching a fighter whose brain and voice are, as it were, part of his physical and muscular development. The movement of his prose is a bodily thing. His sentences do not precisely suggest the swing of an arm or a leg, but they have something in common with it. His style is perhaps the nearest to speech that has really survived.[34]

> It may be said of most poets that they love men and Nature more than words; of Swinburne that he loved them equally. Other poets tend towards a grace and glory of words as of human speech perfected and made divine, Swinburne towards a musical jargon that includes human snatches, but is not and never could be speech.[35]

In the last extract Thomas may have been referring to Matthew Arnold's assertion that 'poetry is nothing less than the most perfect speech of man, that in which he comes nearest to being able to utter the truth.' (It is from his essay on Wordsworth.) It would be difficult to find a more apt description of lines such as these from 'Wind and Mist':

> 'The flint was the one crop that never failed.
> The clay first broke my heart, and then my back;
> And the back heals not. There were other things
> Real, too. In that room at the gable a child
> Was born while the wind chilled a summer dawn:
> Never looked grey mind on a greyer one
> Than when the child's cry broke above the groans . . .
> But flint and clay and childbirth were too real
> For this cloud-castle.'

Thomas had progressed from his own 'inhuman and yet imperfect refinement' (witness his 'grey' period in *Horae Solitariae*) to the 'ordinary mortal speech' of a man shaped and worn by 'work and pain'. There is nothing forced about this 'grey' mind.

When he finished his *Pater* in 1912, Thomas informed his younger brother that he wished thereafter to keep his work 'as near akin as possible to the talk of a Surrey peasant'. 'He was thinking, no doubt,' recalled Julian, 'of George Sturt's *Bettesworth*.'[36] Thomas enlarged on this idea in a long essay published as *The Country* (1913). In it he sketched such a peasant:

> He was probably made by hard work, beer and women, but I should like to live another seventy years to see if this generation produces anything as fit for living on the earth. . . . You may be sure there were hundreds like him in Shakespeare's time and in Wordsworth's, and if there aren't a good sprinkling of them, generation after generation, I do not know what we shall come to, but I have my fears. I warrant, every man who was ever any good had a little apple-faced man or woman like this somewhere not very far back in his pedigree. Where else will he get his endurance, his knowledge of the earth, his feeling for life and for what that old man called God? When a poet writes, I believe he is often only putting into words what such another old man puzzled out among the sheep in a long lifetime.[37]

Both Thomas and Frost had at least one such 'apple-faced man' in their pedigree—in Nicholas Frost of Devonshire and Edward Eastaway, also of Devon blood, whose name Thomas was to adopt as a poet. It was in his poetry that the elemental humour and pithiness of the countryman were to be consummated—in thoughts which might have been 'puzzled out among the sheep in a long lifetime':

> 'Then the hills of the horizon—
> That is how I should make hills had I to show
> One who would never see them what hills were like.'
> ('Wind and Mist')

> When earth's breath, warm and humid, far surpasses
> The richest oven's . . .
> ('April')

> Next Spring
> A blackbird or a robin will nest there,
> Accustomed to them, thinking they will remain
> Whatever is for ever to a bird . . .
> ('Fifty Faggots')

> Over the land freckled with snow half-thawed
> The speculating rooks at their nests cawed
> And saw from elm-tops, delicate as flower of grass,
> What we below could not see, Winter pass.
> ('Thaw')

The accent of common speech is caught and, at the same time, the accent of uncommon poetry. Thomas was at last writing very much as he spoke.

3

In his criticism he consistently deplored a spectatorial attitude towards life. Pater, when he used '*sordes*' instead of 'dung', betrayed an aloofness, an ultra-refinement which, for Thomas, was often absurd, sometimes chilling:

> When he speaks in dreamy monologue about the beauty of the Reserved Sacrament and how it gives the Roman churches all the sentiment of a house where a dead friend lies, it arouses curiosity as to whether Pater had experienced the loss of a friend. The phrase suggests 'a dead friend' as part of the stock-in-trade of an artist—like a rustic bridge or a crescent moon.[38]

Drily, Thomas moved from a specific to a general condemnation:

> He hardly distinguishes between life and art: as they reach his mirror they are alike. . . . He is a spectator. His aim is to see; if he is to become something it is by seeing. . . . Thinking of the noble attitudes of men—heroes of novels—in their strife with circumstance, he asked whether men would fret against their chains if they could see at the end 'these great experiences', these noble attitudes, these tragical situations which thrilled the Fellow of Brasenose. That is nearly pure spectatorship. One more step and he would bid the dying gladiator be comforted by the stanzas of Childe Harold.[39]

Such writing was based on the thin quality of Pater's experience, his 'sober, almost ascetic life at Oxford, varied by tours in continental churches and galleries with his sisters'. Lafcadio Hearn's life was rather more adventurous, and his work occasionally reveals his personal involvement:

> The book [*Chita*] is not without humanity, but the attitude towards human things, the most tragic and the most simple, is usually spectatorial. He describes, for example, the jetsam of a storm which destroyed an island and all its holiday population: the sheep, casks, billiard tables, pianos, children's toys, clothes, and dead bodies. The impression given by the passage is that Hearn had never got beyond the point of view that this scene was a good subject for description. He was writing as a detached aesthetic artist and this cold figure is as conspicuous as the storm and its havoc. In a different key is the description of yellow fever which ends the book. Hearn himself had nearly died of the disease in New Orleans: in *Chita* it kills a man but it gives some life to the style, because the author is writing of what he knows and has mastered too well to regard it as a subject for decoration.[40]

The 'detached aesthetic artist' was as conspicuous in some of Thomas's work as in that of Hearn and Pater. The following review of *Horae Solitariae* appeared in *The Athenaeum* for August 1902, and of all the reviews that his book received it pleased him the most:[41]

> Mr. Edward Thomas produces a very delicate example of old-fashioned essay-writing. He has no gospel to deliver or message to proclaim, but is content to walk in the ways of De Quincey and Charles Lamb, and has evidently come into the world to see, to meditate, and to dream, rather than to do. A Celt of Wales, he

> stands a little aloof from the bustle of the dominant race, and loves sunrise and sunset, anglers, gardners, the outline of trees against the sky, and the unrevealed secrets of unknown women's faces. Above all, in an age which puts strenuous life before literature, he loves books, has the grave Virgilian accents always on his lips, and confesses that 'when I speak a line of Greek, I seem to taste nectar and ambrosia'. . . .this is one of the books which keep alive in unfriendly days a tradition of scholarship and philosophic living to which we trust the world will return.[42]

The world has not returned to it and neither did Thomas once he had emerged from his aesthetic shell. If, in 1902, he had 'come into the world to see, to meditate, and to dream, rather than to do', in 1913 he could criticize Pater for the shortcomings inherent in that ambition:

> That the end of life is contemplation, not action, being, not doing, is, he says, 'the principle of all higher morality'. . . . It is impossible not to regard this aim, as Pater expressed it, as a kind of higher philately or connoisseurship. He speaks like a collector of the great and beautiful. He collected them from books, and pictures, not from life.[43]

That he had in mind more than Pater is obvious from the (now) derisive philately image from *Oxford*. Thomas's admiration was slowly being realigned with those who participated in a strenuous life, as is shown by his introduction to Cobbett's *Rural Rides* (1912) and his study of *George Borrow* (1912). Cobbett and Borrow were the very antithesis of the detached aesthete; in their work they live as eminently robust presences:

> He could write from the first in sentences that express a plain thought or feeling as clearly and swiftly as the flash of an eye or a bang of the fist on a table. . . . To the age of Pater, Cobbett's style is something of a curiosity. But it is an age of tolerant connoisseurs and does not despise Cobbett even though he does soil the carpet with his thick shoes.[44]

> He succeeds not only in evoking things that are very much alive, but in suggesting an artist that is their equal, instead of one, who like so many more refined writers, is a more or less pathetic admirer of living things . . . [Borrow was] a big truculent outdoor wizard, who comes to our doors with a marvellous company of Gypsies and fellows whose like we shall never see again and could not invent.[45]

Some of these attitudes were concentrated in Thomas's poetic comment on 'spectatorship' in 'The Watchers':

> By the ford at the town's edge
> Horse and carter rest:
> The carter smokes on the bridge
> Watching the water press in swathes about his
> horse's chest.
>
> From the inn one watches, too,
> In the room for visitors
> That has no fire, but a view
> And many cases of stuffed fish, vermin, and
> kingfishers.

The poem is about various kinds of living. The carter and his horse are sharing a moment of repose. Their companionship is instinctive and elemental, and the carter watches with sympathy the creature on whom he depends. The horse, in turn, enjoys the pause from work allowed him by his master on whom he too relies. It is a restorative pause, betokening further effort. Even in rest there is activity: the carter smokes and the horse breasts the water.

The traveller does not share their ease or their companionship. He is the impersonal 'one' whose rest is not repose but inactivity. The room he is in lacks a fire (an implied contrast with the carter who is smoking) and is not congenial to social intercourse. 'A tenanted fireplace,' Thomas wrote in *The Heart of England*, 'is better than a cold one on any day of the year, and it is cool in the window-seat between the ale and the wind.'[46] He is reminiscent of the *cold* conspicuous figure in the passage from *Lafcadio Hearn*, the 'more or less pathetic admirer of living things' from *George Borrow*. He shares the room with even colder creatures, the dead stuffed ones in their cases, things more than creatures, simulacra of life. While the horse is breast-high in the water, the fish and the kingfisher are detached from their natural element. Their inactivity is immobility, and the physicality of 'swathes' in the last line of the first stanza contrasts with the 'dry catalogue-effect'[47] in the last line of the second.

The stuffed creatures are watching the visitor from behind their glass cases; the visitor is watching the carter through the glass window; the carter is watching his horse. The watching in each case is from a different world which reflects critically on the others. The fish stare with dead glassy eyes; the visitor contemplates the view which includes the carter and his horse, but his gaze has something in common with the dead stare of the fish, lacking the warmth of the carter's regard for his horse. He too is detached from the 'real life' outside the window.

That the end of life was contemplation, not action, being, not doing, was for Pater 'the principle of all higher morality'. In 'The Watchers' Thomas portrayed it as a sterile occupation, a kind of death-in-life, and as an attitude which could lead only to a falsification or distortion of experience, since it was based on a lack of real sympathy and understanding. Thomas's last word on the subject came in a letter to his wife from the front. In it he said he wished he felt like writing there, but added: 'It is the most impossible thing in this new disturbing world where I am so far *only a spectator*.'[48]

4

The intimate relation of his critical judgments to his habits as a poet may be further illustrated with reference to the theme 'feminine influence on the poet'. In the last chapter mention was made of the infatuation he often displayed for imaginary, legendary or literary maidens. In his *Swinburne*, he reviewed these romantic tendencies more critically:

> It is even more true of *Poems and Ballads* than of *Chastelard* that there is less love in it than love of love, more passionateness than passion. Yet in another sense it is all love and all passion, pure and absolute love and passion that have found 'no object worth their constancy', and so have poured themselves out on light loves, dead women, women that never were alive except in books, and 'daughters of dreams'. Few other books are as full of the learning, passing at times into pedantry, of love: experience, fancy, and books have been ransacked to store it, nor could anything but a divine vitality have saved it from rancidity, putrescence, dust . . . he is not directly expressing a personal emotion or experience. Few of the completely characteristic poems of this volume are or could have been addressed to one woman: it is quite likely that the poet seldom felt monogamous 'three whole days together', and that if he knew the single-hearted devotion to one woman often expressed by Shakespeare, Burns, Shelley, Wordsworth, or Rossetti, he never expressed it,

> unless it was in 'A Leave-Taking'. Instead of 'Margaret and Mary and Kate and Caroline', he celebrates Faustine, Fragoletta, Aholibah, Dolores, Azubah, Aholah, Ahinoam, Atarah. . . . As his poems are seldom personal, so they are not real as Donne's or Byron's or Browning's are, though often 'realistic' at certain points. They are magnificent, but more than human.[49]

Two years earlier in *Feminine Influence on the Poets*, Thomas had set out fully to explore the affinity between love poetry and personal experience.[50] Though he never insisted upon first-hand experience as the foundation for a poem, he was always eager to point out any connections, especially since he found so much love poetry worthless and unreal, such as Herrick's 'lyrics for marionettes'[51] or Landor's 'marmoreal nothings'.[52] For him the superiority of Shakespeare's sonnets over those of his contemporaries lay in the strength of their *particular* passion:

> The lack of anything that might even seem to be decoration gives the series to the Dark Lady an extreme power, exchanging for Shakespeare's customary sensuousness of language the undraped sensuousness and still greater sensuality of the man himself. . . . They do not, or hardly at all, make any appeal to the indolent love of poetry. They refer to a passion for the one particular woman who inspired them, and there is no general interest in them. . . . The poems worthy to stand with them as the expression of love, not heavenly love, but love body and soul, can be counted, when they are found, on the fingers of the two hands.[53]

The poets worthy to stand with Shakespeare in this respect are those to whom he referred in the Swinburne extract—Donne, Byron, Burns and Browning:

> It was Donne's distinction to be the first after Shakespeare, and almost at the same time as Shakespeare, to write love poems in English which bear the undeniable signs not only of love but of one moment of love and for one particular woman. His poems to his wife are of the same kind. There is none of the old-fashioned generalization in them at all.[54]

Byron puts his own case for us, as we should expect, in a clear downright manner. He was writing to Moore in 1816 in reply to a request for a dirge upon a dead girl. 'But how,' he asks, 'can I write on one

> I have never seen or known?' He could not write upon anything without a personal experience and foundation. . . . All but everything he writes is perfectly substantial and at blood heat. He never makes us lift more than one foot out of this very world of every day. Whatever is said, acted or described, hints at the immediate parentage of actual life as it was in the years between 1788 and 1824.[55]

> It is one of the chief glories of Burns that he wrote love poems which every age, and not only his own, must recognize as equally true at once to the spirit of life and to the spirit of poetry. With his songs upon our lips Chloe seems a paper girl, and even Stella but a woman looking out of a picture, an old picture, on a wall. . . . He liked women and could not be without one—one present, one past, and one future. . . . But lover of individual women as Burns was, his poems do not individualize: they call up images only of woman, of youth and of desire.[56]

> Browning is one of the few poets to make poetry out of a matured passion that has passed through the fulfilment of marriage, and 'One Word More' is most likely the proof that he found it difficult.[57]

One other poet worthy to stand alongside those above is Cowper. In *Feminine Influence*, his 'single-hearted devotion' to Mary Unwin received Thomas's unstinted approval:

> The stanzas 'To Mary' succeed in making all other love poems seem airy, fantastical, and written not so much for love of woman, but for love of love. Not only Sidney but even Wordsworth is—for the moment only, be it said—slight and painted beside this poem, so earthly and homely in all detail, yet in sense divine.[58]

Thomas's critical judgments were to stimulate an entirely new approach in his own work. By 1909 he had finished many of the sketches which appeared in *Light and Twilight* in 1911. That is, they were written before *Feminine Influence* though they were published after it. In 'The End of a Day', after a 'young proud girl' had crossed his path, he could still write in this vein:

> The unaccomplished hours hovered about her as she went. She might some day be a Helen, a Guinevere, a Persephone, an Electra, an Isoud, an Eurydice, an Antigone, a Nimue, an Alcestis, a Dido a Lais, a Francesca, a Harriet. She was a violet-eyed maid walking alone. Yet these were the spirits that attended her. Helen whispered

> to her of Theseus, Menelaus, Paris, Ulysses, of calm Lacedaemon, and burning Troy; Persephone of the lone Sicilian meadows, and the dark chariot and Dis; Dido of Carthage and Æneas and the sweet knife of despair; Eurydice of Orpheus and Hades and the harp and silence. . . . And there were many more upon the grass under the western light . . . all drawn after her whithersoever she went, all praising her for her sweet lips, her long brown hair and its gloom and hidden smouldering fires, her eyes and her eyelids that were as the violet opened flower and the white closed bud, her breath sweet as the earth's, her height, whiteness, her swift limbs, and her rippling arms and wrists and hands, made for love and all fair service. . . .[59]

Like Swinburne's *Poems and Ballads*, it is 'full of the learning, passing at times into pedantry, of love', and all Thomas's literary experience has been ransacked to store it. He is the spectator still, the collector from books and pictures, not from life. Only two sketches in *Light and Twilight*, 'Hawthornden' and 'The Attempt', strike the more realistic, domestic note which his preferences in *Feminine Influence* confirmed. 'Hawthornden' is the portrait of a man who is failing in his social and personal relationships. He reads many books, and though he is fond of the poetry of passion he realizes that he is becoming incapable of passion himself:

> He would look up from a poem sometimes and see his wife reading or embroidering, and then take his eyes away with a sigh and only the faintest dissatisfied recognition that he was becoming more and more incapable of being passionate himself and of meeting the passion of another.[60]

The same man is the subject of 'The Attempt'. The story—that of Thomas's own attempted suicide—ends quietly as the protagonist returns home:

> He opened the door. The table was spread for tea. His wife, divining all, said:
> 'Shall I make tea?'
> 'Please,' he replied, thinking himself impenetrably masked.[61]

Helen Thomas reported the same episode in *World Without End:*

> 'Hello,' I called, though the word came out like a croak. He was safe. When I could control my voice and face I went to the study.

He was taking off his shoes by the fire, and I saw they were coated with mud and leaves. He did not look up.
'Shall I make the tea?' I said.
'Please,' he answered, and in his voice I was aware of all he had suffered and overcome, and all that he asked of me.[62]

This sober, unromantic approach is the essence of the poetry. The conclusion to 'These Things that Poets Said' is an extension of Hawthornden's frame of mind:

Only, that once I loved
By this one argument
Is very plainly proved:
I, loving not, am different.

It was out of 'loving not' that Thomas eventually wrote his love poems. The most poignant of all is 'No One So Much As You':

No one so much as you
Loves this my clay,
Or would lament as you
Its dying day.

You know me through and through
Though I have not told,
And though with what you know
You are not bold.

None ever was so fair
As I thought you:
Not a word can I bear
Spoken against you.

All that I ever did
For you seemed coarse
Compared with what I hid
Nor put in force.

My eyes scarce dare meet you
Lest they should prove
I but respond to you
And do not love.

We look and understand,
We cannot speak
Except in trifles and
Words the most weak.

For I at most accept
Your love, regretting
That is all: I have kept
Only a fretting

That I could not return
All that you gave
And could not ever burn
With the love you have,

Till sometimes it did seem
Better it were
Never to see you more
Than linger here

With only gratitude
Instead of love—
A pine in solitude
Cradling a dove.

From an inventory of his reading Thomas has passed to the quintessence of his emotional life, a transition largely prepared for by his criticism. For 'No One So Much As You' has been governed in style and content by his earlier findings: it has 'a personal experience and foundation' (Byron); it is addressed to 'one particular woman' (Donne); it is 'a matured passion that has passed through the fulfilment of marriage' (Browning). It lacks 'anything that might even seem to be decoration' (Shakespeare) and is 'earthly and homely in all detail, yet in sense divine' (Cowper). 'Many, if not most, of the separate lines and separate sentences are plain and, in themselves, nothing. But they are bound together and made elements of beauty by a calm eagerness of emotion' (Frost). The single clinching image perfectly summarizes his attitude. The bare statement would be that as the pine (characteristically 'in solitude') accepts without response the nesting dove (which, in 'Beauty', 'slants unswerving to its home and love'), so Thomas felt that he accepted the love of his wife: 'For I at most accept/Your love, regretting/That is all'. The poetic statement, however, is not so reserved. This pine is '*cradling*' the dove, a 'living and social word' (Pater) with irrepressible connotations of warmth, security and tenderness. (How much would have been lost had an impersonal verb such as 'sheltering' or 'harbouring' been used.) The pine is not as insensate as it might appear, or wish to appear.

'It often happens,' wrote an anonymous contributor to *A Bibliography of Modern Poetry* in 1920, 'that a man who has very definite views on a subject himself produces work that is an absolute negation of the theory he may have spent his life in shaping. This is not the case with Edward Thomas. His poetry will remain as an example of those principles which he took so much time to discover and to present in all his critical essays on the works of his contemporaries.'[63] Thomas himself hinted as much in his *George Borrow*. There he wrote: 'We run after biographies of extraordinary monarchs, poets, bandits, prostitutes, and see in them magnificent expansions of our *fragmentary, undeveloped, or mistaken selves.*'[64] Frequently the reader of his eight critical studies is conscious of the close identification he makes with his subject—especially with Richard Jefferies. Two such passages span the whole of that writer's career. The first concerns the office of the imagination and the work of the youthful Jefferies: 'The seeing eye of child or lover, the poet's verse, the musician's melody, add . . . continually to the richness of the universe. Jefferies early possessed such an eye, such an imagination, though not for many years could he reveal some of its images by means of words. In fact, he was very soon to bear witness to the pitiful truth that the imagination does not supply the words that shall be its expression; he was to fill much paper with words that revealed almost nothing of his inner and little more of his outer life.'[65] No doubt Thomas was painfully aware how relevant this was to his own experience. Yet it is possible that he never intended any self-identification with a second passage which concerns the older, mature Jefferies. In retrospect, however, it bears an uncanny likeness: 'The mood, the very vocabulary, of these early country books was against the revelation of which he was in search. . . . But now, at the age of thirty-four, with five more years to die in—disease already strong upon his body, yet powerless to deny him the pleasure of the north wind on the hills—he was not shy of speaking out in his own person, of going back to the fields of his youth to glean where he had already reaped and harvested—fairy gleanings gathered so late by the ghost of the reaper.'[66]

8

LIKE EXILES HOME

Prose into Poetry

> And now in age I bud again,
> After so many deaths I live and write;
> I once more smell the dew and rain,
> And relish versing . . .
>
> GEORGE HERBERT: 'The Flower'

I

'Now *there* is a clarity. There *is* the harvest of having written twenty novels first.' Ezra Pound's acclamation of the *Collected Poems* of Thomas Hardy is particularly apposite to those of Edward Thomas. For his poetry is the harvest of more than thirty books of prose, and though, in a sense, all are early poems, they are endowed with the lifetime's experience of a writer, an assured critical instinct, and seasons of observation. They were, as he says in 'The Other', 'powers/Coming like exiles home again'.

The first stage in his transformation was a rough prose sketch entitled 'The White House', which was written on 16 November 1914. It was never published:

> Tall beeches overhang the inn, dwarfing, half hiding it, for it lies back a field's breadth from the by-road. The field is divided from the road by a hedge and only a path from one corner and a cart-track from the other which meet under the beeches connect the inn with the road. But for a sign-board or rather the post and empty cross-frame of a sign-board close to the road behind the hedge a traveller could not guess it an inn. The low dirty-white building looks like a farmhouse, with a lean-to, a rick and a shed of black boarding at one side; and in fact the landlord is more than half farmer. Except from the cottages scattered far around, only one of them visible from the inn, customers are few. And yet it is almost at a crossing of roads. One field away from the field with the sign-post the by-road crosses a main road at a high point on the table

land: the inn itself stands so high that its beeches mark it for those who know, and form a station for the eyes of strangers, many miles away on three sides. But both roads lack houses. The main road runs for one length of four miles without a house in sight, and travellers, especially on the main road, are motorists from the ends of the earth and farmers from remote villages going to market. Once the land was all common. Many acres of it are still possessed by gorse and inhabited chiefly by linnets and a pair of stone-curlews. The name of common clings to it though it is hedged. Gorse and bracken mingle with the hedgerow hawthorns and keep memories of the old waste alive. Few trees of any age stand alongside the road, and as the hedges are low and broken, and everywhere gorse is visible, even the stranger has whiffs of the past and tastes something like the olden sensation of journeying over wide common, high and unpopulated, higher than anything except the [ ] far behind him and [ ] far before him northwards. The farmhouses naturally then are placed far behind the gorse or the fields once blazing with it and are reached by lanes of various lengths all off the main road. Once, I think, the roads crossed in the midst of a tract of common which ended perhaps where now the inn is. But as things are it might well seem to have been hidden there out of someone's generosity. 'I should like to wring the old girl's neck for coming away here.' So said the woman who fetched my beer when I found myself at the inn first. She was a daughter of the house, fresh from a long absence in service in London, a bright wildish slattern with a cockney accent and her hair half-down. She spoke angrily. If she did not get away before long, she said, she would go mad with the loneliness. She looked out sharply: all she could see were the beeches and the tiny pond beneath them and the calves standing in it drinking, alternately grazing the water here and there and thinking, and at last going out and standing still on the bank thinking. Who the 'old girl' was, whether she had built the house here, or what, I did not inquire. It was just the loneliness of the high-placed little inn isolated under those tall beeches that pleased me. Every year I used to go there once or twice, never so often as to overcome the original feeling it had given me. I was always on the verge of turning that feeling, or of having it turned by a natural process, into a story. Whoever the characters would have been I do not think they would have included either the 'old girl' or the landlord's indignant cockney daughter. But the story that was to interpret the look that the house had as you came up to it under the trees never took shape, and the daughter stayed on several years, bearing it so well that her wildish looks and cockney accent seemed to fit the scene and I used to look forward to meeting her again. She would come in with her hair half-down as at first or I would find her scrubbing the bricks or getting drums ready in the taproom which was kitchen also. But before I had learnt anything from her she went. I have to be content with what the landlord told me years afterwards, when he left his wheelbarrow standing in profile like a pig and came into the taproom out of his farmyard for a glass and stood drinking outside the door.

Originally or as far back as he knew of the house was a blacksmith's, the lean-to taproom was the smithy as you can tell by the height of it, and the man was remembered and still is spoken of for his skill. The landlord spoke of him yet had never seen him. The smith died and left a widow and as she could not use hammer and tongs and as no second smith arrived to marry her she turned the smithy into a shop and had an off-licence to sell beer. Eventually a man came along from the Chiltern beech country with a two-cylinder engine for sawing timber. At that day the land here carried far more woodland. The beech trunks were cut up to make chairs. The branches were burnt for charcoal, and the circular black floors of the charcoal-burners' fires are still now and then cut into by the farmer's plough. The man from the Chilterns came here to saw beech planks and brought with him a little boy, his nephew, who had to pick up chips to feed the fire of the engine. 'My uncle,' said the landlord, 'fell in love, I suppose, with the widow and married her.' He continued to go about the country with his engine sawing timber. But the beeches overhanging the house were spared. The boy stayed on and farmed. The shop was turned into a taproom with a full licence and the widow sold ale until she died. The man grew old and gave up sawing and then he died. Now the nephew farms the land. It is worth a guinea a mile he says. But he has grown fat on the beer which his daughters draw. On the wall of the taproom is a list of the officers of a slate club and also coloured diagrams illustrating certain diseases of the cow. The room smells as much of bacon and boiled vegetables as of ale and shag, and it is often silent and empty except for a familiar wooden clock ticking above the fire. Yet it is one of the pleasantest rooms in Hampshire, well deserv-

> ing the footpaths which lead men to it from all directions over ploughland and meadow, and deserving as good a story as a man could write.[1]

It is obvious from internal evidence that the shorthand impressions of the sketch are an attempt to commit to paper a feeling that had been stored up over a period of time: 'I was always on the verge of turning that feeling, or of having it turned by a natural process, into a story.' How long this brooding process had continued may be judged by a passage published three years earlier in *The Isle of Wight* (1911). At this point the speaker has turned inland towards Hampshire—the location of 'The White House':

> There are other places which immediately strike us as fit scenes for some tragic or comic episode out of the common. I know a little white inn standing far back from the road, behind a double row of noble elms—an extraordinary combination, this house no bigger than a haystack, and these trees fit to lead up to a manor house where Sidney or Falkland was once a guest. You approach the inn from the road by crossing a stile and following a path among a tangle of gorse which is much overgrown by honeysuckle. Well, I never see the place, the gorse, the great trees, the house at their feet, without a story haunting my mind but never quite defining itself. To others more ready of fancy it is no doubt already a scene of some highway robbery, with blunderbusses, masks, pretty ladies, and foaming horses. Most children could not hit upon a better birthplace for some hero of humble origin and heaven-scaling ambition.[2]

If Thomas had forced the 'story' in 1911 it might have appeared as one of the romantic tales in *Light and Twilight*. The impulse was, however, stored in his 'cupboard', where, during the reconsideration of those 'undeveloped selves' in his criticism, it grew with his growth and strengthened with his strength. When at last it developed into 'as good a story as a man could write' on 3 December 1914, it turned out rather different from what he had expected. And one of the longest ever apprenticeships in the trade of poet was over.

'Up in the Wind' marks the change from minor to major. The liberation of the new medium makes all the difference to the following extracts:

'I should like to wring the old girl's neck for coming away here.' So said the woman who fetched my beer when I found myself at the inn first. She was a daughter of the house, fresh from a long absence in service in London, a bright wildish slattern with a cockney accent and her hair half-down. She spoke angrily.

'I could wring the old thing's neck that put it here!
A public house! it may be public for birds,
Squirrels, and such-like, ghosts of charcoal-burners
And highwaymen.' The wild girl laughed. 'But I
Hate it since I came back from Kennington.
I gave up a good place.'

Once the land was all common. Many acres of it are still possessed by gorse and inhabited chiefly by linnets and a pair of stone-curlews, The name of common clings to it though it is hedged. Gorse and bracken mingle with the hedgerow hawthorns and keep memories of the old waste alive.

—the land is wild, and there's a spirit of wildness
Much older, crying when the stone-curlew yodels
His sea and mountain cry, high up in Spring.
He nests in fields where still the gorse is free as
When all was open and common.

She would come in with her hair half-down as at first or I would find her scrubbing the bricks or getting drums ready in the taproom which was kitchen also. . . . The room smells as much of bacon and boiled vegetables as of ale and shag, and it is often silent and empty except for a familiar wooden clock ticking above the fire.

Her eyes flashed up; she shook her hair away
From eyes and mouth, as if to shriek again;
Then sighed back to her scrubbing . . .
The clock ticked, and the big saucepan lid
Heaved as the cabbage bubbled, and the girl
Questioned the fire and spoke . . .

In his own words 'it is poetry because it is better than prose.'

The story of the poem is not 'out of the common' (as it would have been in *The Isle of Wight*) but relatively ordinary. As in 'The White House', the girl has returned from a long absence in London to her

1

'I cd wring the old thing's neck that put it here!
A public house! it may be public for
Squirrels & such like & ghosts of charcoal burners
Or highwaymen.'
The wild girl laughed. 'But I
Loathe it since I came back fr Kennington.
I gave up a good place.' Her Cockney accent
Made her & the place seem wilder
Pausing there in her scrubbing
Only to be subdued at once by wildness
The idea of London here in this forest parlour.
She looked up from her scrubbing
Her eyes flashed up. She shook her hair away
From eyes & mouth and shrieked
As if to shriek again:
Then sighed back to her scrubbing. While I drank
I shd have mused of coaches & highwaymen
For who else wd come here except
A market man or two once every other Wednesday
A motorist from far off north or south
Or a solitary tramp, since very first one
Servant of those hoarders eleven miles.

5. The First Poem: 'Up in the Wind' (first draft, page 1)

birthplace in a lonely part of the country to look after the little isolated inn for her father. The romantic possibilities raised in 1911—'a scene of some highway robbery, with blunderbusses, masks, pretty ladies, and foaming horses'—are no longer relevant and are passed over in one line:

> While I drank
> I might have mused of coaches and highwaymen,
> Charcoal-burners and life that loves the wild.

The coaches and highwaymen are now mentioned not so much for the sake of romance as to evoke the wildness of this ancient outcrop of England, which so fascinates Thomas and so infuriates the girl. She herself is the greatest change of all. In 1911 she would simply not have appeared. Even in 'The White House' Thomas doubted that she would be included in the story proper. But as his interest turned from the story itself to the way in which it was told, the 'indignant cockney girl' came into her own. In the poem she has replaced her father as the central character, and her fitful moods monopolize the poet's attention. She can be sulky, suppressed, simmering:

> 'It all happened years ago. The smith
> Had died, his widow had set up an alehouse—
> I could wring the old thing's neck for thinking of it.
> Well, I suppose they fell in love, the widow
> And my great-uncle that sawed up the timber:
> Leastways they married. The little boy stayed on.
> He was my father.' She thought she'd scrub again—
> 'I draw the ale and he grows fat,' she muttered—
> But only studied the hollows in the bricks
> And chose among her thoughts in stirring silence.

The speech parenthesis ('I could wring the old thing's neck'), the colloquial shrug ('Leastways they married'), the glancing aside ('I draw the ale and he grows fat') perfectly characterize this 'heroine of humble origin'. There is no self-consciousness on Thomas's part and he uses no word that the girl might not, under similar circumstances, use herself. Yet this easy colloquial movement is capable of rising from casual gossip to moments of remarkable dramatic intensity. Here is the girl's unforced response to living 'up in the wind':

'All I ever had to thank
The wind for was for blowing the sign down.
Time after time it blew down and I could sleep.
At last they fixed it, and it took a thief
To move it, and we've never had another:
It's lying at the bottom of the pond.
But no one's moved the wood from off the hill
There at the back, although it makes a noise
When the wind blows, as if a train were running
The other side, a train that never stops
Or ends. And the linen crackles on the line
Like a wood fire rising.'

Again, Thomas had written all the description that is necessary of these lines in reviewing *North of Boston*: 'With a confidence like genius, he has trusted his conviction that a man will not easily write better than he speaks when some matter has touched him deeply, and he has turned it over until he has no doubt what it means to him, when he has no purpose to serve beyond expressing it, when he has no audience to be bullied or flattered, when he is free, and speech takes one form and no other. Whatever discipline further was necessary, he has got from the use of the good old English medium of blank verse.'

The virtues that Frost celebrated in the dramatic narratives of *North of Boston* were those which enable individuals to confront and survive the worst by the strength of affirmative outgoing love. Thomas's cockney girl is no exception. She has none of the 'heaven-scaling ambition' that was foretold for her in 1911; she does not even have the ambition to 'get away before long' of her predecessor in 'The White House' (who actually leaves). She is resigned to her life and determined to stick it out:

She bent down to her scrubbing with 'Not me:
Not back to Kennington. Here I was born,
And I've a notion on these windy nights
Here I shall die. Perhaps I want to die here.
I reckon I shall stay . . .'

Her final acceptance centres round another incidental detail from the prose draft—the calves:

She looked out sharply: all she could see were the beeches and the

> tiny pond beneath them and the calves standing in it drinking, alternately grazing the water here and there and thinking, and at last going out and standing still on the bank thinking.

In the poem she calls attention to them, and for a moment they soften the bleak landscape before her consciousness is again crossed with fear:

'Look at those calves.'
Between the open door
And the trees two calves were wading in the pond,
Grazing the water here and there and thinking,
Sipping and thinking, both happily, neither long.
The water wrinkled, but they sipped and thought,
As careless of the wind as it of us.
'Look at those calves. Hark at the trees again.'

'Up in the Wind' clearly shows a fruition of Frost's influence, but it was an influence that Thomas quickly assimilated into his own more intimate, more ruminatory voice. How swiftly he achieved this is shown by another early poem which has always been regarded as one of his finest. 'Old Man', like 'Up in the Wind', was originally drafted as prose. It was written on 17 November 1914—the day after 'The White House'—and called 'Old Man's Beard':

> Just as she is turning in to the house or leaving it, the baby plucks a feather of old man's beard. The bush grows just across the path from the door. Sometimes she stands by it, squeezing off tip after tip from the branches and shrivelling them between her fingers on to the path in grey-green shreds. So the bush is still only half as tall as she is, though it is the same age. She never talks of it, but I wonder how much of the garden she will remember, the hedge with the old damson trees topping it, the vegetable rows, the path bending round the house corner, the old man's beard opposite the door, and me sometimes forbidding her to touch it, if she lives to my years. As for myself I cannot remember when I first smelt that green bitterness. I, too, often gather a sprig from the bush and sniff it and roll it between my fingers and sniff again and think, trying to discover what it is that I am remembering. I do not wholly like the smell, yet would rather lose many meaningless sweeter ones than this bitter one of which I have mislaid the key. As I hold the sprig to my nose and slowly withdraw it, I think of nothing, I see, I hear nothing; yet I seem too to be listening, lying in wait for whatever

17 XI 14 Old Man's Beard C

Just as she is turning in to the cottage door or leaving it, the baby plucks a feather of old man's beard. The bush grows just across the path from the door. Sometimes she stands by it squeezing off tip after tip from the branches & shrivelling them between her fingers on to the path in grey-green shreds. So the bush is still only half as tall as she is, though it is the same age. She never talks of it, but I wonder how much of the garden she will remember, the hedge with the old damson trees topping it, the vegetable rows, the path bending round the house corner, the old man's beard opposite the door, if she lives to my years. and me sometimes forbidding her to touch it. As for myself I cannot remember when I first smelt that green bitterness. I too often gather a sprig from the bush & sniff it & roll it between my fingers & sniff again & think, trying to discover what it is that I am remembering. I do not wholly like the smell, yet would rather lose many meaningless sweeter ones than this bitter one of which I have mislaid the key. As I hold the sprig to my nose & slowly withdraw it, I think of nothing, I see, I hear nothing; yet I seem too to be listening, lying in wait for whatever it is comes back to me I ought to remember but never do. No garden, no hedge or path, no grey-green bush called old man's beard or lad's love, no figure of mother or father or playmate, only a dark avenue without an end.

6. 'Old Man's Beard'

> it is I ought to remember but never do. No garden comes back to me, no hedge or path, no grey-green bush called old man's beard or lad's love, no figure of mother or father or playmate, only a dark avenue without an end.[3]

He returned to the sketch three weeks later on 6 December 1914 and in two drafts completed the poem.

The main difference between 'Old Man' and 'Old Man's Beard' is the play made on the alternative names of the plant. In the prose their rich potentialities were not exploited but mentioned as after-thought. In the opening lines of the poem Thomas began to realize them more fully as he 'puzzled' over their significance:

> Old Man, or Lad's-love—in the name there's nothing
> To one that knows not Lad's-love, or Old Man,
> The hoar-green feathery herb, almost a tree,
> Growing with rosemary and lavender.
> Even to one that knows it well, the names
> Half decorate, half perplex, the thing it is:
> At least, what that is clings not to the names
> In spite of time. And yet I like the names.

The names 'half decorate, half perplex' the 'thing it is', whose tenacious, if tenuous, nature is established by 'clings'. The passing of time, explicit in the paradox of the plant's double name, is continued in 'hoar-green feathery herb, almost a tree', in which the impression of latent growth in the second half of the line surprises after the initial sense of age. These contradictions are heightened by the apparent contradiction of the poet's response. 'And yet I like the names,' he says, before moving on to another paradox: 'The herb itself I like not, but for certain/I love it . . . .' It is at this point that prose and poem merge:

> as some day the child will love it
> Who plucks a feather from the door-side bush
> Whenever she goes in or out of the house.
> Often she waits there, snipping the tips and shrivelling
> The shreds at last on to the path, perhaps
> Thinking, perhaps of nothing, till she sniffs
> Her fingers and runs off. The bush is still
> But half as tall as she, though it is as old;
> So well she clips it.

6 Nov. 14

Old Man or Lad's Love, — in the name there's nothing
To one that knows not Lad's Love or Old Man.
The hoar green feathered herb, almost a tree,
Growing with rosemary and lavender.
Even to one that knows it well the names
Half decorate, half perplex, the thing it is.
At least what that is clings not to the names
In spite of time. And yet I like the names.
I cannot say I like the herb
The herb itself I like not, but for certain
I love it, as someday the child will love it
Who plucks a feather from the doorside bush
Whenever she goes in or out of the house.
Often she stands there snipping the tips and shrivelling
Shrivelling grey green shreds on to the path,
Between her fingers grey green shreds.

Often she stands there snipping the tips to shrivel
The grey green shreds on to the path, perhaps
Thinking, perhaps of nothing, till she sniffs
Her fingers and runs off. The bush is still
But half as tall as she is, tho' 'tis as old,
So well she clips it. Not a word she says,

7. 'Old Man' (first draft, page 1)

Old Man or Lad's Love — in the name there's nothing
To one that knows not Lad's Love or Old Man,
The hoar-green feathery herb, almost a tree,
Growing with rosemary & lavender.
Even to one that knows it well the names
Half decorate, half perplex, the thing it is.
At least what that is clings not to the names
In spite of time. And yet I like the names.

The herb itself I like not, but for certain
I love it, as someday the child will love it
Who plucks a feather from the doorside bush
Whenever she goes in or out of the house.
Often she ~~stands~~ waits there snipping the tips to shrivelling
The grey green shreds on to the path. perhaps
Thinking, perhaps of nothing, till she sniffs
Her fingers, runs off. The bush is still
But half as tall as she is, tho tis as old,
So well she clips it. Not a word she says

8. 'Old Man' (second draft, page 1)

From the child there is an inevitable transition to 'the most poignant of realizations' as the daughter's present is viewed against a future that may be the same as the father's *now* ('if she lives to my years,' he muses in the prose). The hint of the association 'rosemary for remembrance' in the opening lines, the distinction between *liking* and *loving*, the subdued insistence on youth and age and time, lead naturally into the climax of the poem:

Not a word she says;
And I can only wonder how much hereafter
She will remember, with that bitter scent,
Of garden rows, and ancient damson trees
Topping a hedge, a bent path to a door,
A low thick bush beside the door, and me
Forbidding her to pick.

As for myself,
Where first I met the bitter scent is lost.
I, too, often shrivel the grey shreds,
Sniff them and think and sniff again and try
Once more to think what it is I am remembering,
Always in vain. I cannot like the scent,
Yet I would rather give up others more sweet,
With no meaning, than this bitter one.

I have mislaid the key. I sniff the spray
And think of nothing; I see and I hear nothing;
Yet seem, too, to be listening, lying in wait
For what I should, yet never can, remember:
No garden appears, no path, no hoar-green bush
Of Lad's-love, or Old Man, no child beside,
Neither father nor mother, nor any playmate;
Only an avenue, dark, nameless, without end.

For Thomas it is the 'meaning' evoked by the 'bitter scent' that is important, even though it baffles remembrance. To the end it remains a 'shy intuition on the edge of consciousness',[4] teasing but ungraspable. The last sombre line contrasts with the homely 'bent path to a door'. This avenue has no end; unlike the names of the plant (however ambiguous) it is nameless. As Thomas perfected the line, its emphases became more pointed, more foreboding:

> ... only a dark avenue without an end.
> (prose)
>
> Only a dark avenue: without end or name.
> (1st draft)
>
> Only an avenue dark without end or name.
> (2nd draft)
>
> Only an avenue, dark, nameless, without end.
> (*Collected Poems*)

Not all of his 'imaginings' had been repressed for as long as 'The White House' and 'Old Man's Beard', and occasionally, as we have seen, Thomas would try to write them into the hack books themselves. The following passage, describing his reactions to the sound of the rain as he lay half-asleep at an inn after a day's journey, is taken from *The Icknield Way* (1913). It is the anguished death-wish which has already been mentioned:

> Rain . . . drowned that sweet noise in a mightier sweetness, heavy and straight rain, and no wind except what itself created. For half an hour everything—trees, mud walls, thatch, old weather-boards, pale-coloured, timbered cottages, the old chapel at a crossing railed off as a sign of private possession—everything was embedded in rain. Every sound was the rain. For example, I thought I heard bacon frying in a room near by, with a noise almost as loud as the pig made when it was stuck; but it was the rain pouring steadily off the inn roof. . . .
>
> I lay awake listening to the rain, and at first it was as pleasant to my ear and my mind as it had long been desired; but before I fell asleep it had become a majestic and finally terrible thing, instead of a sweet sound and symbol. It was accusing and trying me and passing judgment. Long I lay still under the sentence, listening to the rain, and then at last listening to words which seemed to be spoken by a ghostly double beside me. He was muttering: the all-night rain puts out summer like a torch. In the heavy, black rain falling straight from invisible, dark sky to invisible, dark earth the heat of summer is annihilated, the splendour is dead, the summer is gone. The midnight rain buries it away where it has buried all sound but its own.

I am alone in the dark still night, and my ear listens to the rain piping in the gutters and roaring softly in the trees of the world. Even so will the rain fall darkly upon the grass over the grave when my ears can hear it no more. I have been glad of the sound of rain, and wildly sad of it in the past; but that is all over as if it had never been; my eye is dull and my heart beating evenly and quietly; I stir neither foot nor hand; I shall not be quieter when I lie under the wet grass and the rain falls, and I of less account than the grass. The summer is gone, and never can it return. There will never be any summer any more, and I am weary of everything. I stay because I am too weak to go. I crawl on because it is easier than to stop. I put my face to the window. There is nothing out there but the blackness and sound of rain. Neither when I shut my eyes can I see anything. I am alone. Once I heard through the rain a bird's questioning watery cry—once only and suddenly. It seemed content, and the solitary note brought up against me the order of nature, all its beauty, exuberance, and everlastingness like an accusation. I am not a part of nature. I am alone. There is nothing else in my world but my dead heart and brain within me and the rain without. Once there was summer, and a great heat and splendour over the earth terrified me and asked me what I could show that was worthy of such an earth. It smote and humiliated me, yet I had eyes to behold it, and I prostrated myself, and by adoration made myself worthy of the splendour. Was I not once blind to the splendour because there was something within me equal to itself? What was it? Love . . . a name! . . . a word! . . . less than the watery question of the bird out in the rain. The rain has drowned the splendour. Everything is drowned and dead, all that was once lovely and alive in the world, all that had once been alive and was memorable though dead is now dung for a future that is infinitely less than the falling dark rain. For a moment the mind's eye and ear pretend to see and hear what the eye and ear themselves once knew with delight. The rain denies. There is nothing to be seen or heard, and there never was. Memory, the last chord of the lute, is broken. The rain has been and will be for ever over the earth. There never was anything but the dark rain. Beauty and strength are as nothing to it. Eyes could not flash in it.

I have been lying dreaming until now, and now I have awakened, and there is still nothing but the rain. I am alone. The unborn is not more weak or more ignorant, and like the unborn I wait and wait, knowing neither what has been nor what is to come, because of the rain, which is, has been, and must be. The house is still and silent, and those small noises that make me start are only the imagination of the spirit or they are the rain. There is only the rain for it to feed on and to crawl in. The rain swallows it up as the sea does its own foam. I will lie still and stretch out my body and close my eyes. My breath is all that has been spared by the rain, and that comes softly and at long intervals, as if it were trying to hide itself from the rain. I feel that I am so little I have crept away into a corner and been forgotten by the rain. All else has perished except me and the rain. There is no room for anything in the world but the rain. It alone is great and strong. It alone knows joy. It chants monotonous praise of the order of nature, which I have disobeyed or slipped out of. I have done evilly and weakly, and I have left undone. Fool! you never were alive. Lie still. Stretch out yourself like foam on a wave, and think no more of good or evil. There was no good and no evil. There was life and there was death, and you chose. Now there is neither life nor death, but only the rain. Sleep as all things, past, present, and future, lie still and sleep, except the rain, the heavy, black rain falling straight through the air that was once a sea of life. That was a dream only. The truth is that the rain falls for ever and I am melting into it. Black and monotonously sounding is the midnight and solitude of the rain. In a little while or in an age—for it is all one—I shall know the full truth of the words I used to love, I knew not why, in my days of nature, in the days before the rain: 'Blessed are the dead that the rain rains on.'[5]

(1913)

It is hardly surprising that in this, the weariest of all his books, Thomas felt it necessary to put the words into the mouth of 'a ghostly double'. Three years later he spoke in his own voice in 'Rain':

Rain, midnight rain, nothing but the wild rain
On this bleak hut, and solitude, and me
Remembering again that I shall die
And neither hear the rain nor give it thanks
For washing me cleaner than I have been
Since I was born into this solitude.
Blessed are the dead that the rain rains upon:
But here I pray that none whom once I loved

Is dying tonight or lying still awake
Solitary, listening to the rain,
Either in pain or thus in sympathy
Helpless among the living and the dead,
Like a cold water among broken reeds,
Myriads of broken reeds all still and stiff,
Like me who have no love which this wild rain
Has not dissolved except the love of death,
If love it be for what is perfect and
Cannot, the tempest tells me, disappoint.

(1916)

'What I have done so far,' Thomas wrote to John Freeman, 'have been like quintessences of the best parts of my prose books—not much sharper or more intense, but I hope a little.'[6] In 'Rain' the essence of four pages of *The Icknield Way* has been concentrated into eighteen lines. Or, more precisely, the essence of those four pages has been concentrated into *less than* eighteen lines. For the poem differs in a number of important ways from the earlier outpouring. One change is in location: he is no longer at an inn but in a 'bleak hut'—almost certainly an army hut. A second change concerns his awareness of death. In *The Icknield Way* it is present though passing; in the poem it is a stark certainty:

> Even so will the rain fall darkly upon the grass over the grave when my ears can hear it no more. . . . I shall not be quieter when I lie under the wet grass and the rain falls, and I of less account than the grass. . . . In a little while or in an age—for it is all one—I shall know the full truth of the words I used to love, I knew not why, in my days of nature, in the days before the rain: 'Blessed are the dead that the rain rains on.'

Remembering again that I shall die
And neither hear the rain nor give it thanks
For washing me cleaner than I have been
Since I was born into this solitude.
Blessed are the dead that the rain rains upon:

There is in 'Rain' a sharpened sense of loss as well as release, and the 'truth' of the last statement (which concluded the prose) is less welcome and more doubtful. Death has become a mixed blessing:

But here I pray that none whom once I loved
Is dying tonight or lying still awake
Solitary, listening to the rain,
Either in pain or thus in sympathy
Helpless among the living and the dead,
Like a cold water among broken reeds,
Myriads of broken reeds all still and stiff,
Like me . . .

The projection of his thoughts in this entirely new direction is the third and major change from the prose. There he was exclusively concerned with his own private afflictions, real or induced, and his introspection had no room for the misfortune of others. The poem has been pressured outwards (as the colon indicates) by the magnitude of suffering borne by 'the living and the dead' in France. He prays that no one is in pain or dying; in particular he hopes that no one shares his own position of being helpless 'in sympathy'. The image of the cold water (himself) among, yet unable to sustain, the reeds that are 'broken' (the dead and dying soldiers) reinforces his feeling of helplessness. 'Myriads' shows an unusual awareness of the slaughter that was taking place, while 'still and stiff' instantly suggests the laid-out corpses. Thomas had previously used the phrase in such a context in *Light and Twilight*:

> I felt as though I were looking out of a grave where I lay still and stiff . . .[7]

'*Cold* water' also suggests his own sense of detachment to reflect the words 'whom *once* I loved'. Now he has

no love which this wild rain
Has not dissolved except the love of death,
If love it be for what is perfect and
Cannot, the tempest tells me, disappoint.

'Death, the ultimate response,' wrote Alun Lewis, 'that he, despite himself, desired.'[8] It is the element of conflict suggested by Lewis's 'despite himself' that is most apparent in the closing lines of the poem. The 'If' is important. So too is the division between 'Cannot' and 'disappoint' which entails an emphasis on the last word even though it is made negative. Death, as a personal solution, had to be 'perfect' (i.e. total) in the manner prescribed in this extract from *Beautiful Wales*:

> As will happen with men who love life too passionately, he was often in love with death. He found enjoyment in silence, in darkness, in refraining from deeds, and he longed even to embrace the absolute blank of death, if only he could be just conscious of it; and he envied the solitary tree on a bare plain high up among the hills, under a night sky in winter where the only touch of life and pleasure is the rain.[9]

In the poem Thomas fears that 'the absolute blank of death' is not certain to be 'perfect'. In 'The Sign-Post' he had accepted the possibility of 'a *flaw* in that heaven'; in 'Home'* he feared 'my happiness there,/ Or my pain, might be dreams of return'; in 'Liberty' he actually settled for 'what is *imperfect* . . . with life and earth'. In all three poems he falls back on a restless but still bearable present, and it is this kind of strength out of despair that informs 'Rain'. Even the love which is dissolved is not the feeble self-love of *The Icknield Way*, but a compassion that the rain cannot entirely erase.

2

Bottomley described Thomas's life up to his thirty-sixth year as 'little more than the agony of a swimmer upstream, and in a strong current against which he could scarcely keep his head cleared.'[10] In December 1914 it was as if he suddenly turned and was thereafter borne along by the flow. 'Its most precious quality,' wrote Frost in 'The Figure a Poem Makes', 'will remain its having run itself and carried away the poet with it.'[11] This quality above all distinguishes Thomas's verse. For him the dam had burst; the poems were in flood.

The reason for this turning-point is not beyond enquiry. Both of Thomas's biographers regard the meeting with Frost as crucial:

> During those weeks in the open air, in the evenings talking of life and people and poetry, Frost's influence on Thomas's intellectual life was profound. . . . Through his friendship with Frost, Thomas regained confidence in himself, a confidence that made possible the final expression of self that he found in writing poetry.[12]
>
> (R. P. Eckert)
>
> Now at the beginning of 1914 Edward began to see much more of this remarkable man whose influence upon him was so profound

* *Collected Poems*, p. 156.

that it might be held that he would never have expressed himself in poetry if he had not met Robert Frost.[13]

(John Moore)

Other critics have accepted these opinions without serious qualification:

> Robert Frost . . . helped to thrust Thomas out of the old nest of prose.[14]
>
> (Edward Garnett)
>
> Perhaps Thomas would have written no poetry, his death coming when it did, if he had not known Frost; it seems certain he would have written less.[15]
>
> (H. Coombes)
>
> He was not the original poet who can work out a new poetic language for himself. It was Robert Frost who found Edward Thomas's tongue for him. So, at last, Thomas the Doubter became Thomas the Rhymer.[16]
>
> (C. Day Lewis)
>
> The debt we owe to Frost is great: had he not been able to persuade Thomas of his true vocation it is more than likely that we would have been wholly deprived of the Englishman's poems.[17]
>
> (Vernon Scannell)

Occasionally the distinction between 'being influenced by' and 'being under the influence of' is lost, and Thomas is miscast in the role of disciple to Frost's saviour:

> His star of hope was about to fade from his sky, when a sudden creative impulse was born in upon him by our New England poet Robert Frost, who pierced the clouds of disillusionment, and the spirit of self-distrust, thus making him see what was native in him.[18]
>
> (Harold Roy Brennan)
>
> Thomas, delicate, airy, almost feminine, sits worshipping his new-found friend. The smoke of conflict still hovers as a wraith about his devoted head.[19]
>
> (Louis Mertins)
>
> While it is true that there is no school of Frost, he has had some effect on some poets. One glances at them not for what they reveal about modern poetry but for what they reveal about Frost's poetry . . . [Thomas's] friendship with Robert Frost and his admiration for

> Frost's poetry seem to have freed him from bondage. He suddenly wrote what he essentially wished to write, poems rather than charming and respectable essays about other writers or the English countryside. . . . One can feel that had Thomas lived his poetry might have asserted its individuality . . .[20]
>
> (Radcliffe Squires)

Thomas's friendship with Frost was important. It was not *that* important.

Frost's own comments on the subject were modest in the extreme. In a letter to John W. Haines after Thomas's death, he wrote: 'We didn't have to wait till he was dead to find out how much we loved him. Others pitied him for his misfortunes and he accepted their pity. I don't know what he looked for from me in his black days when I first met him. All he ever got was admiration for the poet in him before he had written a line of poetry.'[21] His laconic explanation of how he helped transform Thomas's work also made light of any 'profound' influence on his part:

> Edward Thomas had about lost patience with the minor poetry it was his business to review. He was suffering from a life of subordination to his inferiors. Right at that moment he was writing as good poetry as anybody alive, but in prose form where it did not declare itself and gain him recognition. I referred him to paragraphs in his book *In Pursuit of Spring* and told him to write it in verse form in exactly the same cadence. That's all there was to it. His poetry declared itself in verse form, and in the year before he died he took his place where he belonged among the English poets.[22]

Perhaps the following was one of those paragraphs from the abovementioned book to which he referred Thomas:

> All the thrushes of England sang at that hour, and against that background of myriads I heard two or three singing their frank, clear notes in a mad eagerness to have all done before dark; for already the blackbirds were chinking and shifting places along the hedgerows. And presently it was dark, but for a lamp at an open door, and silent, but for a chained dog barking, and a pine tree moaning over the house. When the dog ceased, an owl hooted, and when the owl ceased I could just hear the river Frome roaring steadily over a weir far off.[23]
>
> (1914)

Later that year Thomas followed his advice in 'March':

> What did the thrushes know? Rain, snow, sleet, hail,
> Had kept them quiet as the primroses.
> They had but an hour to sing. On boughs they sang,
> On gates, on ground; they sang while they changed perches
> And while they fought, if they remembered to fight:
> So earnest were they to pack into that hour
> Their unwilling hoard of song before the moon
> Grew brighter than the clouds . . .
>
> (1914)

'All he ever got,' confessed Frost, 'was admiration for the poet in him before he had written a line of poetry.' Certainly the 'frank, clear notes' of *In Pursuit of Spring* are a tribute to Thomas's self-critical faculty which had enabled him to work out that new poetic language *for himself* before he met the American. Moreover, the latter's advice, so often quoted as momentous, amounted to no more than what Thomas's friends had been telling him and each other for years. Compare the conclusions reached by Bottomley in conversation with Thomas, and by Hudson in a letter to Garnett:

> I said as much to him, and that I believed they [paragraphs in *The Heart of England*] would make their effect better if they had been conceived in actual verse from the first. He replied 'It is strange you should say this: I spent the night at de la Mare's on my way North to you, and he said almost the same thing.' I felt sure there was a solution for him on those lines, and that he would find new liberation in verse; and so I urged the experiment on him. He smiled and only said 'I do not know how.'[24]
>
> (Gordon Bottomley)
>
> *The Happy-Go-Lucky Morgans* interested me greatly, but I don't think it will interest the reading public one bit. It interested me because of my esteem and affection for him (and my admiration too), also because I believe he has taken the wrong path and is wandering lost in the vast wilderness . . . he is essentially a poet, one would say of the Celtic variety, and this book shows it, I think, more than any of the others . . . I should say that in his nature books and fiction he leaves all there's best and greatest in him unexpressed . . . and I believe that if Thomas had the courage or the opportunity

> to follow his own genius he could do better things than these. . . . You noticed probably in reading the book that every person described in it . . . are one and all just Edward Thomas. A poet trying to write prose fiction often does this.[25]
>
> (W. H. Hudson)

Frost's advice was no more than what he claimed it was—the appreciation and encouragement of a friend. The decisive influence came from elsewhere.

'Thinking back on my own writing,' Alun Lewis wrote in June 1943, 'it all seemed to mature of a sudden between the winter of 1939 and the following autumn. Can't make it out. Was it Gweno [his wife] and the Army? What a combination! ! ! Beauty and the Beast!'[26] Thomas's poetry matured of a sudden between the winter of 1914 and the following autumn, and the combination that made him a poet was Frost and the war, with the war (as in the case of Alun Lewis) predominant. It broke out in August 1914, while he was staying with Frost in Ledington. The following month he recalled the period in his essay 'This England', which bore the seed of his poem 'The Sun Used to Shine'. As in the poem, Thomas celebrates their friendship by describing their walks, their conversations, and the surrounding Herefordshire countryside. Unlike the poem, the essay ends on this note of urgent soliloquy:

> I thought, like many other people, what things that same new moon sees eastward about the Meuse in France. Of those who could see it there, not blinded by smoke, pain, or excitement, how many saw it and heeded? I was deluged, in a second stroke, by another thought, or something that overpowered thought. All I can tell is it seemed to me that either I had never loved England, or I had loved it foolishly, aesthetically, like a slave, not having realized that it was not mine unless I were willing and prepared to die rather than leave it as Belgian women and old men and children had left their country. Something I had omitted. Something, I felt, had to be done before I could look again composedly at English landscape . . . at the purple-headed wood-betony with two pairs of dark leaves on a stiff stem, who stood sentinel among the grasses or bracken by the hedge-side or wood's edge. What he stood sentinel for I did not know, any more than what I had got to do.[27]

It is astonishing that John Moore can write of the same period: 'So August passed, *like a dream; and the war scarcely touched or disturbed the poets at all. Indeed, they rarely mentioned it.*'[28] 'This England' reveals the *immediate* impact of the war on Thomas. It was for him that 'revolution' or 'catastrophe' or 'improbable development' he had hoped for since 1905. At a blow it unburdened him of most of his hack work and left him with a sense of freedom never before experienced. 'I haven't any work now,' he told Hudson in November, when he was at last being 'thrust out of the old nest of prose'. 'But I don't find the war shuts me up. In fact it has given me time to please myself with some unprofitable writing, and up to now I have not been hard hit as many are.'[29] The following month his poetry was in spate, coinciding with this period of free time under the stress of indecision as to whether he should enlist or accompany Frost to America. If H. Coombes's earlier statement were modified, we might say: 'Perhaps Thomas would have written no poetry . . . if war had not been declared; it seems certain he would have written less.'

For all his wavering, Thomas's ultimate decision was never in doubt. Already his enlistment was being seriously considered in 'This England', where Frost was finally eclipsed by the shadow of the war:

> All I can tell is, it seemed to me that either I had never loved England, or I had loved it foolishly, aesthetically, *like a slave*, not having realized that it was not mine unless I were willing and prepared to die rather than leave it . . .
>
> (1914)

His rising determination points to the justification he gave for enlisting in 'No Case of Petty Right or Wrong':

> lest
> We lose what never *slaves* and cattle blessed.
>
> (1915)

This resolution is mirrored in his very use of words. Once they were chosen purely for their aesthetic appeal:

> In pursuit of words, which soon *enthrall* him, he goes far rather than deep . . .
>
> (1903)

In 'Words' they are

as dear
As the earth which you *prove*
That we love.

(1915)

The poems spring out of his need to prove that love. Writing to Lascelles Abercrombie in 1915, Frost touched the heart of the matter. 'I forgot to mention the war in this letter,' he wrote. 'And I ought to mention it, if only to remark that I think it has made some sort of new man and a poet out of Edward Thomas.'[30] It was an idea he re-worked in his elegy 'To E.T.'—

First soldier, and then poet, and then both

—which is chronologically inaccurate (as he knew), though it does place a certain emphasis where it belongs. Thomas himself testified as much in 'There Was A Time':

There was a time when this poor frame was whole
And I had youth and never another care,
Or none that should have troubled a strong soul.
Yet, except sometimes in a frosty air
When my heels hammered out a melody
From pavements of a city left behind,
I never would acknowledge my own glee
Because it was less mighty than my mind
Had dreamed of. Since I could not boast of strength
Great as I wished, weakness was all my boast.
I sought yet hated pity till at length
I earned it. Oh, too heavy was the cost!
But now that there is something I could use
My youth and strength for, I deny the age,
The care and weakness that I know—refuse
To admit I am unworthy of the wage
Paid to a man who gives up eyes and breath
For what would neither ask nor heed his death.

(1916)

The truth of Frost's remark to Haines that 'others pitied him for his misfortunes and he accepted their pity' is openly admitted: 'I sought yet hated pity till at length/I earned it.' The 'But now' marks the change accomplished by the war. It is from the Edward Thomas whom Pound condescendingly described as 'a mild fellow with no vinegar in his veins'[31] to the Edward Thomas whom Frost recognized as 'some sort of new man and a poet'. The potential strength of his position in 'This England'—'Something had to be done'—is given direction and positive affirmation in the last lines of the poem. He denies his age (he was already old for active military service), and though he would not therefore be asked, he declares himself 'willing and prepared to die'. The poem was written a few months before he volunteered for action in France. Here surely is that new-found 'confidence' which R. P. Eckert attributes to his meeting with Frost, but which both he and Thomas related specifically and solely to the war.

Unlike Alun Lewis, who was a younger man reacting to new experience, Thomas's first response was to his past, with the new experience reacting on the old. John Lehmann writes that it was 'as if, in the last years of his life, under the stress of war and the desperate sense of urgency it gives to the creative artist who is threatened with annihilation by it, he had recovered the whole range of his inspiration over twenty years, so that he could resume and concentrate it in the new medium.'[32] Thomas's own word for this was 'quintessence'. It is the difference between 'unfathomable deep' and 'unfathomable deep/Forest'; between 'Rain' as it might have been written in 1913 and how it was written in 1916; between the initial memory of 'It Was Upon' and its new relation with the present 'after the interval/Of a score years'. Inevitably from the author of such books as *The Heart of England*, *The South Country* and *A Literary Pilgrim in England*, this 'quintessence' involved his own brand of patriotism. C. Day Lewis acknowledged a similar response during the Second War. At that time he was translating Virgil's *Georgics*:

> As I worked on into the summer of 1940, I felt more and more the kind of patriotism which I imagine was Virgil's—the natural piety, the heightened sense of the genius of place, the passion to praise and protect one's roots, or to put down roots somewhere while there is still time, which it takes a seismic event such as a war to reveal to most of us rootless moderns. . . . Again, just as I had never been consciously a patriot, so I had never had much respect for, much sense of obligation to, the past. The inner disturbances created by

> the war threw up my own past before my eyes, giving it new value. . . . A heightened sense of the past—both my own and that which, through the European tradition of Virgil, I shared with many—was added to the enhanced awareness of place, of England, and especially that South-West of England which, because I had been at school there twenty years before, was associated with the *Georgics* I had first read there.[33]

Thomas was another of those 'rootless moderns' though he did have a sense of allegiance to the South Country. In the book of that title, he wrote:

> Yet is this country, though I am mainly Welsh, a kind of home, as I think it is more than any other to those modern people who belong nowhere.[34]

He too had never been 'consciously a patriot'. In *Beautiful Wales*, he declared:

> I do not easily believe in patriotism, in times of peace or war, except as a party cry, or the result of intoxication or an article in a newspaper, unless I am in Wales.[35]

However, with the outbreak of war came 'the passion to praise and protect one's roots,' and this cockney Welshman became a poet more profoundly English than many an Englishman, with a natural piety, a heightened sense of the genius of place ('Older than Clare and Cobbett, Morland and Crome') at the core of his patriotism. So intimately connected are his patriotism and his inspiration that had he followed Frost to America he might have stopped writing altogether.

3

Thomas began to write poetry 'with the inevitable imitation of the forms and tones which he admired in his contemporaries and the older poets, but with an exceptional fidelity to his own thought, feeling, and observation.'* Such 'tones' vary in the following lines from unconscious echo to deliberate allusion:

> My mistress' eyes are nothing like the sun . . .
> (Shakespeare: Sonnet 130)

* His own description of Keats's first book of poems.

There's nothing like the sun as the year dies...
('There's Nothing Like the Sun')

the wandering moon,
Riding near her highest noon...
(Milton: 'Il Penseroso')

the moon on high
Riding the dark surge silently...
('Two Pewits')

Forlorn! the very word is like a bell
To toll me back from thee to my sole self!
(Keats: 'Ode to a Nightingale')

But the end fell like a bell:
The bower was scattered...
('Ambition')

For love, and beauty, and delight,
There is no death nor change: their might
Exceeds our organs, which endure
No light, being themselves obscure.
(Shelley: 'The Sensitive Plant')

How weak and little is the light,
All the universe of sight,
Love and delight,
Before the might,
If you love it not, of night.
('Out in the Dark')

As I can't leap from cloud to cloud, I want to wander from road to road. That little path there by the clipped hedge goes up to the high road. I want to go up that path and to walk along the high road, and so on and on and on, and to know all kinds of people. Did you ever think that the roads are the only things that are endless: that one can walk on and on, and never be stopped by a gate or a wall? They are the serpent of eternity. I wonder they have never been worshipped. What are the stars beside them? They never meet one another. The roads are the only things that are infinite. They are all endless.[36]
(Yeats: *Where There Is Nothing*)

I love roads:
The goddesses that dwell
Far along invisible
Are my favourite gods.

Roads go on
While we forget, and are
Forgotten like a star
That shoots and is gone.

('Roads')

The number of influences which may impinge on Thomas's consciousness in the course of a single poem is evinced by 'October'. In the chapter *The Road Not Taken*, its initial impulse was traced as far back as his first book, published eighteen years earlier when the poetic 'tones' were supplied chiefly by Shelley and Keats. As an adolescent Thomas had tried to outglitter Keats; as a mature critic he rejected those poems of his which were 'crammed with loveliness and love of loveliness', praising them only when 'the verse disencumbers itself, running fresh as well as full.'[37] In his *Keats* (1916), he quoted the whole of the opening paragraph of *Hyperion* (which includes the passage below) as an example of 'pure Keats, though even farther than the odes from the sumptuousness of "St. Agnes".'[38] In 1897 he had imitated the lines in *The Woodland Life* (see page 110); in 1915 he returned to them as a poet:

No stir of air was there,
Not so much life as on a summer's day
Robs not one light seed from the feather'd grass,
But where the dead leaf fell, there did it rest.

(Keats)

and the wind travels too light
To shake the fallen birch leaves from the fern;
The gossamers wander at their own will.

(Thomas)

The echo 'no stir'/'stirless' shows that the young prose writer had Keats in mind. In 'October' a light wind *is* present to suggest the delicacy and fragility of the scene, at once out of time ('fresh again and new/As Spring') and yet not timeless.

Keats's influence is slight and blends with that of Wordsworth. In *The Happy-Go-Lucky Morgans* Thomas had casually borrowed a phrase from 'Lines Composed upon Westminster Bridge'; in the poem he brilliantly adapted it:

The river glideth at his own sweet will.

(Wordsworth)

. . . gardens where everything tall, old-fashioned, and thick grew at their own sweet will.[39]

The gossamers wander at their own will.

(Thomas)

'Sweet' has been omitted, making the line sound at first like four-stress instead of the five-stress of the other lines—'The góssamers wánder at their ówn wíll'. But, as C. Day Lewis observes, if the last syllable of 'gossamers' is accented we get 'a sort of airy sustaining of the word, and a movement in the whole line which remarkably suggests the light, erratic, wayward flight of gossamers, changing speed at the slightest variation of the wind's force—"The góssamérs wánder at their ówn wíll".'[40]

As the poem moves from its richly detailed opening to focus on the poet's inward mood, it does so with the help of a momentary echo from Frost's 'In the Home Stretch':

'I think you see
More than you like to own to out that window.'

'No; for besides the things I tell you of,
I only see the years. They come and go
In alternation with the weeds, the field,
The wood.'

(Frost)

. . . and now I might
As happy be as earth is beautiful,
Were I some other or with earth could turn
In alternation of violet and rose,
Harebell and snowdrop, at their season due,
And gorse that has no time not to be gay.

(Thomas)

In the remaining lines this raw, personal feeling struggles towards generalized statement. If the opening of the poem derived from *The Woodland Life*, the germ of its conclusion lay in a passage from *The South Country* concerning memories and happiness. Here again is the 'exceptional fidelity to his own thought, feeling, and observation':

I do not recall happiness in them, yet the moment that I return to them in fancy I am happy. Something like this is true also of much later self-conscious years. I cannot—I am not tempted to—allow what then spoiled the mingling of the elements of joy to reappear when I look back. The reason, perhaps, is that only an inmost true self that desires and is in harmony with joy can perform these long journeys, and when it has set out upon them it sheds those gross incrustations which were our curse before.[41]

> But if this be not happiness—who knows?
> Some day I shall think this a happy day,
> And this mood by the name of melancholy
> Shall no more blackened and obscured be.

Of all his contemporaries it was Frost to whom he came closest, in friendship and in practice, and it would be as unwise to underestimate as to exaggerate his influence. The debt in the following lines is obvious. In each case the first extract is from Frost:

> There is a singer everyone has heard . . .
> ('The Oven Bird')
> Everybody has met one such man as he . . .
> ('Lob')

> Each circling each with vague unearthly cry . . .
> ('Waiting')
> Each facing each as in a coat of arms . . .
> ('Cock-Crow')

> 'Warren,' she said, 'he has come home to die:
> You needn't be afraid he'll leave you this time.'
>
> 'Home,' he mocked gently.
>
> 'Yes, what else but home?
> It all depends on what you mean by home . . .'
> ('The Death of the Hired Man')

> 'How quick,' to someone's lip
> The words came, 'will the beaten horse run home!'
>
> The word 'home' raised a smile in us all three,
> And one repeated it, smiling just so
> That all knew what he meant and none would say.
> (' "Home" ')

A more extended comparison illustrates several further correspondences. 'Mowing' was a poem to which Frost drew Thomas's particular attention:

> There was never a sound beside the wood but one,
> And that was my long scythe whispering to the ground.
> What was it it whispered? I knew not well myself;
> Perhaps it was something about the heat of the sun,
> Something, perhaps, about the lack of sound—
> And that was why it whispered and did not speak.
> It was no dream of the gift of idle hours,
> Or easy gold at the hand of fay or elf:
> Anything more than the truth would have seemed too weak
> To the earnest love that laid the swale in rows,
> Not without feeble-pointed spikes of flowers
> (Pale orchises), and scared a bright green snake.
> The fact is the sweetest dream that labour knows.
> My long scythe whispered and left the hay to make.

In 'The Manor Farm' there is a direct verbal echo of the first line of this poem:

> There was no sound but one.
> Three cart-horses were looking over a gate
> Drowsily through their forelocks, swishing their tails
> Against a fly, a solitary fly.

The cadence that rounds off this extract is also Frostian. Compare

> How like a fly, how very like a fly

from 'The White-Tailed Hornet'. Finally, the reticence of the scythe in the fifth line of 'Mowing'

> And that was why it whispered and did not speak

is transferred to the breeze in Thomas's poem 'I Never Saw that Land Before':

> The blackthorns down along the brook
> With wounds yellow as crocuses
> Where yesterday the labourer's hook
> Had sliced them cleanly; and the breeze
> That hinted all and nothing spoke.

This in turn develops into a description of Thomas's poetic method:

if I could sing
What would not even whisper my soul
As I went on my journeying,

I should use, as the trees and birds did,
A language not to be betrayed;
And what was hid should still be hid
Excepting from those like me made
Who answer when such whispers bid.

The sound of the scythe has been fully integrated into his own imagination and personality.

More important in 'Mowing' is the sense of the actual moment—'The fact is the sweetest dream that labour knows'. In 'Swedes' Thomas's reaction was somewhat different:

They have taken the gable from the roof of clay
On the long swede pile. They have let in the sun
To the white and gold and purple of curled fronds
Unsunned. It is a sight more tender-gorgeous
At the wood-corner where Winter moans and drips
Than when, in the Valley of the Tombs of Kings,
A boy crawls down into a Pharaoh's tomb
And, first of Christian men, beholds the mummy,
God and monkey, chariot and throne and vase,
Blue pottery, alabaster, and gold.

But dreamless long-dead Amen-hotep lies.
This is a dream of Winter, sweet as Spring.

Far from dismissing his own 'dream of . . . easy gold', Thomas allows it to expand naturally out of his description of the clamp of swedes. Moreover, he does not merely assert that one element is less vital than the other: he creates the measure of difference between them. Details of the first five lines are paralleled in the second five in order to point to that difference. The house metaphor ('gable', 'roof') is paralleled by the house of death ('tomb'); the common majesty of the swedes ('white and gold and purple') is reflected in the regal treasure hoard ('Blue pottery, alabaster, and gold'); lastly, the promise of 'curled fronds/ Unsunned' finds a sterile counterpart in 'mummy'. This theme is clinched in the concluding lines with the decisiveness of the sonnet's final couplet:

> But dreamless long-dead Amen-hotep lies.
> This is a dream of Winter, sweet as Spring.

The comparison of wonder in the latter half of the poem is drawn from *The Heart of England*. In the relevant passage, Thomas rejoices in the coming dawn after leaving London behind him:

> Suddenly my mind went back to the high dark cliffs of Westminster Abbey, the blank doors and windows of endless streets, the devouring river, the cold gleam before dawn, and then with a shudder forgot them and saw the flowers and heard the birds with such a joy as when the ships from Tarshish, after three blank years, again unloaded apes and peacocks and ivory, and men upon the quay looked on; or as, when a man has mined in the dead desert for many days, he suddenly enters an old tomb, and making a light, sees before him vases of alabaster, furniture adorned with gold and blue enamel and the figures of gods, a chariot of gold, and a silence perfected through many ages in the company of death and of the desire of immortality.[42]

'Fact' and 'dream' in the prose are comparable ('with such a joy as when . . .'); in the poem the 'fact' *is* 'the sweetest dream' ('more tender-gorgeous/. . . Than when . . .'). Thomas eventually reaches the same conclusion as Frost, but by an approach that is altogether his own.

Generally these essential differences between the two poets are more pronounced than their superficial resemblances. Thomas, though he told Frost that he was the 'only begetter' of his poetry, soon made a declaration of independence. 'Since the first take off,' he wrote to John Freeman in 1915, 'they haven't been Frosty very much or so I imagine'.[43] 'Take off' could refer to deliberate imitation or to the sudden flight of his poetry. The latter supposition would seem more correct, for Thomas was never pleased if his work was regarded as imitation Frost:

> W. H. Davies never forgave himself for his unintentional blunder in telling Thomas, who showed him three of his earliest poems without disclosing their authorship, that they were certainly the work of Robert Frost—a remark that pained Thomas as it served to confirm his lack of faith in the individuality of his work.[44]

Davies's remark was more likely to irritate Thomas than 'confirm his lack of faith in the individuality of his work'. Certainly there is a shade of irritation rather than resignation in this reply to W. H. Hudson: 'I had quite enough ups and downs reading your letter first, though I was really very glad of it all. I would very much rather know that you like or don't wholly like a thing than that somebody else thinks it a pity I ever read Frost, etc.'[45]

Thomas lacked nothing in artistic spirit and his poetry reveals a mind and personality quite distinct from the American's. W. W. Gibson's first-hand portraits in 'The Golden Room' sharply distinguish the two men. Frost was invariably the life and soul of the occasion as he

> kept on and on and on,
> In his slow New England fashion, for our delight,
> Holding us with shrewd turns and racy quips,
> And the rare twinkle of his grave blue eyes.

It is not difficult to imagine him relating a 'stretcher' such as this from 'New Hampshire':

> I knew a man who failing as a farmer
> Burned down his farmhouse for the fire insurance,
> And spent the proceeds on a telescope
> To satisfy a life-long curiosity
> About our place among the infinities.
> And how was that for other-worldliness?

The anecdote was alien to Thomas's deeply introspective nature that 'hinted all and nothing spoke'. Gibson portrayed his occasional contribution as 'a murmured dry half-heard aside'—the tone of such a poem as 'When He Should Laugh':

> When he should laugh the wise man knows full well:
> For he knows what is truly laughable.
> But wiser is the man who laughs also,
> Or holds his laughter, when the foolish do.

A second example should underline this contrast. First, 'The Wrights' Biplane', followed by a stanza from 'Tall Nettles':

> This biplane is the shape of human flight.
> Its name might better be First Motor Kite.

Its makers' name—Time cannot get that wrong,
For it was writ in heaven doubly Wright.

(Frost)

This corner of the farmyard I like most:
As well as any bloom upon a flower
I like the dust on the nettles, never lost
Except to prove the sweetness of a shower.

(Thomas)

Frost's poem is a public epigram and its heavy-handed pun presupposes and depends for its effect upon a listener (or reader) just as much as the rhetorical question in the 'New Hampshire' extract. In Gibson's words, Frost talked and wrote 'for *our* delight'. The pun was as alien to Thomas as the anecdote. 'Tall Nettles' is in an undertone, overheard rather than heard. It is more hesitant, moving to a subdued revelation that unfolds by surprise in the last line. Nothing could be further from the public epigram.

Frost's tone denotes his greater all-round confidence, in himself, in others, and in the world he inhabits. What Gibson called his 'rich and ripe philosophy' contrasts in these examples with the brooding, sceptical nature of Thomas's thoughts:

The mind—is not the heart.
I may yet live, as I know others live,
To wish in vain to let go with the mind—
Of cares, at night, to sleep; but nothing tells me
That I need learn to let go with the heart.

('Wild Grapes')

Here love ends,
Despair, ambition ends;
All pleasure and all trouble,
Although most sweet or bitter,
Here ends in sleep that is sweeter
Than tasks most noble.

('Lights Out')

'Men work together,' I told him from the heart,
'Whether they work together or apart.'

('The Tuft of Flowers')

Every one of us
This morning at our tasks left nothing said,

In spite of many words. We were sealed thus,
Like tombs.

('That Girl's Clear Eyes')

Earth's the right place for love:
I don't know where it's likely to go better.

('Birches')

'I did not know it was the earth I loved
Until I tried to live there in the clouds
And the earth turned to cloud.'

('Wind and Mist')

And were an epitaph to be my story
I'd have a short one ready for my own.
I would have written of me on my stone:
I had a lover's quarrel with the world.

('The Lesson for Today')

I sit and frame an epitaph—
'Here lies all that no one loved of him
And that loved no one.'

('Beauty')

The speeding of devoted souls
Which God makes his especial care.

('The Trial by Existence')

And God still sits aloft in the array
That we have wrought him, stone-deaf and stone-blind.

('February Afternoon')

Frost was, of course, prone to his own darker moods, of fear and loneliness ('Bereft'), alienation ('Acquainted with the Night'), plaintive regression ('To Earthward'), and even scepticism ('Stars'). In his poetry, however, such moods are fitful in comparison with the force and persistence of Thomas's bleaker vision, and they tend most often to revitalize Frost's general theme of acceptance. Even in those poems where he wishes to steal away, as in 'Birches', he implies only a temporary withdrawal and resists any other interpretation:

So was I once myself a swinger of birches.
And so I dream of going back to be.
It's when I'm weary of considerations,
And life is too much like a pathless wood
Where your face burns and tickles with the cobwebs

Broken across it, and one eye is weeping
From a twig's having lashed across it open.
I'd like to get away from earth awhile
And then come back to it and begin over.
May no fate wilfully misunderstand me
And half grant what I wish and snatch me away
Not to return. Earth's the right place for love:
I don't know where it's likely to go better.
I'd like to go by climbing a birch tree,
And climb black branches up a snow-white trunk
Toward heaven, till the tree could bear no more,
But dipped its top and set me down again.
That would be good both going and coming back.
One could do worse than be a swinger of birches.

It was this psychological theme of attempted escape and necessary return that first attracted Thomas to Frost's verse (and which became a dominant theme in his own poetry). Compare his conclusion to 'Liberty':

If every hour
Like this one passing that I have spent among
The wiser others when I have forgot
To wonder whether I was free or not,
Were piled before me, and not lost behind,
And I could take and carry them away
I should be rich; or if I had the power
To wipe out every one and not again
Regret, I should be rich to be so poor.
And yet I still am half in love with pain,
With what is imperfect, with both tears and mirth,
With things that have an end, with life and earth,
And this moon that leaves me dark within the door.

Frost's impulse was to retreat for strength—so long as he could have it both ways ('good both going and coming back'); Thomas's strength lay in his refusal to retreat. 'Liberty' is characterized by what Leavis in his discussion of the 'Ode to a Nightingale' described as 'an extremely subtle and varied interplay of motions, directed now positively, now negatively. . . . Keats is strictly only half in love with death.'[46] Thomas is just as fastidious as Keats in 'half in love . . . with life and earth'. It is a clarification of life he has made during the course of the poem and 'half in love' is as far as he was ever prepared to go. Yet 'Liberty', for all its apparent darkness, leaves us with a sense of positive assertion; 'Birches', for all its whole-hearted affirmation, leaves us with a curious sense of timidity.

There were other shared psychological traits which Frost preferred not to handle or even to reveal. 'I have written to keep the over-curious out of the secret places of my mind in both my verse and in my letters,' he once told Sidney Cox.[47] Yet one of the most compelling glimpses he did give us of those 'secret places' was in a letter to Susan Hayes Ward dated 10 February 1912:

> Two lonely cross-roads that themselves cross each other I have walked several times this winter without meeting or overtaking so much as a single person on foot or on runners. The practically unbroken condition of both for several days after a snow or a blow proves that neither is much travelled. Judge then how surprised I was the other evening as I came down one to see a man, who to my own unfamiliar eyes and in the dusk looked for all the world like myself, coming down the other, his approach to the point where our paths must intersect being so timed that unless one of us pulled up we must inevitably collide. I felt as if I was going to meet my own image in a slanting mirror. Or say I felt as we slowly converged on the same point with the same noiseless yet laborious strides as if we were two images about to float together with the uncrossing of someone's eyes. I verily expected to take up or absorb this other self and feel the stronger by the addition for the three-mile journey home. But I didn't go forward to the touch. I stood still in wonderment and let him pass by: and that, too, with the fatal omission of not trying to find out by a comparison of lives and immediate and remote interests what could have brought us by crossing paths to the same point in the wilderness at the same moment of nightfall. Some purpose I doubt not, if we could but have made it out. I like a coincidence almost as well as an incongruity.[48]

At first Frost scares himself as this 'convergence of the twain' presages disaster—'unless one of us pulled up we must inevitably collide'. His apprehension is quickened by the familiarity of the apparition:

> I felt as if I was going to meet my own image in a slanting mirror.

The most interesting comparison is the *doppelgänger* in Poe's 'William Wilson', in which two selves do 'inevitably collide':

> A large mirror—so at first it seemed to me in my confusion—now stood where none had been perceptible before, and, as I stepped up to it in extremity of terror, mine own image, but with features all pale and dabbled in blood, advanced to meet me with a feeble and tottering gait.

Frost shies away from so daunting a prospect to consider a more favourable alternative:

> Or say I felt as we slowly converged on the same point with the same noiseless yet laborious strides as if we were two images about to float together with the uncrossing of someone's eyes.

He used a similar image of integration in 'Two Tramps in Mud Time':

> But yield who will to their separation,
> My object in living is to unite
> My avocation and my vocation
> As my two eyes make one in sight.

Similarly, in the letter, his primary object is 'to unite':

> I verily expected to take up or absorb this other self and feel the stronger by the addition for the three-mile journey home.

The threat of collision has been successfully eliminated ('collide . . . float together . . . absorb'). But even at what promises to be the most opportune moment Frost remains apart ('I didn't go forward to the touch'), shrugs his shoulders ('Some purpose I doubt not . . .'), and passes off the experience ('I like a coincidence . . .'). He reduces it finally to a casual encounter.

Thomas's 'secret places' were equally disturbing. In 1911, on the verge of complete mental breakdown, he wrote to MacAlister of the latest remedy prescribed for him (vegetarianism!):

> I hope it will cure my head, which is almost always wrong now—a sort of conspiracy going on in it which leaves me only a joint tenancy and a perpetual scare of the other tenant and wonder what he will do.[49]

'The other tenant' became 'The Other Man' in *In Pursuit of Spring*[50] and simply 'The Other' in the poem of that title. At an inn the narrator of the poem realizes that ahead of him is a man so like himself that others cannot tell the difference between them. At once he gives chase:

> I travelled fast, in hopes I should
> Outrun that other. What to do
> When caught, I planned not. I pursued
> To prove the likeness, and, if true,
> To watch until myself I knew.

Even the syntax makes him the pursuer of himself. It is as if the poem begins at the point where Frost dismissed the experience. His reaction was to '*stand still* in wonderment' and so let the opportunity for greater self-knowledge ('a comparison of lives and immediate and remote interests') slip through his fingers; Thomas's poem has an acute sense of urgency which can only be satisfied by some measure of understanding:

> I was more eager than before
> To find him out and to confess,
> To bore him and to let him bore . . .

The background shifts from forest to inn, street to country road, as the scent is picked up. At last there is as near a confrontation as is possible. For a moment it seems that they too must 'inevitably collide':

> —amid a tap-room's din
> Loudly he asked for me, began
> To speak, as if it had been a sin,
> Of how I thought and dreamed and ran
> After him thus, day after day:
> He lived as one under a ban
> For this: what had I got to say?

'Under a ban' is again reminiscent of 'William Wilson':

> 'Scoundrel!' I said, in a voice husky with rage, while every syllable I uttered seemed as new fuel to my fury, 'scoundrel! accursed villain! you shall not—you *shall not* dog me unto death!'

There is nothing fortunate after all in their meeting and Thomas does not go forward to the touch—'I said nothing. I slipped away.' But it is out of a fuller recognition of the situation than was gained by Frost.

He has learnt that his two selves, though irrevocably linked, are irrevocably hostile:

And now I dare not follow after
Too close. I try to keep in sight,
Dreading his frown and worse his laughter.
I steal out of the wood to light;
I see the swift shoot from the rafter
By the inn door: ere I alight
I wait and hear the starlings wheeze
And nibble like ducks: I wait his flight.
He goes: I follow: no release
Until he ceases. Then I also shall cease.

It was not until 1914 that Frost turned his own experience into poetry. 'The Road Not Taken' seems, however, at first sight to have little connection with it:

Two roads diverged in a yellow wood,
And sorry I could not travel both
And be one traveller, long I stood
And looked down one as far as I could
To where it bent in the undergrowth;

Then took the other, as just as fair,
And having perhaps the better claim,
Because it was grassy and wanted wear;
Though as for that the passing there
Had worn them really about the same,

And both that morning equally lay
In leaves no step had trodden black.
Oh, I kept the first for another day!
Yet knowing how way leads on to way,
I doubted if I should ever come back.

I shall be telling this with a sigh
Somewhere ages and ages hence:
Two roads diverged in a wood, and I—
I took the one less travelled by,
And that has made all the difference.

'You have to be careful of that one; it's a tricky poem—very tricky,' was one of Frost's favourite warnings. And after its publication in *The Atlantic Monthly* for August 1915, he wrote to Louis Untermeyer: 'Even here I am only fooling my way along as I was in the poems in the Atlantic (particularly in The Road Not Taken). . . . The best of your parody of me was that it left me in no doubt as to where I was hit. I'll bet not half a dozen people can tell who was hit and where he was hit by my Road Not Taken.'[51] He subsequently explained that the origin of the poem lay in his amusement at the familiar mannerism of a friend, who would often regret the choice of direction he had made for one of their walks, sighing for what he might have shown Frost if they had taken a 'better' direction. He hoped that the poem would pivot on the phrase 'I shall be telling this with a sigh', the 'sigh' being alien to his own puritan nature. The subject of the poem was, in short, meant to be Thomas.[52]

This 'explanation' seems no more than a further attempt to veil those 'secret places' of his mind from the over-curious. For although basic changes have been made, there is still sufficient evidence to suggest that the actual origin of the poem precedes his friendship with Thomas and owes more to the strange meeting with his other self. The opening of letter and poem are similar:

> Two lonely cross-roads that themselves cross each other . . .
>
> (1912)
>
> Two roads diverged in a yellow wood . . .
>
> (1914)

The isolation is the same:

> The practically unbroken condition of both for several days after a snow or a blow proves that neither is much travelled.
>
> And both that morning equally lay
> In leaves no step had trodden black.

The anticipation of the first narrator is not unlike the regret of the second:

> I verily expected to take up or absorb this other self and feel the stronger by the addition for the three-mile journey home.
>
> And sorry I could not travel both
> And be one traveller . . .

Even the 'sigh' on which Frost claimed the poem should pivot is latent in the letter:

> I stood still . . . and let him pass by . . . with the fatal omission of not trying to find out . . . what could have brought us . . . to the same point in the wilderness at the same moment of nightfall.

> I shall be telling this with a sigh
> Somewhere ages and ages hence:
> Two roads diverged in a wood, and I—
> I took the one less travelled by,
> And that has made all the difference.

Frost sighs for a 'fatal omission' which, in the poem, 'has made all the difference'. This last phrase introduces a more positive force than either context seems to warrant. Is it used in a negative sense to prolong the note of wistful regret? Or is Frost allowing the natural affirmation of the phrase to emerge—and, if so, why 'sigh' at all?

The remoteness of 'The Road Not Taken' from Thomas's predicament is shown by 'The Sign-Post', in which he faces a similar choice:

> I read the sign. Which way shall I go?
> A voice says: You would not have doubted so
> At twenty. Another voice gentle with scorn
> Says: At twenty you wished you had never been born.

In this poem two sides of his nature are brought together in minor conflict as a contemptuous ironic voice is directed against the melancholic 'first voice'. Again the question of age is central. The first voice looks back to an illusory youth ('At twenty') when there was no uncertainty; the scornful retort of the second voice immediately dispels that illusion. The first then looks to age ('sixty') with a wish to know what the future holds. The second voice answers with customary realism:

> 'You shall see; but either before or after,
> Whatever happens, it must befall,
> A mouthful of earth to remedy all
> Regrets and wishes shall freely be given;
> And if there be a flaw in that heaven
> 'Twill be freedom to wish, and your wish may be
> To be here or anywhere talking to me,
> No matter what the weather, on earth,
> At any age between death and birth . . .'

The only certainty is death, but if even oblivion ('heaven') is not total and he is free to wish, he may long to be on earth '*At any age*', despite the attendant difficulties and the uncertainty of life. The poem ends as it began with the difficulty of choice, the uncertainty of direction. He is still left 'Wondering where he shall journey, O where?' It was a question he was beginning to answer in his poetry.

9. Corporal, April 1916

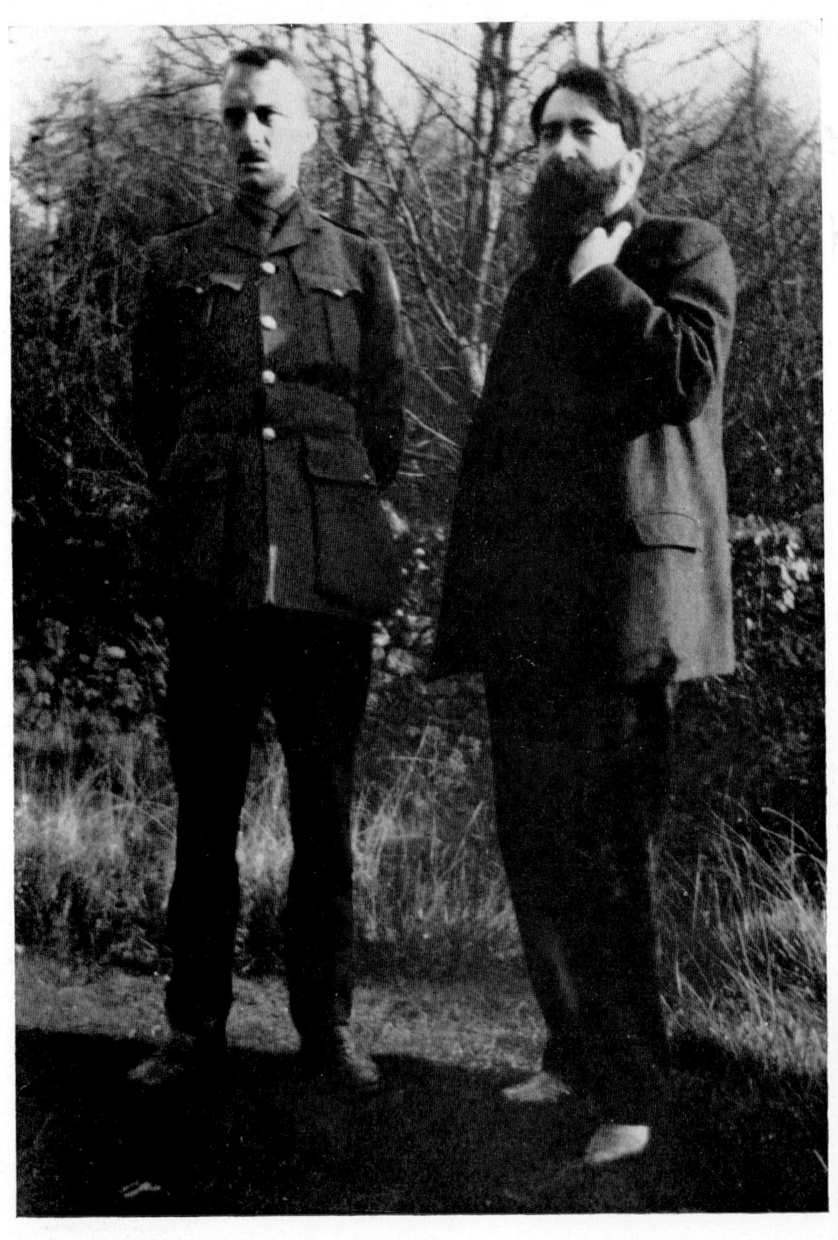

10. The Last Photograph: Edward Thomas and Gordon Bottomley at the Sheiling, November 1916

9

ROADS TO FRANCE

The War Poetry

> I knew the voice that called you
> Was soft and neutral as the sky . . .
> growing clearer,
> More urgent as all else dissolved away . . .
> Till suddenly, at Arras, you possessed that hinted land.
> ALUN LEWIS: 'To Edward Thomas'

I

As a war poet Thomas is virtually ignored. His poems are seldom included in anthologies of war poetry, and if his name is mentioned in critical studies it is largely for the sake of comprehensive appearances. The general feeling was summarized in 1947 by Athalie Bushnell:

> Although the background to his writing was often an army hut or trench, yet very little of his poetry actually takes war or war incidents as its subject. His poetry is nature poetry, taking simplicity, wonder and longing as its keynotes.[1]

In *Edward Thomas* (1956), H. Coombes categorized 'between eighty and ninety' of his poems as 'nature poems' (this description is qualified) but found only 'six or seven war poems'.[2] John H. Johnston in *English Poetry of the First World War* (1964) dismissed him in a single reference:

> Unlike Francis Ledwidge and Edward Thomas, who refused to let the conflict interfere with their nostalgic rural visions, Blunden successfully adapted his talent for unpretentious landscape description to the scenes of war.[3]

Only a year later in *Heroes' Twilight* (1965), Bernard Bergonzi compared Thomas with Blunden:

> . . . like Blunden he found a therapeutic and sanative value in contemplating nature, or remembering rural England, in the midst of

violence and destruction. But very few of Thomas's poems are actually about the war, even obliquely: in his loving concentration on the unchanging order of nature and rural society, the war exists only as a brooding but deliberately excluded presence.[4]

The inadequacy of these comments may be seen if they are considered alongside extracts from poems already discussed:

His poetry is nature poetry, taking simplicity, wonder and longing as its keynotes.

(Athalie Bushnell)

wondering,
What of the lattermath to this hoar Spring?

('It Was Upon')

Before the might,
If you love it not, of night.

('Out in the Dark')

Edward Thomas . . . refused to let the conflict interfere with [his] nostalgic rural visions.

(Johnston)

Tall reeds
Like criss-cross bayonets . . .

('Bright Clouds')

Now all roads lead to France
And heavy is the tread
Of the living; but the dead
Returning lightly dance . . .

('Roads')

. . . very few of Thomas's poems are actually about the war, even obliquely: in his loving concentration on the unchanging order of nature and rural society, the war exists only as a brooding but deliberately excluded presence.

(Bergonzi)

And when the war began
To turn young men to dung.

('Gone, Gone Again')

Helpless among the living and the dead,
Like a cold water among broken reeds,
Myriads of broken reeds all still and stiff . . .

('Rain')

Even those anthologists who consider Thomas worthy of inclusion have unwittingly given a false impression of his significance and development. Brian Gardner includes 'No Case of Petty Right or Wrong' and 'No One Cares Less Than I' in his anthology *Up The Line To Death* (1964), and then makes this statement as part of his biographical note:

> Joined the Artists' Rifles, *and was soon in the trenches;* transferred to the Royal Garrison Artillery. *He continued to write his favourite poems of nature and the countryside, even when in the front line, and he wrote few war poems.*[5]

The italicized lines are inaccurate.

I. M. Parsons divides his anthology *Men Who March Away* (1965) into seven sections, each representative of a mood or a subject connected with the war. This allows him 'to try to reflect not only the chronological progress of the war, but also the changing attitude of poets to it.'[6] His first section *Visions of Glory* is introduced by Thomas's poem 'The Trumpet', which is followed by such poems as Julian Grenfell's 'Into Battle', Hardy's 'Men Who March Away' and Brooke's 'Peace'. This section represents

> the mood of optimistic exhilaration with which so many writers, young and old, greeted the outbreak of war. This was the period of euphoria, when it was still possible to believe that war was a tolerably chivalrous affair, offering welcome opportunities for heroism and self-sacrifice, and to hope that this particular war would be over in six months.[7]

Afterwards, four more of Thomas's poems are included in three other sections in order to reflect his 'changing' attitude to the war. 'There Was A Time' and 'As the Team's Head-Brass' appear in *The Pity of War*; 'A Private' appears among *The Dead*; and 'Lights Out' (the last poem but one) appears under *Aftermath*. The impression likely to be gained is that Thomas falls neatly into the familiar pattern of romantic idealist disillusioned by experiencing the horror of actual warfare. Though unintentional, this is a complete misrepresentation of his true development. His attitude to the war was, from the outset, remarkably mature and perceptive, and 'The Trumpet' is not one of those early chauvinistic poems—it is not even an early poem. It was written two years after that initial period of euphoria (when it was obvious that the war would not be over in six months) and only a month separates it from 'Lights Out'. So the circular movement of the anthology is misleading. So too is the apparent change in attitude from 'visions of glory' to 'the pity of war'. Thomas did not go through this process of disillusionment simply because he had no illusions to shed, and, in fact, 'There Was A Time', 'As the Team's Head-Brass' and 'A Private' were written *before* 'The Trumpet'. Finally, all his poetry was written between 1914 and 1916 *before he had been to France*. He wrote no poetry at all in the trenches, so quickly was he killed.*

Thus the above comments by various critics and anthologists are doubly misleading, since they are based on a fundamental error of approach. All of them wrongly assume that Thomas lived to become a trench poet. Athalie Bushnell speaks of the background to his writing as 'an army hut or trench'; Johnston dismisses him for his 'refusal' to adapt himself to 'the scenes of war'; Bergonzi imagines him writing therapeutically 'in the midst of violence and destruction'; both Gardner and Parsons refer to him explicitly as a front-line poet. A correct and more meaningful approach would be to explore his decision to enlist and volunteer for action in France. The whole perspective of his poetry needs to be changed.

2

'If they also serve who only sit and write, poets are doing their work well. Several of them, it seems to me, with names known and unknown, have been turned into poets by the war, printing verse now for the first time. Whatever other virtues they show, courage at least is not lacking—the courage to write for oblivion.' With these words Thomas began a review entitled 'War Poetry' in December 1914. He himself was one of those who had been turned into a poet by the war, but he had no desire to write for oblivion by complying with what the age demanded. Already he was writing 'Deceased'[8] over many books:

> No other class of poetry vanishes so rapidly, has so little chosen from it for posterity. One tiny volume would hold all the patriotic poems surviving in European languages, and originally written, as most of these are today, under the direct pressure of public patriotic

* Helen Thomas confirmed that no poetry was written in France. A check-list of the dates of all but seven of the poems is given in Appendix I.

motives. Where are the poems of Marlborough's wars? Where are the songs sung by the troops for Quebec while Wolfe was reading Gray's 'Elegy'? But for the wars against Napoleon English poetry would have been different, but how many poems directly concerning them, addressed to Englishmen at that moment, do we read now? One of the earliest, I believe, was Coleridge's 'Fears in Solitude: written in April, 1798, during the alarm of an invasion.' But no newspaper or magazine, then or now, would print such a poem, since a large part of it is humble. . . . The poem, one of the noblest of patriotic poems, has been omitted from most of the anthologies. Another odd thing is that a poem included in several anthologies, and perhaps the finest of English martial songs—I mean Blake's 'War Song to Englishmen'—was written in or before 1783, by one who became a red-capped Revolutionary and cared nothing for Pitt's England. What inspired him? The war with the American colonies? More likely, the history of England as he felt it when he saw the Kings in Westminster Abbey and Shakespeare's plays. He wrote from a settled mystic patriotism, which wars could not disturb.

Another poet, touched by the outbreak of war, will be disturbed for some time: he will be more fit for taking up work from the past, if only for relief, though it is possible for a mature man who has seen other wars and is not shaken from his balance to seize the new occasion firmly. Mr. Charles M. Doughty might have done so: Mr. Hardy has done. The period of gestation varies, but few younger men who had been moved to any purpose could be expected to crystallize their thoughts with speed. Supposing they did, who would want their poems? The demand is for the crude, for what everybody is saying or thinking, or is ready to begin saying or thinking. I need hardly say that by becoming ripe for poetry the poet's thoughts may recede far from their original resemblance to all the world's, and may seem to have little to do with daily events. They may retain hardly any colour from 1798 or 1914, and the crowd, deploring it, will naturally not read the poems.

It is a fact that in the past but a small number of poems destined to endure are directly or entirely concerned with the public triumphs, calamities, or trepidations, that helped to beget them. The public, crammed with mighty facts and ideas it will never digest, must look coldly on poetry where already those mighty things have sunk

> away far into 'The still sad music of humanity.' For his insults to their feelings, the newspapers, history, they might call the poet a pro-Boer. They want something raw and solid, or vague and lofty or sentimental. They must have Mr. Begbie to express their thoughts, or 'Tipperary' to drown them. . . .
>
> The writer of . . . patriotic verses appears to be a man who feels himself always or at the time at one with a class, perhaps the whole nation, or he is a smart fellow who can simulate or exaggerate this sympathy. Experience, reality, truth, unless suffused or submerged by popular sentiment, are out of place. . . . It is the hour of the writer who picks up popular views or phrases, or coins them, and has the power to turn them into downright stanzas. Most newspapers have one or more of these gentlemen. They could take the easy words of a statesman, such as 'No price is too high when honour and freedom are at stake', and dish them up so that the world next morning, ready to be thrilled by anything lofty and noble-looking, is thrilled. These poems are not to be attacked any more than hymns. Like hymns, they play with common ideas, with words and names which most people have in their heads at the time. Most seem to me bombastic, hypocritical, or senseless. . . .[9]

The review establishes beyond doubt his attitude to the 'rage of gladness' that greeted the outbreak of war. He restated it succinctly in 'No Case of Petty Right or Wrong':

> I hate not Germans, nor grow hot
> With love of Englishmen, to please newspapers.

The review also explains why he was to remain unpublished during his lifetime (and why he is still read today):

> I need hardly say that by becoming ripe for poetry the poet's thoughts may recede far from their original resemblance to all the world's, and may seem to have little to do with daily events. They may retain hardly any colour from 1798 or 1914, and the crowd, deploring it, will naturally not read the poems.

His own poetry had nothing in common with the rampant patriotism of the 'bardic' phase, and, indeed, seemed to have little to do with the events that were its inspiration. As a result he met with the neglect he foresaw. 'He offered some of these poems to various editors,' his wife recalled, 'but no one had any room for such quiet meditative verse, in which the profound love and knowledge of his country were too subtle in their patriotism for the nation's mood.'[10]

The distinction between subtle (private) patriotism and deliberate (public) patriotism was one that Thomas himself drew several times. In a second review of 1914 he wrote:

> The worst of the poetry being written today is that it is too deliberately, and not inevitably, English. It is for an audience: there is more in it of the shouting of rhetorician, reciter, or politician than of the talk of friends and lovers.[11]

In his essay 'England', he declared that *The Compleat Angler* was for him the most patriotic of books:

> Since the war began I have not met so English a book, a book that filled me so with a sense of England, as this, though I have handled scores of deliberately patriotic works. There, in that sort of work, you get, as it were, the shouting without the crowd, which is ghastly. In Walton's book I touched the antiquity and sweetness of England—English fields, English people, English poetry, all together.[12]

It was this 'inevitable' English quality that he looked for when he compiled his *This England: An Anthology from her Writers* in 1915:

> Building round a few most English poems like 'When icicles hang by the wall'—excluding professedly patriotic writing because it is generally bad and because indirect praise is sweeter and more profound—never aiming at what a committee from Great Britain and Ireland might call complete—I wished to make a book as full of English character and country as an egg is of meat. If I have reminded others, as I did myself continually, of some of the echoes called up by the name of England, I am satisfied.[13]

Into that anthology he slipped 'Haymaking' and 'The Manor Farm' by Edward Easatway. They were among the first of his poems that he ever saw in print, and the occasion was never more suitable. For their inclusion was not a mischievous act by which 'he had his own back'[14] for his numerous rejections. He was rather placing himself in the tradition of writers who had celebrated England, in peace and war. Even the position he gave to his poems is significant. They appear immediately after Coleridge's 'Fears in Solitude', which he described in his earlier review as 'one of the noblest of patriotic poems' though 'no newspaper or magazine, then or now, would print such a poem, since a large part of it is humble.' The same applied to his own instinctive patriotism:

> The ages made her that made us from dust:
> She is all we know and live by, and we trust
> She is good and must endure, loving her so:
> And as we love ourselves we hate her foe.

His cool, tolerant assessment agreed with the spirit of the age no more than Coleridge's in 1798.

'Lob' is the apotheosis of all that he sought for his *This England* anthology and must surely be one of the most patriotic poems ever written. It is 'as full of English character and country as an egg is of meat':

> This is tall Tom that bore
> The logs in, and with Shakespeare in the hall
> Once talked, when icicles hung by the wall.
> (Chaucer—Wordsworth and all true poets were
> His friends, and Cobbett, Bunyan and Latimer . . .)*
>
> He is English as this gate, these flowers, this mire.
> And when at eight years old Lob-lie-by-the-fire
> Came in my books, this was the man I saw.
> He has been in England as long as dove and daw,
> Calling the wild cherry tree the merry tree,
> The rose campion Bridget-in-her-bravery;
> And in a tender mood he, as I guess,
> Christened one flower Love-in-idleness . . .
> From him old herbal Gerard learnt, as a boy,
> To name wild clematis the Traveller's-Joy.
> Our blackbirds sang no English till his ear
> Told him they called his Jan Toy 'Pretty dear' . . .
> 'Twas he first called the Hog's Back the Hog's Back.
> That Mother Dunch's Buttocks should not lack
> Their name was his care. He too could explain
> Totteridge and Totterdown and Juggler's Lane:
> He knows, if anyone. Why Tumbling Bay,
> Inland in Kent, is called so, he might say . . .

* The two lines in parenthesis are so marked on the MS. They were omitted from the printed version.

The poem readily assimilates the line 'when icicles hang by the wall' from *Love's Labour's Lost*, around which he wished to 'build' his anthology. There was also a good reason why Cobbett's name should have been included. 'It was an altogether English name to begin with,' Thomas had written in his introduction to *Rural Rides* in 1912, 'thoroughly native and rustic; and English it remains, pure English, old English, merry English . . . he is one of the few thorough-going countrymen in our literature. . . . His open-air scenes take us back to Chaucer.'[15] The fructifying association of such writers and poets with Lob was closely foreshadowed in *The Country*, where, extolling the lore of one old countryman, Thomas averred: 'You may be sure there were hundreds like him in Shakespeare's time and in Wordsworth's, and if there aren't a good sprinkling of them, generation after generation, I do not know what we shall come to, but I have my fears.'

Such fears are groundless in the poem, for Lob's wisdom is seen to be passed down the ages. In *This England*, Thomas had anthologized an extract from John Gerard's *The Herball* naming Traveller's-Joy:

> It is called commonly *Viorna quasi vias ornans*, of decking and adorning ways and hedges, where people travel, and thereupon I have named it the Traveller's-Joy.[16]

In the poem Lob became that informing master spirit:

> From him old herbal Gerard learnt, as a boy,
> To name wild clematis the Traveller's-Joy.

The couplet immediately following—

> Our blackbirds sang no English till his ear
> Told him they called his Jan Toy 'Pretty dear'

—alludes to the work of another countryman whom Thomas greatly admired, his contemporary Thomas Hardy. His poem 'The Spring Call' was also chosen for *This England*:

> Down Wessex way, when spring's a-shine,
> The blackbird's 'pret-ty de-urr!'
> In Wessex accents marked as mine
> Is heard afar and near . . .
>
> Yes, in this clime at pairing time,
> As soon as eyes can see her

At dawn of day, the proper way
To call is 'pret-ty de-urr!'[17]

Another latter-day inheritor was the eighteenth-century antiquarian William Stukeley. In his introduction to Isaac Taylor's *Words and Places* in 1911, Thomas wrote of him:

> These were the men who made England great, fearing neither man nor God nor philology. There are some such still with us. . . . We have need of men like that to explain 'Eggpie' Lane near the village of Sevenoaks Weald, or Tumbling Bay in a neighbouring parish far inland.[18]

The last name was enshrined in the poem:

He too could explain
Totteridge and Totterdown and Juggler's Lane:
He knows, if anyone. Why Tumbling Bay,
Inland in Kent, is called so, he might say.

The other names to which Thomas refers had all previously appeared in his prose books. 'Totteridge' was mentioned in *A Literary Pilgrim*,[19] 'Totterdown' in *Richard Jefferies*,[20] and 'Juggler's Lane' in *The Icknield Way*.[21] More than any of his poems, 'Lob' was the *quintessence* of the best parts of his work.

Yet it is not a golden treasury of nostalgia. 'Lob' has such sardonic moments as:

Hob being then his name,
He kept the hog that thought the butcher came
To bring his breakfast. 'You thought wrong,' said Hob.

The 'hog' is perhaps an oblique reference to the 'fat patriot' in 'No Case of Petty Right or Wrong':

Beside my hate for one fat patriot
My hatred of the Kaiser is love true.

Wilfred Owen used the same image in 'And I Must Go':

I see a food-hog whet his gold-filled tusk
To eat less bread, and more luxurious rusk.

He too wished on them a savage retribution:

> I wish the Boche would have the pluck to come right in and make a clean sweep of the pleasure boats, and the promenaders on the Spa, and all the stinking Leeds and Bradford war-profiteers now reading *John Bull* on Scarborough Sands.[22]

Lob carries out part of that wish. In all his exploits he shows an admirable sagacity and social conscience:

> And while he was a little cobbler's boy
> He tricked the giant coming to destroy
> Shrewsbury by flood . . .
> . . . as Jack the giant-killer
> He made a name. He too ground up the miller,
> The Yorkshireman who ground men's bones for flour.

Thomas is not far from Owen's 'Leeds and Bradford war-profiteers' (or those at Sheffield whom he had discovered himself in 'Tipperary') in the last lines of this extract. Lob is the spirit which rises above such hypocrisy. It is he who faces the German threat, submerged in the image of the giant who comes with 'earth for damming Severn'. Thomas borrowed the fable from Charlotte S. Burne's *Shropshire Folk-Lore*[23] and gave it a 'new reality'.[24] In his essay 'It's a Long, Long Way', he reported that the countrypeople had made up their minds about invasion:

> They not only imagined themselves suffering like Belgian peasants, but being specially attacked in the Forest of Dean by German aeroplanes. Napoleon, a hundred years ago, was expected to sail up the Severn and destroy the Forest: now it was feared that the Germans were coming.[25]

On the next page, describing some of the adventures of the old shepherd 'Hobbe' against German spies and infiltrators, he wrote that before the war 'it was almost in vain that the newspapers had been erecting a *German Colossus* to terrify us.'[26] The image was to persist throughout the war, and 'The Prussian Bully 1857–1914' (a supplement of *Punch*) amply demonstrates how it was used.* The essence of these pages went into the image of 'the giant coming to destroy/Shrewsbury by flood',

* Robert Graves's poem 'Goliath and David' is an offshoot of this idea. In his version David fails, and the giant moves in for the kill:

> spike-helmeted, grey, grim,
> Goliath straddles over him.

though by becoming ripe for poetry it seemed to have little to do with daily events.

These undertones of war resound in a final affirmation of English character and tradition that had outfaced danger on so many occasions:

> 'Do you believe Jack dead before his hour . . . ?
> One of the lords of No Man's Land, good Lob—
> Although he was seen dying at Waterloo,
> Hastings, Agincourt, and Sedgemoor too—
> Lives yet. He never will admit he is dead
> Till millers cease to grind men's bones for bread . . .'

Lob had to be both warrior and sage to protect what he held in trust. It was an example that his creator would inevitably follow.

The climax of 'Lob' is more deliberately patriotic than usual in Thomas's poetry. Ordinarily, he preferred that 'indirect praise' which he considered 'sweeter and more profound'. A starting-point for three of his poems was this excerpt from his essay 'England':

> A writer in *The Times* on patriotic poetry said a good thing lately: 'There may be pleasanter places, there is no *word* like home.' A man may have this feeling even in a far quarter of England. One man said to me that he felt it, that he felt England very strongly, one evening at Stogumber under the Quantocks. His train stopped at the station which was quite silent, and only an old man got in, bent, gnarled, and gross, a Caliban; 'but somehow he fitted in with the darkness and the quietness and the smell of burning wood, and it was all something I loved being part of.' We feel it in war-time or coming from abroad, though we may be far from home: the whole land is suddenly home.[27]

This feeling was the inspiration for 'Adlestrop', 'Home', and 'Good-Night', poems which are, in his own phrase, 'inevitably English'; in Leavis's, they 'seem to happen':

> Yes. I remember Adlestrop—
> The name, because one afternoon
> Of heat the express-train drew up there
> Unwontedly. It was late June. . . .
>
> And for that minute a blackbird sang
> Close by, and round him, mistier,

Farther and farther, all the birds
Of Oxfordshire and Gloucestershire.

('Adlestrop')

Often I had gone this way before:
But now it seemed I never could be
And never had been anywhere else;
'Twas home; one nationality
We had, I and the birds that sang,
One memory.

('Home')

The friendless town is friendly; homeless, I am
  not lost;
Though I know none of these doors, and meet but
  strangers' eyes.
Never again, perhaps, after tomorrow, shall
I see these homely streets, these church windows
  alight,
Not a man or woman or child among them all:
But it is All Friends' Night, a traveller's good-night.

('Good-Night')

A more complex response emerges from 'Tears', written on the same day as 'Adlestrop'. Like 'Swedes', the poem is composed of two disparate experiences which are fused in an unexpected relationship. The first is a vivid recollection of a fox-hunt:

When twenty hounds streamed by me, not yet combed out
But still all equals in their rage of gladness
Upon the scent, made one, like a great dragon
In Blooming Meadow that bends towards the sun
And once bore hops . . .

The second, equally as English, is of the changing of the guard:

They were changing guard,
Soldiers in line, young English countrymen,
Fair-haired and ruddy, in white tunics. Drums
And fifes were playing 'The British Grenadiers'.
The men, the music piercing that solitude
And silence, told me truths I had not dreamed,
And have forgotten since their beauty passed.

An incident which Charles Sorley described in a letter from Germany shortly before the war makes an interesting parallel to the poem:

> I was coming back from a long walk with the Frau last night and we passed a couple of companies of military returning from a field day of sorts. It is truth that we could hear them a mile off. Were they singing? They were roaring—something glorious and senseless about the Fatherland (in England it would have been contemptible Jingo: it wasn't in Deutschland). . . . And when I got home, I felt I was a German, and proud to be a German: when the tempest of the singing was at its loudest, I felt that perhaps I could die for Deutschland—and I have never had an inkling of that feeling about England, and never shall. And if the feeling died with the cessation of the singing—well I had it, and it's the first time I have had the vaguest idea what patriotism meant—and that in a strange land.[28]

'Tears' offers an 'inkling' of that feeling for England without becoming the 'contemptible Jingo' that Sorley feared. It relies on the 'settled mystic patriotism' of Blake and Jefferies—indeed, a passage from Jefferies which Thomas had quoted in his study could stand as an epigraph to the poem:

> So subtle is the chord of life that sometimes to watch troops marching in rhythmic order, undulating along the column as the feet are lifted, brings tears into my eyes.[29]

That chord is struck in Thomas by the troops ('soldiers in line') *and* by the hounds ('still all equals') as they participate in their separate rituals. Yet not only do the two memories reflect in each other but *on* each other. For despite their superficial splendour, both hounds and soldiers also suggest a less attractive reality. The hounds are out to kill ('upon the scent') and merge into one menacing animal—'a great dragon'; the troops have lost some of their individuality by being 'in line' and 'in white tunics', while it is a martial air that 'pierces' the silence. The profound ambiguity of the poem's basic emotion is caught in that astonishing paradox 'rage of gladness'.

'The Owl' (later re-titled 'Those Others') provides another mood, another step towards his enlistment:

> Downhill I came, hungry, and yet not starved;
> Cold, yet had heat within me that was proof
> Against the North wind; tired, yet so that rest
> Had seemed the sweetest thing under a roof.

Then at the inn I had food, fire, and rest,
Knowing how hungry, cold, and tired was I.
All of the night was quite barred out except
An owl's cry, a most melancholy cry

Shaken out long and clear upon the hill,
No merry note, nor cause of merriment,
But one telling me plain what I escaped
And others could not, that night, as in I went.

And salted was my food, and my repose,
Salted and sobered, too, by the bird's voice
Speaking for all who lay under the stars,
Soldiers and poor, unable to rejoice.

The impact of the poem lies in that repeated word 'salted', an example of 'the awkwardness and the irresistibleness of absolute sincerity'[30] in Thomas's verse. Firstly, the bird's voice 'salts' (i.e. flavours) his refuge at the inn by making him aware of his privileged position over others less fortunate. But almost immediately less comfortable connotations surface when the word is repeated. For 'salted' has that 'rich inheritance' which Thomas could not detect in Pater's 'sterilized words' nor in Swinburne's 'self-contained words'. It certainly means 'flavoured' or 'spiced', but it also evokes 'the harshness of salt, the salt in the wound, the taste of bitterness, and of tears.'[31] This self-chastening element introduces a sense of his own 'guilt' and pity for those 'unable to rejoice'. Their sacrifice was, for Thomas, the inescapable fact of war:

'Many a man sleeps worse tonight
Than I shall.' 'In the trenches.' 'Yes, that's right . . .'
('Man and Dog')

where now at last he sleeps
More sound in France—that, too, he secret keeps.
('A Private')

The flowers left thick at nightfall in the wood
This Eastertide call into mind the men,
Now far from home, who, with their sweethearts, should
Have gathered them and will do never again.
('In Memoriam (Easter, 1915)')

The cherry trees bend over and are shedding,
On the old road where all that passed are dead,
Their petals, strewing the grass as for a wedding
This early May morn when there is none to wed.
('The Cherry Trees')

The 'unchanging order of . . . rural society' is not as unchanging as Bergonzi maintains; nor are these 'nostalgic rural visions' as remote from the conflict as Johnston would have us believe. Thomas was that rare poet for whom the division between the 'two Englands' did not exist, and he faced the tragedy of war, the waste and the pity, with an awareness beyond most of his contemporaries.* In reading his poetry we are reminded not of Francis Ledwidge nor Edmund Blunden, but of Wilfred Owen. A friend of Owen's wrote that the keynote of his character was 'an intense pity for suffering humanity—a need to alleviate it, wherever possible, and an inability to shirk the sharing of it, even when this seemed useless.'[32] It is the keynote of such poems as 'The Owl', 'In Memoriam (Easter, 1915)' and 'The Cherry Trees'. 'The pity of war' entered Thomas's poetry before Owen had even enlisted.

'You have let me follow your thought in almost every twist and turn toward this conclusion,' Frost replied, when Thomas acquainted him with his decision to enlist. 'I know pretty well how far down you have gone and how far off sideways.'[33] That decision culminates in a little-known poem called 'For These'. It was written at a time when Frost was urging him to go over to America, and it might almost have been on this theme. The first three stanzas depict a 'nostalgic rural vision' such as his critics have visualized:

An acre of land between the shore and the hills,
Upon a ledge that shows my kingdoms three,
The lovely visible earth and sky and sea
Where what the curlew needs not, the farmer tills:

A house that shall love me as I love it,
Well-hedged, and honoured by a few ash trees
That linnets, greenfinches, and goldfinches
Shall often visit and make love in and flit:

* The date of 'In Memoriam'—Easter, 1915—was the occasion when Brooke's sonnet 'The Soldier' was eulogized by Dean Inge in St. Paul's Cathedral.

PUNCH, OR THE LONDON CHARIVARI.—MAY 31, 1916.

INJURED INNOCENCE.

THE GERMAN OGRE. "HEAVEN KNOWS THAT I HAD TO DO THIS IN SELF-DEFENCE; IT WAS FORCED UPON ME." *(Aside)* "FEE, FI, FO, FUM!"

[According to the Imperial Chancellor's latest utterance Germany is the deeply-wronged victim of British militarism.]

11. 'Injured Innocence' (see p. 219)

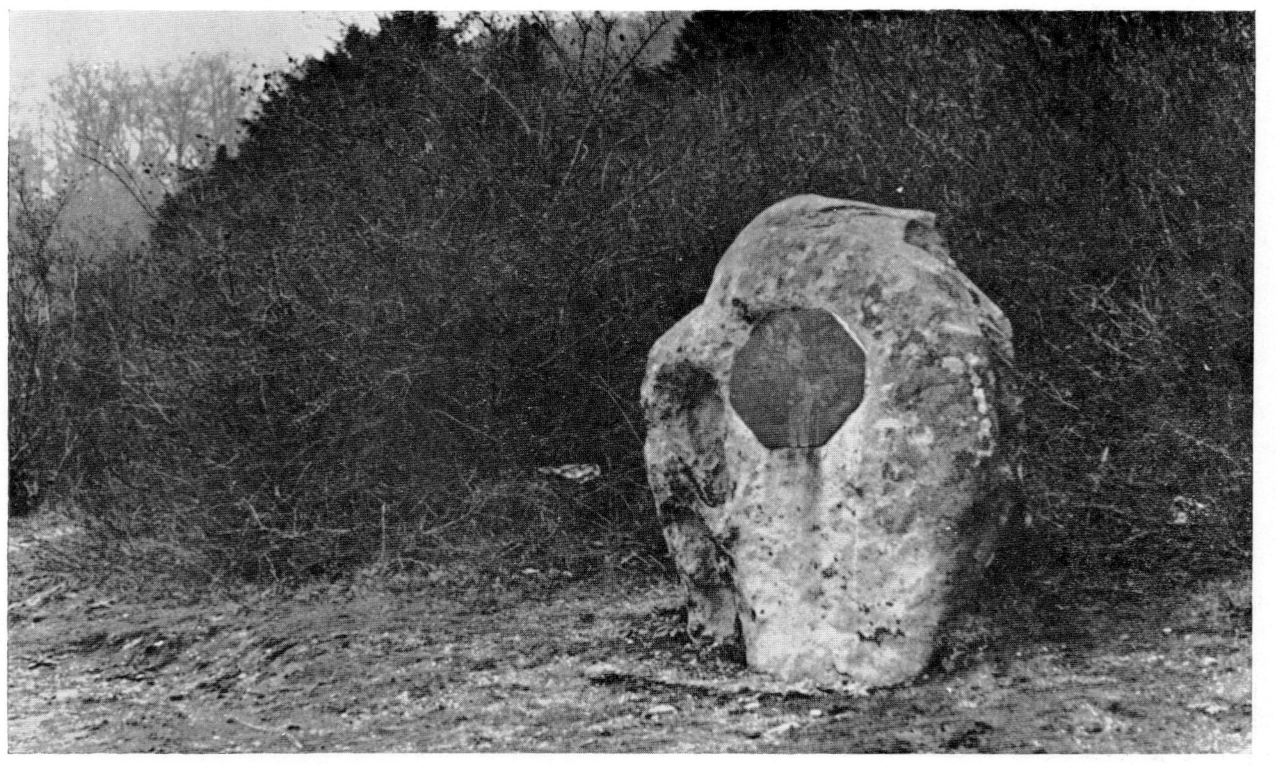

12. The Memorial Stone above Steep in Hampshire

A garden I need never go beyond,
Broken but neat, whose sunflowers every one
Are fit to be the sign of the Rising Sun:
A spring, a brook's bend, or at least a pond:

A dream of retiring to 'the simple life' is typical of much Georgian verse (cf., e.g., W. H. Davies's 'Truly Great' or de la Mare's 'I Dream of a Place')—an impression that most people seem to retain of Thomas's poetry. Yet the title 'For These' is deceptive. The fourth and final stanza completely reverses our expectations:

For these I ask not, but, neither too late
Nor yet too early, for what men call content,
And also that something may be sent
To be contented with, I ask of Fate.

The poem ends with the mental urgency that Alun Lewis stressed in 'To Edward Thomas'. For Thomas that 'hinted land' lay not in America but in France. On the same day as he wrote 'For These', he voluntarily enlisted.

3

He described his enlistment as 'not a desperate nor purposed resolution but the natural culmination of a long series of moods and thoughts.'[34] That resolution, the moods and thoughts which preceded and succeeded it, have long been misunderstood. Even allowing for the critics' chronological error, it is difficult to see why they are unanimous in dismissing him as a 'nostalgic nature poet', unaffected by 'the march of events'. The epithet 'nostalgic' is, of course, no more than 'a conveniently non-committal derogatory label'[35] which confers on the user a kind of aloof superiority. The term probably gained critical acceptance with reference to Thomas from an article which appeared in *Scrutiny* in 1932, entitled 'A Note on Nostalgia' by D. W. Harding. In it Harding gives examples of three kinds of nostalgic writing and discusses the causes for that nostalgia. The first kind stems from the frustrated desire for an adequate social group (e.g. Synge's periodic escapes from 'civilization' to the primitive islanders in *Aran Islands*); the second frequently expresses the writer's longing for his home (e.g. D. H. Lawrence's 'Piano'); the third, an extension of the second, is the 'welcoming of death'. In connection with the last variety, Harding quotes a passage from *Problems in Dynamic Psychology*:

> J. T. MacCurdy points out that the welcoming of death as a rest and a sleep is one expression of the tendency: the underlying impulse is not to go forward to meet death, but to go back to a state of freedom from effort, a state which has been approximated to only in pre-natal life. 'If reality is difficult to endure, and if acute consciousness is developmentally connected with the recognition of external reality, and if contact with the environment is essentially a function of consciousness . . . then a most natural regression would appear with a dissolution of consciousness associated with some expression of return to the earlier type of existence. One would expect the latter to be formulated as ideas of death and, in fact, this is a universal phenomenon. Suicide is common, death is frequently portrayed as a release from life. . . .'[36]

Two illustrations given are Edward Shanks's 'The Grey Land' and Brooke's 'Retrospect'. In the second the 'mother' references are very prominent:

> There was a man who loved a wood so well,
> Each separate tree, each flower, each climbing weed,
> That at the last he thither went to dwell
> And mixed himself with all those quiet things.
> Then gradually left him thought and deed
> And dead were all his soul's imaginings . . .
> Where being sleeps and is not curst or blest,
> Where hands can never feel and eyes not see,
>   Where life and death alike are grey,
> In this grey land that sucks my life away.
>
> (Shanks)

> O mother quiet, breasts of peace,
> Where love itself would faint and cease!
> O infinite deep I never knew,
> I would come back, come back to you,
> Find you as a pool unstirred,
> Kneel down by you, and never a word,
> Lay my head, and nothing said,
> In your hands, ungarlanded;
> And a long watch you would keep;
> And I should sleep, and I should sleep!
>
> (Brooke)

Harding then makes this important qualification:

> The fact of experiencing the tendency towards regression means nothing. It is the final attitude towards the experience that has to be evaluated, and in literature this attitude may be suggested only very subtly by means of the total context. In 'The Grey Land' and in 'Piano' the writer's attitude is clear. Shanks obviously finds a tranquil pleasure in the thought of throwing up the sponge. In Lawrence's poem the impulse seems to have been equally strong and is certainly expressed more forcefully, but the attitude is different. Lawrence is adult, stating the overwhelming strength of the impulse but reporting resistance to it and implying that resistance is better than yielding:
>
> In spite of myself the insidious mastery of song
> Betrays me back . . .
> The glamour
> Of childish days is upon me, my manhood is cast
> Down in the flood of remembrance, I weep like a child
> for the past.
>
> There are of course several connecting links between regression and nostalgia. One is the likelihood that regressive tendencies will be especially strong in people who have found no adequate social group and tend to be nostalgic. Another is the fact that the longing for some remoter period than the present may unite both tendencies; regressive because the ideal period seems to have been free from difficulties that have to be met in the present, and nostalgic because the difficulties of the present are seldom unrelated to the difficulty of living with an uncongenial group.[37]

Such tendencies are clearly recognizable in Thomas's work and several —the dissolution of consciousness ('Liberty'), the attraction of an ideal period ('Sedge-Warblers'), the death-wish ('Rain')—have already been touched on. However, Thomas's nostalgia is of a complex nature and, as Harding emphasizes, it is the *final* attitude towards the experience that has to be evaluated, which may be suggested only by means of the *total context* (as in 'For These'). Thomas is always as adult as Lawrence, experiencing 'the overwhelming strength of the impulse but reporting resistance to it and implying that resistance is better than yielding.' Harding fails to acknowledge this, claiming that 'in Edward Thomas's poetry the feeling of nostalgia is pervasive'.[38] He quotes the first two stanzas of 'Home' as one example:

Not the end: but there's nothing more.
Sweet Summer and Winter rude
I have loved, and friendship and love,
The crowd and solitude:

But I know them: I weary not;
But all that they mean I know.
I would go back again home
Now. Yet how should I go?

Out of context they seem to illustrate perfectly his second kind of nostalgia ('the writer's longing for his home'), merging into the third kind as 'home' comes to be equated with 'a welcoming of death'. The underlying impulse is to go back ('I would go *back* again home') to a state of freedom from effort rather than forward to meet death. An extract from 'The Attempt' (the story of his own attempted suicide from *Light and Twilight*) makes this quite explicit:

> He was called to death, but hardly to an act which could procure it. Death he had never feared or understood; he feared very much the pain and the fear that would awake with it. . . . Death was an idea tinged with poetry in his mind—a kingly thing which was once only at any man's call. After it came annihilation. . . . To escape from the difficulties of life, from the need of deliberating on it, from the hopeless search for something that would make it possible for him to go on living like anybody else without questioning, he was eager to hide himself away in annihilation, just as, when a child, he hid himself in the folds of his mother's dress or her warm bosom, where he could shut out everything save the bright patterns floating on the gloom under his closed eyelids.[39]

As in Brooke's 'Retrospect', the 'mother' references are prominent. Yet 'Home' differs considerably from the prose extract and from its own first two stanzas. Death is still an idea 'tinged with poetry in his mind', but the allusions are now specific and relevant. The title is taken from a poem by George Herbert called 'Home'* in which he longs to quit 'this world of wo'. Herbert had the confidence of his faith but Thomas

* Thomas included the poem in his edition of Herbert's poetry in 1908.

was an agnostic, and as he ponders 'the pain and the fear' that might awaken with death, the movement of the poem is given a new direction by way of a second allusion:

> This is my grief. That land,
> My home, I have never seen;
> No traveller tells of it,
> However far he has been.
>
> And could I discover it,
> I fear my happiness there,
> Or my pain, might be dreams of return
> Here, to these things that were.

'I suppose every man thinks that Hamlet was written for him,' he told Eleanor Farjeon, 'but I *know* he was written for me.'[40] The allusion is to Hamlet's renowned soliloquy in Act III:

> But that the dread of something after death—
> The undiscovered country, from whose bourn
> No traveller returns—puzzles the will,
> And makes us rather bear those ills we have
> Than fly to others that we know not of...

It is the final attitude of 'Home' that has to be evaluated, for the poem ends with a stoicism ('forward to meet death') absent from its opening:

> No: I cannot go back,
> And would not if I could.
> Until blindness come, I must wait
> And blink at what is not good.

'Home' is a pre-enlistment poem; '"Home"' is post-enlistment. Harding quotes its conclusion as a further example of 'pervasive nostalgia':

> Never a word was spoken, not a thought
> Was thought, of what the look meant with the word
> 'Home' as we walked and watched the sunset
>   blurred.
> And then to me the word, only the word,
> 'Homesick', as it were playfully occurred:
> No more.

If I should ever more admit
Than the mere word I could not endure it
For a day longer: this captivity
Must somehow come to an end, else I should be
Another man, as often now I seem,
Or this life be only an evil dream.

Harding presumably understands 'this captivity' to mean 'everyday life' and equates the 'homesickness' with similar regressive tendencies as in the earlier poem.* But by 'captivity' Thomas surely means 'everyday *army* life'. The 'cold roofs' for which they are making in the poem are army huts (cf. 'bleak hut' in 'Rain'), and when the word 'home' is applied to them it is in wryly ironic inverted commas (this is the point of the title):

'How quick,' to someone's lip
The words came, 'will the beaten horse run home!'

The word 'home' raised a smile in us all three,
And one repeated it, smiling just so
That all knew what he meant and none would say.

Several letters to Eleanor Farjeon throw an additional light on the poem. On 11 March 1916 he wrote from a camp in Romford: 'It is fine and wintry here, very dirty though underfoot. The hills look impassable and make me think they must have looked like that 2000 years ago.'[41] The opening lines of the poem, written at exactly the same time, reflect the wildness of the scene:

Fair was the morning, fair our tempers, and
We had seen nothing fairer than that land,
Though strange, and the untrodden snow that made
Wild of the tame, casting out all that was
Not wild and rustic and old . . .

In other letters telling of the boredom of camp life, Thomas had mentioned the homesickness which, in this situation, is generally recognized to be legitimate: 'Somebody said something about homesickness the other day. It is a disease one can suppress but not do without

* Cf. C. Day Lewis's reading of the same lines: 'It is clear at last what he was chafing at—the limitations of life itself . . . .' 'The Poetry of Edward Thomas', *Essays by Divers Hands*, vol. XXVIII (London, 1956), p. 91.

under these conditions . . . the new rule against going more than two miles out of camp makes Saturday and Sunday days of imprisonment.'[42] It is this 'captivity' against which he is chafing in the poem. Here too is the homesickness which is necessary, but which is suppressed ('If I should ever more admit/Than the mere word I could not endure it'). Harding places too great an emphasis on the impulse rather than on the resistance which Thomas makes to it. In both poems called 'Home' there are hints of the 'new man' of 'There Was A Time'.

Harding's discussion of his first type of nostalgia ('the frustrated desire for an adequate social group') likewise suffers from an incomplete evaluation. He writes:

> In most of the poems there is no recognition of any underlying social cause for his feeling. Yet the quality of the melancholy so often suggests nostalgia that it is hard not to suppose that the unadmitted craving for an adequate social group lay behind his most characteristic moods. . . . It is symptomatic too that his happier and more satisfying moments are often associated with an escape from other people, as though normally he never felt free from the pressure of a social group with which he could make no satisfying contact.[43]

Certainly this is one aspect of his nature:

> Once the name I gave to hours
> Like this was melancholy, when
> It was not happiness and powers
> Coming like exiles home again,
> And weaknesses quitting their bowers,
> Smiled and enjoyed, far off from men,
> Moments of everlastingness.
>
> ('The Other')

However, it is only one aspect, and there are social instincts and impulses in a number of poems which completely contradict Harding's assertion. For instance, there is little that is *unadmitted* about his craving for an adequate group. His own epitaph in 'Beauty'—'Here lies all that no one loved of him/And that loved no one'—would seem candidly to admit it. Similarly, in his letters to Garnett, Thomas showed that he was only too aware of his social insecurity:

> I can only say now that at first sight you seem to ask me to try to turn over a new leaf and be some one else. I can't help dreading

people both in anticipation and when I am among them and my only way of holding my own is the instinctive one of turning on what you call coldness and a superior manner.* That is why I hesitated about America.[44]

Perhaps it is worth while assuring you I am aware of my deficiency and that being aware of it only exaggerates it, for it is all due to self-consciousness and fear. What you call superiority is only a self-defence unconsciously adopted by the most faint-hearted humility—I believe. It goes on thickening into a callosity which only accident—being left to my own devices perhaps—can ever break through. I long for the accident but cannot myself arrange to produce it! However perhaps landing in New York quite alone, and under some stress, may do the trick and I almost feel inclined to go if only to see whether it will happen so.[45]

Enclosed with the second letter was a poem written on the same day entitled 'I Built Myself a House of Glass':

I built myself a house of glass:
It took me years to make it:
And I was proud. But now, alas!
Would God someone would break it.

But it looks too magnificent.
No neighbour casts a stone
From where he dwells, in tenement
Or palace of glass, alone.

For Thomas the 'callosity' ('glass') was to be broken not by landing in New York but by enlisting—an act which temporarily encouraged a sense of unity with an adequate group:

But with the best and meanest Englishmen
I am one in crying, God save England . . .
('No Case of Petty Right or Wrong')

His awareness of, and resignation to, the transient nature of that alliance was not, however, overlooked. 'I am really lucky to have such

* Cf. his *Childhood*, p. 147: 'Shyness made me terribly severe and reticent and gave me an appearance of great calm which was perhaps useful to me and was certainly annoying to others.'

a crowd of people always round and these two or three nearer,' he wrote to Frost. 'You might guess from ' "Home" ' how much nearer':

> Between three counties far apart that lay
> We were divided and looked strangely each
> At the other, and we knew we were not friends
> But fellows in a union that ends
> With the necessity for it, as it ought . . .
>
> (' "Home" ')

When he returned to the more general theme in one of his last poems, the agony of 'I Built Myself' was sublimated in a vision which did not admit the entire hopelessness of that former position. 'What Will They Do?' is one of the happier moments in Thomas's poetry, the result not of an escape from other people as Harding declares, but of a sense of fruitful contact with them:

> What will they do when I am gone? It is plain
> That they will do without me as the rain
> Can do without the flowers and the grass
> That profit by it and must perish without.
> I have but seen them in the loud street pass;
> And I was naught to them. I turned about
> To see them disappearing carelessly.
> But what if I in them as they in me
> Nourished what has great value and no price?
> Almost I thought that rain thirsts for a draught
> Which only in the blossom's chalice lies,
> Until that one turned back and lightly laughed.

Above all he desires some sort of reciprocity between the crowd ('the rain') and himself ('the blossom's chalice'—a reference to his poetry?). But realizing that such a wish involved a certain self-importance, he half-surrenders the vision to his humility.

4

Thomas described his enlistment as 'the natural culmination of a long series of moods and thoughts.' The same might be said of his decision to volunteer for France, though these moods and thoughts were perceptibly darker. The uncertainty of 'The Sign-Post' was sharpened into foreboding in 'It Was Upon'; the mental fretting towards his enlistment in 'This England' and 'For These' was matched by the chafing of' "Home" ' and 'Bright Clouds'; pity for suffering humanity in 'The Owl' and 'In Memoriam (Easter, 1915)' was more bleakly reflected in 'Rain'. Finally, the need to participate in 'No Case of Petty Right or Wrong' developed into a determination to prove himself and face death if necessary in 'There Was A Time'. The very titles of the poems—'The Dark Forest', 'Out in the Dark', 'Lights Out'—point only in one direction.

In 'No Case of Petty Right or Wrong' Thomas had condemned the futility of chauvinism and the murderous requirements of war. At the same time he had asserted a willingness to accept them by identifying himself with the Cause, thereby providing a sanction for the same acceptance by those waiting to be encouraged to commit themselves. 'The Trumpet' appears to be that encouragement:

> Rise up, rise up,
> And, as the trumpet blowing
> Chases the dreams of men,
> As the dawn glowing
> The stars that left unlit
> The land and water,
> Rise up and scatter
> The dew that covers
> The print of last night's lovers—
> Scatter it, scatter it!
>
> While you are listening
> To the clear horn,
> Forget, men, everything
> On this earth new-born,
> Except that it is lovelier
> Than any mysteries.
> Open your eyes to the air
> That has washed the eyes of the stars
> Through all the dewy night:
> Up with the light,
> To the old wars;
> Arise, arise!

It is not a good introduction to Thomas's poetry, yet it has retained its position as first poem in almost every collection of his work. Possibly it is for this reason that it is sometimes read as a poem of the 'visions of glory' category. It is, however, wholly different from such poems and testifies more to the ambiguity of Thomas's commitment. It was as if he had to pervert his own nature to adapt himself to the war, and the impotent climax of the first stanza

Rise up and scatter
The dew that covers
The print of last night's lovers

amounts almost to an act of desecration against the lovers, who represent a norm of sanity in his other poems. In the second stanza he urges

Forget, men, everything
On this earth new-born,
Except that it is lovelier
Than any mysteries

—as if exhilaration in the Cause were to be had only at the expense of thought. Even the poetry flags, and Thomas is guilty of making the vaguest of gestures. Finally, in

Up with the light,
To the old wars;
Arise, arise!

the long vowel sounds suggest a note of weary resignation rather than joyful acceptance.

A phrase like 'the old wars' cuts right across any optimistic belief in 'a war to end war'. Probably Thomas's historical training had encouraged his healthy scepticism in this regard. 'I have read a great deal of history,' he wrote in *The South Country*, 'in fact, a university gave me a degree out of respect for my apparent knowledge of history—but I have forgotten it all, or it has got into my blood and is present in me in a form which defies evocation or analysis.'[46] It is not wholly beyond analysis in 'The Sun Used to Shine':

The war
Came back to mind with the moonrise
Which soldiers in the east afar
Beheld then. Nevertheless, our eyes

> Could as well imagine the Crusades
> Or Caesar's battles.

At first he seems to infer the impossibility of imagining the present war—or any war. However, his *Marlborough* had shown him quite capable of imagining its true condition, and a second reading emerges from the lines which is not so innocent. His apparently casual reference to the 'Crusades' reminds us that the First War had been welcomed as a modern 'crusade'. He then ironically juxtaposes the Holy Wars with 'Caesar's battles', implying that they could as well imagine those old wars as this 'new' one, since war was basically the same whether it was waged to reclaim under the cross or subjugate under the imperial standard. Out of this context came Thomas's version of the millennium in 'February Afternoon':

> Men heard this roar of parleying starlings, saw,
> A thousand years ago even as now,
> Black rooks with white gulls following the plough
> So that the first are last until a caw
> Commands that last are first again—a law
> Which was of old when one, like me, dreamed how
> A thousand years might dust lie on his brow
> Yet thus would birds do between hedge and shaw.
>
> Time swims before me, making as a day
> A thousand years, while the broad ploughland oak
> Roars mill-like and men strike and bear the stroke
> Of war as ever, audacious or resigned,
> And God still sits aloft in the array
> That we have wrought him, stone-deaf and stone-blind.

The ageless 'roar' of the starlings is associated with the 'roar' of the oak, and both suggest peaceful activities of man ('following the plough', 'Roars mill-like'). Yet both in turn are contrasted with the impulse in man's nature to wage war. The natural rhythm of the rooks and gulls ('so that first are last') is reflected in the unnatural rhythm of the human world ('men strike and bear the stroke'); this is simultaneously contrasted with the nature of the oak through internal rhyme ('mill-like'—'strike') and end rhyme ('oak'—'stroke'). The last two lines utterly refute any misplaced faith in the war as a crusade, watched over by a benevolent deity.

No less sceptical is a companion-piece to 'The Trumpet' called 'No One Cares Less Than I':

> 'No one cares less than I,
> Nobody knows but God,
> Whether I am destined to lie
> Under a foreign clod,'
> Were the words I made to the bugle call in the
> morning.
>
> But laughing, storming, scorning,
> Only the bugles know
> What the bugles say in the morning,
> And they do not care, when they blow
> The call that I heard and made words to early this
> morning.

John Moore's superficial consideration of the poem is less than helpful:

> In September he was transferred for further training to the Royal Artillery Barracks at Trowbridge, where 'the trumpet blew for everything' and where one day he set some more words to the brave bugle-call:
>
> 'No one cares less than I,
> Nobody knows but God,
> Whether I am destined to lie
> Under a foreign clod.'
>
> These were the words he made to the bugle-call in the morning.[47]

The impression which is conveyed (and which is certainly intended from that transferred epithet 'brave') is that Thomas was careless of personal risk and eager to join the fray. In fact he is saying no such thing. The romantic response of the first stanza is deliberately undercut by the heavy 'God'—'clod' rhyme. Significantly, it is 'a foreign clod', which may have been Thomas's personal reaction to Brooke's 'corner of a foreign field/That is for ever England'. The second stanza points to the possible discrepancy (in the conjunction 'But') between the words he makes to that call and what the bugles may really be saying. Consequently, 'laughing, storming, scorning' may be read not only as the stimulus for the cavalier attitude portrayed in the first verse, but also as a criticism of it. For '*they*' do not care: the single bugle of the earlier lines now includes all the morning bugles, collectively referred to as 'they'—the pronoun used by the common soldier to incriminate the politicians and generals responsible for the war (Thomas used it in this way in his very next poem). And that 'they' do not care what they are saying when they make the call suggests their irresponsibility and the ambiguous nature of that call, at once stimulating and hollow.

'As the Team's Head-Brass', written directly afterwards, gives the lie to the 'no one cares less than I' attitude as far as Thomas was concerned. His reply to a ploughman's question is exceptional for its common sense:

> 'Have you been out?' 'No.' 'And don't want to,
>   perhaps?'
> 'If I could only come back again, I should.
> I could spare an arm. I shouldn't want to lose
> A leg. If I should lose my head, why, so,
> I should want nothing more . . .'

It is difficult to see how I. M. Parsons can read this as a trench poem. In *Men Who March Away*, his introductory comment to the section *The Pity of War* begins:

> It was not necessary to have been in the trenches to appreciate 'the pity war distilled' or to understand, if one had the heart and wit, the larger implications of the conflict. Thus two of the most remarkable poems in this group—Hardy's 'I Looked Up From My Writing', and de la Mare's 'Motley'—are by older poets who wrote of it at a distance.[48]

It is in this context that Thomas's name should appear. But Parsons, after mentioning 'Tommies in the Train' and 'Bombardment' by the 'non-combatant' D. H. Lawrence (two other poems which are to be found in this section), goes on to make this distinction:

> But it is still the front-line poets who, understandably, have most to say on this subject and who interpret it most diversely and movingly. Here the prevalent mood is meditative and reflective, rather than assertive or denunciatory. Typical of it are two gifted but very different poets, Edward Thomas and Edmund Blunden, who found it possible to construct, out of their varied experiences, if not 'something upon which to rejoice' at least something with which to solace

> themselves and others: poems like Thomas's 'As the Team's Head-Brass' or Blunden's 'Zillebeke Brook', whose quiet rhythms and perceptive insights create a sense of pastoral calm which, by antithesis, make their message all the more effective.[49]

Parsons seems to be reading 'As the Team's Head-Brass' as some sort of therapeutic activity ('to solace themselves and others') by which Thomas sustained himself in the front line. This is exactly what he was *not* doing. Blunden was the front-line poet for whom the muddy French stream suddenly recalled

> a glassy burn
> Ribanded through a brake of Kentish fern.
> ('Zillebeke Brook')

He was writing in France, in April 1917. Thomas's poem was written in England, in May 1916, and he is creating not a sense of 'pastoral calm' but a sense of the rural community undergoing serious disruption from the effects of the war:

> 'Have many gone
> From here?' 'Yes.' 'Many lost?' 'Yes, a good few.
> Only two teams work on the farm this year.
> One of my mates is dead. The second day
> In France they killed him . . .'

The 'pastoral calm' is not as prevalent as Parsons imagines. It is the sterility of the scene ('charlock', 'fallow', 'the fallen elm') that is most evident.

Even stranger is Hoxie N. Fairchild's discussion of the poem in *Religious Trends in English Poetry* (1962). He begins by making the common mistake of regarding Thomas as a trench poet:

> He wrote almost no 'war poetry' in the ordinary sense . . . the nature poems which he *stubbornly* continued to produce . . . were attempts to remind himself and his countrymen of what England was fighting to preserve.[50]

His subsequent exposition of 'As the Team's Head-Brass' may be quoted in full:

> The war . . . is firmly kept in its place as an insane detour from the highway of the great eternal sanities.

> As the team's head-brass flashed out on the turn
> The lovers disappeared into the wood.
>
> The observer talks about the war with the ploughman, who shows no awareness that it is more important than his ploughing. He would be willing enough to join up if he could be quite sure of coming back. Several men of the neighbourhood will never do so. 'One of my mates is dead.' But, adds the farmer, 'If we could see all all might seem good.' As if in corroboration of these words, the lovers emerge from the grove, while
>
> The horses started and for the last time
> I watched the clods tumble* and topple over
> After the ploughshare and the stumbling team.
>
> That and the lovers are what really matter.
>
> More often, however, the war is kept in its place simply by writing as if it did not exist. . . .[51]

Fairchild confuses the dialogue as though it were the observer (obviously Thomas) who asks 'Have you been out?' Surely it is the ploughman, who shows more awareness than Fairchild credits him with. Moreover, it is not a question of 'joining up' but of 'going out'—to provoke the question the observer must *already* be in uniform. Finally, Fairchild insists that the ploughing and the lovers are what really matter. Yet the poem ends on an ominous note—'for the last time'—which does not offer any of the consolation that he seemingly derives from it. His comments are more appropriate to Thomas Hardy's 'In Time of "The Breaking of Nations"':

I

Only a man harrowing clods
  In a slow silent walk
With an old horse that stumbles and nods
  Half asleep as they stalk.

II

Only thin smoke without flame
  From the heaps of couch-grass;
Yet this will go onward the same
  Though Dynasties pass.

* Misquotation: read 'crumble'.

III

Yonder a maid and her wight
  Come whispering by:
War's annals will cloud into night
  Ere their story die.

The poem sets out to create Parson's sense of 'pastoral calm' and Bergonzi's 'unchanging order of nature and rural society'. The ploughman and lovers are, for Hardy, what really matter. But in Thomas's poem those 'great eternal sanities' are shown to be under pressure and actually disappearing.

In 'As the Team's Head-Brass' Thomas deliberated on the possibility of his own death. It is introduced so often in the poems, first as an intuition prior to his enlistment, then as a certainty as the time of his embarkation approached. In *Rose Acre Papers* in 1904, he wrote that 'sleep is a novitiate for the beyond'.[52] In 'Lights Out' in 1916, he faced that beyond. It is one of the quietest and most haunting of leave-takings:

I have come to the borders of sleep,
The unfathomable deep
Forest where all must lose
Their way, however straight,
Or winding, soon or late;
They cannot choose.

Many a road and track
That, since the dawn's first crack,
Up to the forest brink,
Deceived the travellers,
Suddenly now blurs,
And in they sink.

Here love ends,
Despair, ambition ends;
All pleasure and all trouble,
Although most sweet or bitter,
Here ends in sleep that is sweeter
Than tasks most noble.

There is not any book
Or face of dearest look
That I would not turn from now
To go into the unknown
I must enter, and leave, alone,
I know not how.

The tall forest towers;
Its cloudy foliage lowers
Ahead, shelf above shelf;
Its silence I hear and obey
That I may lose my way
And myself.

'His poetry is so brave,' wrote Frost after his friend's death, 'so unconsciously brave. He didn't think of it for a moment as war poetry, though that is what it is. It ought to be called Roads to France.'[53] His remark leaves no doubt as to the true origin of Thomas's poetry.

Appendix 1

DATES OF THE POEMS IN ORDER OF COMPOSITION

The following abbreviations have been used to indicate the source of the date of each poem:

B: The Bodleian.

BC: Berg Collection of the New York Public Library.

BM: The British Museum.

LML: Lockwood Memorial Library, State Univ. of New York at Buffalo.

No MSS of seven poems could be traced: 'When First', 'The Mountain Chapel', 'The Glory', 'The Other', 'Birds' Nests', 'Interval', and 'After Rain'. Copies of the last two poems were sent to Eleanor Farjeon on 6 January 1915 (see *The Last Four Years*, pp. 109–10), and have been dated thus approximately in the list below (abbrev. source *EF*). 'The Lane' is the only undated MS poem. It is probable, however, that these are the fifteen lines which were written on 15 December 1916, to which ET referred in a further letter to Eleanor Farjeon (p. 235).

1914

3 December	'Up in the Wind'	(*LML*)
4	'November'	(*LML*)
5	'March'	(*LML*)
6	'Old Man'	(*LML*)
7	'The Sign-Post'	(*LML*)
24	'The Manor Farm'	(*BM*)
25	'An Old Song' ('I was not apprenticed . . .')	(*BM*)
26	'An Old Song' ('The sun set . . .')	(*BM*)
30	'The Combe'	(*BM*)
31	'The Hollow Wood'	(*BM*)

1915

1 January	'The New Year'	(*BM*)
4	'The Source'	(*BM*)
5	'The Penny Whistle'	(*BM*)
6 (?)	'Interval'	(*EF*)
	'After Rain'	(*EF*)
6–7	'A Private'	(*BM*)
7	'Snow'	(*BM*)
8	'Adlestrop'	(*BM*)
	'Tears'	(*BM*)
9	'Over the Hills'	(*BM*)
10	'The Lofty Sky'	(*BM*)
15	'The Cuckoo'	(*BM*)
	'Swedes'	(*BM*)
17	'The Unknown Bird'	(*BC/BM*)
18	'The Mill-Pond'	(*BC/BM*)
20	'Man and Dog'	(*BC/BM*)
21	'Beauty'	(*BM*)
22	'The Gypsy'	(*BC/BM*)
23	'Ambition'	(*BC/BM*)
3–4 February	'House and Man'	(*BM*)
11	'Parting'	(*BM*)
	'First Known when Lost'	(*BM*)
15	'May the Twenty-third'	(*BM*)
22	'The Barn'	(*BM*)
23	'Home' ('Not the end . . .')	(*BM*)
24	'The Owl'	(*BM*)
11 March	'The Child on the Cliffs'	(*BM*)
12	'The Bridge'	(*BM*)
16	'Good-Night'	(*BM*)
18	'But These Things Also'	(*BM*)
19	'The New House'	(*BM*)
22–3	'The Barn and the Down'	(*BM*)
23	'Sowing'	(*BM*)
	'March the Third'	(*BM*)
24	'Two Pewits' (Revised version 4 May 1915)	(*BM*)

25	'Will You Come?'	(*BM*)
26	'The Path'	(*BM*)
27	'The Wasp Trap'	(*BM*)
28	'A Tale' (Revised version 31 March 1915)	(*BM*)
1 April	'Wind and Mist'	(*BM*)
2	'A Gentleman'	(*BM*)
3–4	'Lob'	(*BM*)
4	'Digging' ('Today I think...')	(*BM*)
5	'Lovers'	(*BM*)
6	'In Memoriam (Easter, 1915)'	(*BM*)
14	'Head and Bottle'	(*BM*)
17	'Home' ('Often I had gone ...')	(*BM*)
18	'Health'	(*BM*)
20	'The Huxter'	(*BM*)
21	'She Dotes'	(*BM*)
22	'Song'	(*BM*)
24	'A Cat'	(*BM*)
25	'Melancholy'	(*BM*)
30	'To-night'	(*BM*)
2 May	'April'	(*BM*)
7	'July'	(*BM*)
8	'The Chalk-Pit'	(*BM*)
13	'Fifty Faggots'	(*BM*)
23–4	'Sedge-Warblers'	(*BM*)
25 June	'I Built Myself a House of Glass'	(*B*)
26–8	'Words'	(*B*)
5 July	'The Word'	(*B*)
	'Under the Woods'	(*B*)
6–8	'Haymaking'	(*B*)
7–8	'A Dream'	(*B*)
10	'The Brook'	(*B*)
11	'Aspens'	(*B*)
12	'The Mill-Water'	(*B*)
13–14	'For These'	(*B*)
21	'Digging' ('What matter makes my spade ...')	(*B*)

22	'Two Houses'	(*B*)
23	'Cock-Crow'	(*B*)
15–16 October	'October'	(*B*)
18–19 November	'There's Nothing Like the Sun'	(*B*)
26	'Liberty'	(*B*)
[ ]	'The Thrush'	(*B*)
26 December	'This is No Case of Petty Right or Wrong'	(*B*)

1916

7 January	'Rain'	(*B*)
15	'The Clouds that are so Light'	(*B*)
22	'Roads'	(*B*)
4–9 February	'The Ash Grove'	(*B*)
7–8	'February Afternoon'	(*B*)
8	'P.H.T.'	(*B*)
9	'These Things that Poets Said'	(*B*)
11	'No One So Much As You'	(*B*)
14	'The Unknown'	(*B*)
4 March	'Celandine'	(*B*)
7–10	' "Home" '	(*B*)
10	'Thaw'	(*B*)
6 April	'If I Should Ever by Chance'	(*B*)
7	'If I were to Own'	(*B*)
8	'What Shall I Give?'	(*B*)
9	'And You, Helen'	(*B*)
30	'The Wind's Song'	(*B*)
	'Like the Touch of Rain'	(*B*)
1 May	'When We Two Walked'	(*B*)
	'Tall Nettles'	(*B*)
	'The Watchers'	(*B*)
5	'I Never Saw that Land Before'	(*B*)
7–8	'The Cherry Trees'	(*B*)
11–13	'It Rains'	(*B*)
13–14	'Some Eyes Condemn'	(*B*)

22	'The Sun Used to Shine'	(*B*)
25–6	'No One Cares Less Than I'	(*B*)
27	'As the Team's Head-Brass'	(*B*)
3 June	'After You Speak'	(*B*)
4–5	'Bright Clouds'	(*B*)
8–11	'Early One Morning'	(*B*)
21	'It Was Upon'	(*B*)
22	'Women He Liked'	(*B*)
23	'There Was A Time'	(*B*)
28	'The Green Roads'	(*B*)
1–10 July	'The Dark Forest'	(*B*)
3–4	'The Gallows'	(*B*)
15	'When He Should Laugh'	(*B*)
10 August	'How at Once'	(*B*)
3 September	'Gone, Gone Again'	(*B*)
10	'That Girl's Clear Eyes'	(*B*)
15	'What Will They Do?'	(*B*)
26–8	'The Trumpet'	(*B*)
[ ] October	'The Child in the Orchard'	(*B*)
[ ] November	'Lights Out'	(*B*)
[ ]	'The Long Small Room'	(*B*)
23	'The Sheiling'	(*B*)
15 December (?)	'The Lane'	(*EF*)
24	'Out in the Dark'	(*B*)

Appendix 2

A NOTE ON THE MANUSCRIPT POEMS

Edward Thomas never had the privilege of publishing his own poetry. During his lifetime he saw only twelve of his poems in print, and though he knew that eighteen were to appear in *An Annual of New Poetry* (1917), the selection had been made largely by Gordon Bottomley. His own selection of sixty-four poems for *Poems* (1917) was published after his death, and he never saw the proofs. Over the years the number of his *Collected Poems* (hereafter referred to as *CP*) has risen to a hundred and forty-one, all of which were written in just two years. Doubtless, if he had lived, Thomas would have suppressed some (e.g. 'April') and modified others (e.g. 'Health'). The MS poems themselves suggest the haste in which they were written and the little time that was available for any concentrated revision. Sometimes a title is repeated, as with 'Home' (three times). Most often the poems are untitled and simply record the name of the place where they were written. 'Fifty Faggots' is headed 'British Museum'—written there during his final spell as a hack; 'Words' was composed on a bicycle tour and has the phrase 'Hucclecote—on the road from Gloucester to Coventry' instead of a title. Many later poems bear the names of the camps where he trained as a soldier. 'Gone, Gone Again' originated at 'Handel Street'; 'Bright Clouds' and '"Home"' at 'Harehall'; 'The Trumpet' and 'Lights Out' at 'Trowbridge'. They were written in any spare moments that came to hand, and 'The Thrush'* has the additional information below its title: 'Harehall XI. 15. The day I was in as hut-orderly while the rest went to South Weald'; 'How at Once' has 'Hospital, Harehall'; 'No One So Much As You' tells that he was 'going home on sick leave'. In spite of such evidence, as F. R. Leavis found, 'the greater part of the collected poems is good'.

Several variant readings have already been noted in the course of this study, and some need to be considered at greater length, particularly

* MS title 'A Thrush'.

as the printed text occasionally hints that the poet had no part in the proof-reading. Titles, punctuation, even the form of poems vary somewhat from edition to edition. Moreover, not all of Thomas's corrections were consistently carried out. The fair copy of 'October' has this alteration in line 10 (italics indicate ET's deletions):

> late year
> The ~~rich scene~~ has grown fresh again and new . . .

Except for the *CP* (1928), the earlier version of the line has always been printed.

Lines 3–6 of 'As the Team's Head-Brass' are another example. When he was in camp Thomas used to send new poems to Eleanor Farjeon in order to obtain typescripts, and corrections often followed on the heels of the poem. The lines which he originally sent read:

> I sat among the boughs of the fallen elm
> That strewed the angle of the fallow, and
> Watched the plough narrowing the yellow square
> Of charlock.

His subsequent revision eliminated two of the definite articles:

> At the beginning 'the angle' should be 'an angle' and 'the yellow square' 'a yellow square'.*

As they were first printed in *Poems* (1917) and the *CP* (1920), the lines appeared according to his wishes:

> I sat among the boughs of the fallen elm
> That strewed an angle of the fallow, and
> Watched the plough narrowing a yellow square
> Of charlock.

In the *CP* (1928), however, 'the angle' reappears, a half-corrected version that has persisted to the 1965 edition.

Such discrepancies make a closer look at the MSS more meaningful and necessary. There are three main public collections, at the Lockwood Memorial Library of the State University of New York at Buffalo, the British Museum, and the Bodleian. The exercise book in Lockwood

* Eleanor Farjeon obviously misplaces this letter in *The Last Four Years* by printing it on page 144 under the postmark 4 June 1915. The date should be 4 June 1916, and the letter should appear on page 198. If this is correct, the mysterious illness referred to in the letter would be her whooping cough of 1916 (see p. 198).

Library is one of the most important, showing Thomas's transition from prose to poetry. It contains 'The White House' (prose), 'Up in the Wind' (two drafts), 'November' (two drafts), 'March' (one draft), 'Old Man's Beard' (prose), 'Old Man' (two drafts), and 'The Sign-Post' (two drafts). All the work is dated, but only the prose pieces are titled. They are the only MS versions of these poems extant.

From the contents of this exercise book (which was discussed in the chapter *Like Exiles Home*), it is possible to determine Thomas's method of composition. He himself testified that under the sheer intensity of production his poems did 'not ask or get much correction on paper', and from the evidence of the Lockwood MSS it appears that he took his first poems through only a single working draft before making a fair copy. Thereafter these second drafts could be copied from the scraps of paper on which they were written into a manuscript book, during which process further revision might take place. Additional MS 44990 in the Department of Manuscripts of the British Museum is such a book. It contains sixty-two poems, all of which are in chronological order and dated. The majority are certainly fair copies: a slightly earlier version of 'The Manor Farm' was included in his anthology *This England* (1915), and working drafts of five poems—'The Unknown Bird' (two drafts), 'Ambition' (one draft), 'The Mill-Pond' (one draft), 'The Gypsy' (one draft), and 'Man and Dog' (one draft)—are extant in the New York Berg Collection. Nevertheless many poems are corrected, and in nine cases—'The Penny Whistle', 'A Private', 'Snow', 'Adlestrop', 'Swedes', 'The Barn and the Down', 'Two Pewits', 'A Tale', and 'Sedge-Warblers'—a poem is taken through a further draft. In one case—'The Hollow Wood'—there are three separate versions. Many even of those copies which are here corrected underwent subsequent correction. Hardly any of the poems as first written down correspond exactly with the printed text.

Variations range in significance from minor details of punctuation to alternative versions of some poems. For example, the original version of 'A Tale' was written on 28 March 1915:

> There once the walls
> Of the ruined cottage stood.
> The periwinkle crawls
> With flowers in its hair into the wood.

In flowerless hours
Never will the bank fail,
With everlasting flowers
On fragments of blue plates, to tell the tale.

This is the version of the poem as it has always been printed, yet it is *cancelled* in this MS book in favour of a later version written on 31 March 1915:

Here once flint walls,
Pump, orchard and woodpile stood.
Blue periwinkle crawls
From the lost garden down into the wood.

The flowerless hours
Of winter cannot prevail
To blight those other flowers,
Blue china fragments scattered, that tell the tale.

'A Private' exists in two earlier drafts, neither of which are cancelled. They were written on 6 and 7 January 1915, and both are untitled:

A labouring man lies hid in that bright coffin
Who slept out many a frosty night and kept
Good drinkers and bedmen tickled with his scoffing:
'At Mrs. Greenland's Hawthorn Bush I slept.'

The labouring man here lying slept out of doors
Many a frosty night, and merrily
Answered good drinkers and bedmen and all bores:
'At Mrs. Greenland's Hawthorn Bush' said he,
'I slept.' None knew which bush. Above the town,
Beyond 'The Drover' a hundred spot the down.

The printed poem is a reworking at an unknown date of this vignette of rural life and death:

This ploughman dead in battle slept out of doors
Many a frozen night, and merrily
Answered staid drinkers, good bedmen, and all bores:
'At Mrs. Greenland's Hawthorn Bush,' said he,

'I slept.' None knew which bush. Above the town,
Beyond 'The Drover', a hundred spot the down
In Wiltshire. And where now at last he sleeps
More sound in France—that, too, he secret keeps.

The earlier drafts are not concerned with the war at all, and there is no reason to suspect that the countryman has not died a natural death. In the final version the influence of the war is paramount: the labourer/ploughman has become 'a private'; he is 'dead in battle'; and the closing lines introduce and exploit the euphemism of 'sleeps/More sound' with a grim irony.

Not all of Thomas's revisions were nearly so radical, and as a rule the poems required little beyond the smoothing out of certain lines. The conclusion of 'May the Twenty-third' originally read:

A fine day was May the 20th,
The day of Old Jack Noman's death.

This was printed as:

That fine day, May the twenty-third,
The day Jack Noman disappeared.

'Digging' began with a false start:

Except with scents
I cannot think,—scents dead . . .

Immediately he began again:

To-day, with scents
Only, I think,—scents dead leaves yield,
And sage,—the wild carrot's seed,
And the square mustard field . . .

The printed text reveals a later modification:

To-day I think
Only with scents,—scents dead leaves yield,
And bracken, and wild carrot's seed,
And the square mustard field.

The third stanza of 'The Penny Whistle' underwent this successful revision:

8.1.15.

Adlestrop

Yes I remember Adlestrop.
At least the name. One afternoon
The train slowed & drew up
There unexpectedly. 'Twas June.

Of heat

The steam hissed. Someone cleared his throat.
No one left & no one came
On the bare platform. What I saw
Was Adlestrop, only the name,

And willows, willow herb & grass,
And meadowsweet. The haycocks dry
Were not less still & lonely fair
Than the high cloudlets in the sky.

And all that minute a blackbird sang
Close by, and round him, mistier,
Farther & farther, all the birds
Of Oxfordshire & Gloucestershire.

13. 'Adlestrop' (first draft)

Adlestrop

Yes, I remember Adlestrop —
At least the name. One afternoon
Of heat ~~[illegible]~~ the express train drew up there
~~[illegible]~~ against its custom. It was June.

The steam hissed. Someone cleared his throat.
No one left & no one came
On the bare platform. What I saw
Was Adlestrop — only the name,

And willows, willow herb & grass,
And meadowsweet. The haycocks dry
Were not less still & lonely fair
Than the high cloudlets in the sky.

And all that minute a blackbird sang
Close by, and round him, mistier,
~~Farther~~ & farther, all the birds
Of Oxfordshire & Gloucestershire.

Yes, I remember Adlestrop —
The name, because ~~[illegible]~~. One afternoon
Of heat, the express train drew up there
~~[illegible]~~
Unwontedly. It was late June...

14. 'Adlestrop' (second draft)

But the caravan hut up in the clearing
Still gleams like a kingfisher:
Round the mossed old hearths of the charcoal-
  burners
There are primroses, I aver.

(1st draft)

But still the caravan-hut by the hollies
Like a kingfisher gleams between:
Round the mossed old hearths of the charcoal-
  burners
First primroses ask to be seen.

(2nd draft)

'Adlestrop' is unusual in that its first stanza went through four versions in the two MS drafts of the poem, which otherwise needed little correction before it was printed:

~~Yes I remember Adlestrop,~~
~~At least the name. One afternoon~~
~~train~~
~~The express slowed down there & drew up~~
~~Quite~~

Yes, I remember Adlestrop,
At least the name. One afternoon
Of heat The ~~steam~~ train slowed ~~down~~ & drew up
There unexpectedly. 'Twas June.

The steam hissed. Someone cleared his throat.
~~But no one left~~ No one left & no one came
On the bare platform. What I saw
Was Adlestrop, only the name,

And willows, willow herb & grass,
And meadowsweet. The haycocks dry
Were not less still & lonely fair
Than the high cloud tiers in the sky.

And all that minute a blackbird sang
Close by, and round him, mistier,
Farther & farther ~~off,~~ all the birds
Of Oxfordshire & Gloucestershire.

(1st draft)

Yes, I remember Adlestrop—
At least the name. One afternoon
the express train
Of heat ~~the train slowed &~~ drew up there
Against its custom.
~~There unexpectedly~~. It '~~T~~was June.

Yes, I remember Adlestrop—
The name, because
~~At least the name.~~ One afternoon
Of heat, the express train drew up there
~~Against the custom—~~
Unwontedly. It was late June.

The steam hissed. Someone cleared his throat.
No one left & no one came
On the bare platform. What I saw
Was Adlestrop, only the name,

And, willows, willow herb & grass,
And meadowsweet. The haycocks dry
Were not less still & lonely fair
Than the high cloudlets ~~tiers~~ in the sky.

And all that minute a blackbird sang
Close by, and round him, mistier,
Farther & farther, all the birds
Of Oxfordshire & Gloucestershire.

(2nd draft)

Occasionally a poem was lengthened before publication. The last thirteen lines of the printed version of 'The Chalk-Pit' are represented in the MS book by no more than three:

'Mild and yet wild too. You may know the breed.'
'Some literary fellow, I suppose.
I shall not mix my fancies up with him.'

Usually, however, the printed text is shorter, and stanzas have been eliminated from two poems before publication. 'Song' originally had three four-lined stanzas instead of the two of the *CP*. The additional (first) stanza read:

She is beautiful
With happiness invincible:
If cruel she be
It is the hawk's proud innocent cruelty.

'Sowing' had an additional fifth stanza. The last two MS verses ran:

And now, hark at the rain
Windless and light,
Half a kiss, half a tear,
Saying good-night:

A kiss for all the seeds'
Dry multitude,
A tear of ending this
March interlude.

The *CP* omits the last stanza and places a full stop instead of a colon at the end of stanza four.

The third major collection of MS poems is that of the Bodleian. Don. d. 28 is an exercise book containing sixty-seven poems. All but 'The Lane' are dated, and all but four of the poems are in chronological order. They are fair copies, and Eleanor Farjeon prints earlier versions of a number of these poems in *The Last Four Years* which have been revised before being copied up here. There are no alternative versions of any poems; thirty-four are identical with the *CP*; other variations are slight and not numerous.

REFERENCES

The following abbreviations have been used in the notes to indicate sources of unpublished material:

ACL: Academic Center Library, Univ. of Texas.

BC: Berg Collection of the New York Public Library.

DCL: Dartmouth College Library, New Hampshire.

LML: Lockwood Memorial Library, State Univ. of New York at Buffalo.

MUL: Marquette Univ. Library.

Introduction

1 H. W. Nevinson, 'Fame Too Late', *Life and Letters To-day*, March 1940, p. 272.
2 H. G. Wright, *Studies in Contemporary Literature* (Bangor, 1918), p. 105.
3 Quoted in Louis Mertins, *Robert Frost: Life and Talks—Walking* (Norman, Oklahoma, 1965), p. 136.
4 *The Bookman*, April 1919, p. 22.
5 *The Dial*, 20 Dec. 1917, p. 631.
6 *The Times Literary Supplement*, 18 Oct. 1917, p. 502.
7 F. R. Leavis, *New Bearings in English Poetry* (London, 1932), p. 69 (my italics).
8 See, e.g., C. K. Stead, *The New Poetic* (London, 1964), p. 101n.
9 Lawrance Thompson (ed.), *Selected Letters of Robert Frost* (London, 1965), p. 217.

1. How I Began

1 A rough family tree drawn up by Thomas has two notes concerning the original Marendaz, who came from Switzerland. The first tells that he was 'a courier to the Talbots [who] received on his marriage

with a Miss Evans, a clergyman's daughter, the farm of Tydraw at Margam, at peppercorn rent: fair-haired.' The second concerns his nationality: 'reputed a "German", but presumably Spanish—a man who knew many languages.' *BC*.

2 *The Childhood of Edward Thomas* (London, 1938), p. 17.
3 'Addenda to Autobiography', *BC*.
4 Ibid.
5 Gordon Bottomley, 'A Note on Edward Thomas', *The Welsh Review*, vol. I, no. 3 (Sept. 1945), 177.
6 ET to H. N. Sturmer, 4 April 1900, *BC*.
7 *Childhood*, pp. 52–3.
8 Ibid., p. 85.
9 Ibid., p. 134.
10 Ibid., p. 105.
11 Quoted in a letter from ET to his parents, 13 July[1892], *BC*. The address on the letter is 61 Shelgate Road, Battersea Rise, where the Thomas family lived from 1889. They later moved to 13 Rusham Road, Balham.
12 *Childhood*, p. 104.
13 Quoted in G. K. Chesterton, *Autobiography* (London, 1937 edn.), p. 71.
14 E. C. Bentley, *Those Days* (London, 1940), p. 58.
15 G. K. Chesterton, op. cit., pp. 60–1.
16 *Childhood*, pp. 142–3.
17 'Addenda to Autobiography', *BC*.
18 Helen Thomas, *As It Was* and *World Without End* (London, 1956), p. 22—hereafter cited as *World Without End*.
19 *Childhood*, p. 144.
20 *Richard Jefferies* (London, 1909), p. 56.
21 Helen Noble to Janet Aldis, 6 Jan. 1896. All correspondence cited between Helen Noble (afterwards Helen Thomas) and Janet Aldis (afterwards Janet Hooton) is by kind permission of Mrs. Patricia M. Rogers.
22 Helen Noble to Janet Aldis, 1 April 1896.
23 Helen Noble to Janet Aldis, 23 May 1896.

2. The Divided Self

1 I am indebted to Mr. F. W. Oser of the New York Public Library

for typescripts of a number of poems from ET's early notebooks. Dr. John D. Gordan wrote with reference to these poems: 'The poetry in the notebooks is far less frequent than the prose, and without exhaustive examination it is not possible to be certain whether the poetry is Thomas's own or little-known poetry that he copied out. Examples of both—including a famous stanza of Byron's—can be found in vol. VI (1896), showing how far back Thomas's desire to express himself in verse can be traced. Vol. XIX contains the earliest dated poem, 14. ii. '98'. 'New in the Berg Collection', *Bulletin of the New York Public Library*, vol. LXVIII, no. 2 (Feb. 1964), 74.

Such examples disprove the theory that ET wrote no poetry until middle life. The one referred to above in vol. XIX runs as follows:

Cottage on the turbid Wye
Often had I past thee by;—
Often saw, but spoke not thee
(As they say of ships at sea!)
Thee I saw, as sunset's rose
Withered sadly into snows,
And while all the earth was still
To watch the moonrise o'er the hill
Lightly on the brink of night,—
Pave her lonely footsteps white.
Ever since in penance mild
I go to thy dim garden wild;
And when in storm the ivies fall
Restore them fondly to the wall;
And often Cold Wye! for thy sake
Loyal from thy ruins take,
Underneath the chestnut arch,
Lustrous celandines of March.

The lines referred to in vol. VI are in quotation marks and are most likely a copy from his reading. The two poems quoted in the text are from vol. XIX (1897). They are almost certainly ET's own, for they express characteristic moods and impulses which were reworked in his mature verse.

2 Quoted in John Moore, *The Life and Letters of Edward Thomas* (London, 1939), p. 41—hereafter cited as *Letters*.

3 Loc. cit.

4 Norman G. Brett-James to Alun John, 15 July 1950. Quoted in Alun John's unpublished thesis 'The Life and Work of Edward Thomas' (Univ. College of South Wales and Monmouthshire, 1952–3), p. 16. For permission to quote two short extracts from the thesis I am indebted to the Librarian, Mr. R. J. Bates.

5 'Olivia Patterson', *BC.*

6 E. S. P. Haynes, *The Lawyer* (London, 1951), p. 168.

7 *Walter Pater* (London, 1913), p. 10.

8 'Wit and Dalliance', *The Daily Chronicle*, 13 April 1908, p. 3.

9 ET to E. S. P. Haynes, 12 Aug. 1899, *ACL.*

10 *Oxford* (London, 1903), p. 117.

11 T. Russell in conversation with Alun John. See note 4 above.

12 'Notes on the Life and Ancestry of Edward Thomas by his Father', included in H. G. Wright's *Studies in Contemporary Literature*, pp. 108–9.

13 John Moore, *Letters*, p. 279.

14 H. W. Nevinson, *Changes and Chances* (London, 1923), p. 195.

15 ET to Edna (surname unknown), undated, *BC.*

16 John Moore, *Letters*, p. 62.

17 ET to Jesse Berridge, 12 March 1902. All Thomas—Berridge correspondence cited is by kind permission of Mr. Christian Berridge.

18 Helen Thomas to Janet Hooton, 7 June 1902.

19 Helen Thomas, *World Without End*, p. 111.

20 In an interview with Patric Dickinson, broadcast on the Third Programme on 8 April 1967, Helen Thomas maintained that 'No One So Much As You' was written for ET's mother. It is, however, far more satisfactory to read the poem as addressed to her.

21 ET to Helen Thomas, *c.* April 1916. The original letter is in Lincoln College Library. It was published by W. W. Robson in *The Times Literary Supplement* for 23 March 1962, p. 208.

22 Extracts from Helen Thomas's diary are included in 'A Golden Book', a private anthology in the Bodleian.

23 John Moore, *Letters*, p. 103.

24 ET to Jesse Berridge, 14 June 1903.

25 ET to Jesse Berridge, 22 Dec. 1903.

26 Helen Thomas, *World Without End*, pp. 90–1 (my italics).

27 ET to Jesse Berridge, 6 June 1902.

28 John Moore, *Letters*, p. 300.

29 Ibid., p. 303.
30 Ibid., p. 292.
31 Ibid., p. 297.
32 Sir Ian MacAlister, 'I Knew Edward Thomas', *The Listener*, 5 Jan. 1939, p. 32.
33 Helen Thomas, *World Without End*, p. 108 (my italics).
34 *The Happy-Go-Lucky Morgans* (London, 1913), pp. 122–7.
35 Ibid., p. 124.
36 *Selected Letters of Robert Frost*, p. 164.
37 John Moore, *Letters*, p. 290.
38 Ibid., pp. 289–90.
39 ET to Jesse Berridge, 10 Sept. 1904.
40 J. C. Squire, 'Books of the Day', *The Observer*, 21 Nov. 1926.
41 W. H. Davies, 'Memories', *School*, vol. I, no. 3 (Nov. 1933), 19.
42 Norman Douglas, *Looking Back* (London, 1934), pp. 175–6.
43 John Moore, *Letters*, p. 120.
44 Helen Thomas, *World Without End*, p. 108.
45 Ibid., p. 107.

3. Promises to Keep

1 John Moore, *Letters*, pp. 295–7.
2 Ibid., p. 124.
3 ET to Jesse Berridge, 25 July 1905.
4 ET to Jesse Berridge, 8 Aug. 1905.
5 *Beautiful Wales* (London, 1924 edn.), p. 44.
6 Ashley Gibson, *Postscript to Adventure* (London, 1930), p. 12.
7 John Moore, *Letters*, pp. 299–300.
8 See his 'Preface' to *The Autobiography of a Super-Tramp*.
9 R. J. Stonesifer, *W. H. Davies: A Critical Biography* (London, 1963), p. 69.
10 'A Poet at Last', *The Daily Chronicle*, 21 Oct. 1905, p. 3.
11 Quoted in Lawrence W. Hockey, 'Edward Thomas and W. H. Davies', *The Welsh Review*, vol. VII, no. 2 (1948), 83.
12 'A Poet and Mr. Shaw', *The Daily Chronicle*, 23 April 1908, p. 3.
13 John Moore, *Letters*, p. 132.
14 R. J. Stonesifer (op. cit., p. 239, n. 2) wrote that he was unable to locate any Davies–Thomas correspondence of this period. Nineteen such letters, from March 1908 to July 1911, are in Yale Univ. Library.

15 Quoted in Lawrence W. Hockey, op. cit., pp. 86–7.
16 ET to Edward Garnett, 30 March 1909, *ACL.*
17 Review of *Farewell to Posey*, *The Morning Post*, 7 April 1910, p. 2.
18 A copy of the petition, signed by Hilaire Belloc, is in the *ACL.*
19 John Moore, *Letters*, p. 302.
20 'Edward Thomas's Letters to W. H. Hudson', *London Mercury*, vol. II, no. 10 (Aug. 1920), 436–7.
21 ET to Jesse Berridge, 1 Jan. 1907.
22 Mrs. Q. D. Leavis, *Scrutiny*, vol. VI, no. 4 (March 1938), 436.
23 ET to Jesse Berridge, 8 Aug. 1908.
24 'Happy Hampshire', *The Daily Chronicle*, 1 May 1908, p. 3.
25 *The Athenaeum*, 22 July 1911, p. 98.
26 'Two Poets', *The English Review*, vol. II, no. 3 (June 1909), 627–30.
27 Edgar Jepson, *Memories of an Edwardian and Neo-Georgian* (London, 1938), pp. 140–1.
28 Helen Thomas, *World Without End*, p. 133.
29 ET to Jesse Berridge, 26 Dec. 1909.
30 Harry Hooton to Janet Hooton, 15 Jan. 1910.
31 ET to Jesse Berridge, 8 Dec. 1910.
32 Rupert Brooke to ET, 10 Sept. 1910, *MUL.*
33 'A Brilliant Group', *The Daily Chronicle*, 9 April 1912, p. 3.
34 John Moore, *Letters*, p. 313.
35 ET to Harold Monro, 19 May 1911, *LML.*
36 *The Athenaeum*, 26 April 1913, pp. 454–5.
37 *Letters from W. H. Hudson to Edward Garnett* (London, 1925), p. 118.
38 Helen Thomas, *World Without End*, p. 116.
39 ET to Harold Monro, 26 Dec. 1911, *LML.*
40 Helen Thomas to ET, 10 Nov. [1911].
41 ET to Edward Garnett, 5 Nov. and 2 Dec. 1911, *ACL.*
42 *George Borrow* (London, 1912), p. 206.
43 Quoted in R. P. Eckert, *Edward Thomas: A Biography and a Bibliography* (London, 1937), p. 126—hereafter cited as *A Biography.*

4. Elected Friends

1 ET to Harold Monro, 3 Jan. 1913, *LML.*
2 'Georgian Poets', *The Daily Chronicle*, 14 Jan. 1913, p. 4. For his second review of *G.P.* I, see *The Bookman*, March 1913, p. 330.
3 ET to Harold Monro, 24 Feb. 1913, *LML.*

4 'Ella Wheeler Wilcox', *Poetry and Drama*, vol. I, no. 1 (March 1913), 42.

5 Joy Grant, *Harold Monro and the Poetry Bookshop* (London, 1967), p. 55.

Thomas's contributions to the eight numbers of *Poetry and Drama* were as follows:

No. 1 (March 1913):	'Ella Wheeler Wilcox', pp. 33–42. Review of *Poems* by W. B. Yeats, pp. 53–6.
No. 2 (June 1913):	'Thomas Hardy of Dorchester', pp. 180–4.
No. 3 (Sept. 1913):	Review of *Poems* by John Gould Fletcher, pp. 363–5. Review of *Poems* by John Alford, p. 366. Review of *Eve and Other Poems* by Ralph Hodgson, pp. 370–1.
No. 4 (Dec. 1913):	Review of *Oxford Poetry 1910–1913* and *Cambridge Poets 1900–1913*, pp. 489–91.
No. 5 (March 1914):	'Reviewing: An Unskilled Labour', pp. 37–41. Review of 'New Editions, Reprints, and Anthologies', pp. 62–5.
No. 6 (June 1914):	Review of 'Reprints and Anthologies', pp. 185–8.
No. 7 (Sept. 1914):	Review of 'Reprints and Anthologies', pp. 299–301.
No. 8 (Dec. 1914):	'War Poetry', pp. 341–5. Review of 'Anthologies and Reprints', pp. 384–8.

6 'ET's Letters to W. H. Hudson', *London Mercury*, p. 439.

7 Eleanor Farjeon, *Edward Thomas: The Last Four Years* (London, 1958), p. x.

8 Ibid., p. 13.

9 *In Pursuit of Spring* (London, 1914), p. 50.

10 Rupert Brooke to ET, undated (but *c.* May 1913), *MUL*.

11 James Guthrie, 'Edward Thomas in Sussex', *Sussex County Magazine*, Sept. 1939, p. 591.

12 Eleanor Farjeon, op. cit., p. 27.

13 Review of *Peacock Pie*, *The Bookman*, Sept. 1913, p. 260.

14 Eleanor Farjeon, op. cit., p. 28.

15 Ibid., p. 13.

16 *Four-and-Twenty Blackbirds* (London, 1915), pp. 67–9.
17 Eleanor Farjeon, op. cit., p. 28. For a variation of his reply, see Ernest Rhys, *Letters From Limbo* (London, 1936), p. viii.
18 Eleanor Farjeon, op. cit., p. 37.
19 Lawrance Thompson, *Robert Frost: The Early Years 1874–1915* (London, 1967), p. 464.
20 ET to Robert Frost, 24 Feb. 1914, *DCL.*
21 ET to Edward Garnett, 7 Jan. 1914, *ACL.*
22 The fragments of which are now in the *B.C.*
23 *Selected Letters of Robert Frost*, p. 126.
24 'Robert Frost', *The New Weekly*, 8 Aug. 1914 p. 249
25 Review of *North of Boston*, *The English Review*, vol. XVIII, no. 1 (Aug. 1914), 142–3.
26 For one of Frost's characteristic tributes to Thomas, see Louis Mertins, *Robert Frost*, p. 136.
27 ET to Robert Frost, 19 May 1914, *DCL.*
28 ET to Robert Frost, 6 June 1914, *DCL.*
29 Eleanor Farjeon, op. cit., p. 79.
30 Ibid., p. 81.
31 In connection with this incident Lawrance Thompson (op. cit., p. 452) wrote that 'Thomas was aware that he might be drafted into military service at any time.' In fact enlistment was still voluntary, and conscription was not introduced until 1916. The age limit was raised from 35 to 40 shortly after the outbreak of the war, but this age barrier was arbitrarily lowered and raised to meet the demands of the Front. (I am indebted to the Imperial War Museum for the above information.)
32 Eleanor Farjeon, op. cit., p. 88.
33 Helen Thomas, *World Without End*, p. 159.
34 When not otherwise indicated, biographical details concerning Robert Frost are drawn from Lawrance Thompson's *The Early Years.*
35 Lawrance Thompson, op. cit., p. 310.
36 Walter de la Mare, 'Foreword', *Collected Poems of Edward Thomas* (London, 1965 edn.), p. 12.
37 John W. Haines, 'As I Knew Him', *In Memoriam: Edward Thomas* (London, 1919), p. 18.
38 Helen Thomas, 'Poets' Holiday in the Shadow of War', *The Times*, 3 Aug. 1963, p. 8.

39 Edward Thomas, 'Rupert Brooke', *The English Review*, vol. XX, no. 3 (June 1915), 325.
40 Quoted in Louis Mertins, *Robert Frost*, p. 136.
41 Mrs. Lascelles Abercrombie, 'Memories of a Poet's Wife', *The Listener*, 15 Nov. 1956, p. 794.
42 Christopher Hassall, *Rupert Brooke: A Biography* (London, 1964), p. 459.
43 The essays originally appeared in *The English Review* during 1914–15. All three were reprinted in *The Last Sheaf* (London, 1928), pp. 91–149.
44 Eleanor Farjeon, op. cit., p. 95.
45 *The Last Sheaf*, p. 113.
46 Ibid., p. 141.
47 Ibid., p. 124.
48 Ibid., p. 147.
49 Ibid., p. 116.
50 Ibid., pp. 119–20.
51 Ibid., pp. 117–18.
52 ET to Jesse Berridge, 3 Sept. 1914.
53 'ET's Letters to W. H. Hudson', *London Mercury*, pp. 439–40.
54 Loc. cit.
55 Ernest Rhys, *Letters From Limbo*, p. 139.
56 ET to Robert Frost, 15 Dec. 1914, *DCL.*
57 *Selected Letters of Robert Frost*, p. 209.
58 ET to Harold Monro, 15 Dec. 1914, *LML.*
59 Thomas had reviewed *Des Imagistes* under the title 'Exotic Verse' in *The New Weekly* for 9 May 1914. He declared that the book 'sticks out of the crowd like a tall marble monument'. Pound, he felt, had contributed 'the most impressive-looking poems' and had 'seldom done better than here under the restraint imposed by Chinese originals or models.' F. S. Flint's work, however, remained 'the most attractive'.
60 ET to Harold Monro, undated (but *c.* Dec. 1914), *LML.*
61 Eleanor Farjeon, op. cit., p. 104.
62 Ibid., p. 114.
63 See *This England: An Anthology from her Writers* (London, 1915), pp. 111–12.

Thomas, of course, felt extremely vulnerable as far as his poetry was concerned. Giving his reason for the pseudonym to Garnett, he wrote: 'I don't want people to be confused by what they know or think of me already, although I know I shall lose the advantage of some friendly prejudice.' (ET to Edward Garnett, 17 March 1915, *ACL.*)

64 Eleanor Farjeon, op. cit., p. 114.
65 *Selected Letters of Robert Frost*, pp. 217–20.

5. Lights Out

1 ET to Robert Frost, 3 May 1915, *DCL.*
2 ET to Robert Frost, 22 April 1915, *DCL.*
3 *Selected Letters of Robert Frost*, p. 165.
4 H. Coombes, *Edward Thomas* (London, 1956), p. 42.
5 *The Life of the Duke of Marlborough* (London, 1915), p. 118.
6 Ibid., pp. 11–12.
7 Ibid., pp. 95–6.
8 Eleanor Farjeon, *The Last Four Years*, p. 119.
9 ET to Jesse Berridge, 1 June 1915.
10 ET to Edward Garnett, 17 March 1915, *ACL.*
11 Eleanor Farjeon, op. cit., p. 142.
12 ET to Robert Frost, 18 June 1915, *DCL.*
13 Eleanor Farjeon, op. cit., p. 148.
14 ET to Robert Frost, 11 July 1915, *DCL.*
15 ET to Robert Frost, 28 Aug. 1915, *DCL.*
16 ET to Robert Frost, 3 Oct. 1915, *DCL.*
17 ET to Robert Frost, 12 Oct. 1915, *DCL.*
18 ET to Robert Frost, 3 Oct. 1915, *DCL.*
19 Wilfred Owen trained at the camp at approximately the same time, but there is no evidence that they ever met. Mr. Harold Owen wrote to me that 'Wilfred Owen never mentioned ET in conversation nor yet in any of his letters home.'
20 Eleanor Farjeon, op. cit., p. 171.
21 R. P. Eckert, *A Biography*, pp. 165–6.
22 John Moore, *Letters*, p. 228.
23 H. W. Nevinson, *Changes and Chances*, pp. 195–6.
24 ET to Robert Frost, 13 Nov. 1915, *DCL.*
25 ET to Robert Frost, 21 May 1916, *DCL.*
26 Claude Colleer Abbott and Anthony Bertram (eds.), *Poet and Painter. Being the Correspondence between Gordon Bottomley and Paul Nash 1910–1946* (London, 1955), p. 89.

27 For details see Christopher Hassall, *Edward Marsh, Patron of the Arts* (London, 1959), p. 211. Hassall mistakenly says that this was the first time that Thomas and Brooke met.
28 ET to Robert Frost, 6 Dec. 1915, *DCL*.
29 Christopher Hassall, op. cit., pp. 422–3.
30 Quoted in Robert H. Ross, *The Georgian Revolt* (London, 1967), p. 177.
31 Gordon Bottomley, *The Welsh Review*, p. 177.
32 ET to Jesse Berridge, 17 Sept. 1916.
33 Eleanor Farjeon, op. cit., p. 154.
34 *Selected Letters of Robert Frost*, p. 217.
35 Mrs. Joseph Conrad, *The Bookman*, Sept. 1930, p. 324.
36 Helen Thomas to Janet Hooton, 29 Jan. 1920.
37 Quoted in a letter from Roger Ingpen to Robert Frost, 17 April 1917, *DCL*.
38 Eleanor Farjeon, op. cit., p. 244.
39 Ibid., p. 253.
40 John Moore, *Letters*, p. 255.
41 ET to Robert Frost, 6 March 1917, *DCL*.
42 ET to Robert Frost, 8 March 1917, *DCL*.
43 Eleanor Farjeon, op. cit., p. 254.
44 Ibid., p. 257.
45 ET to Robert Frost, 2 April 1917, *DCL*.
46 *The Times Literary Supplement*, 29 March 1917, p. 151.
47 R. G. Thomas (ed.), *Letters from Edward Thomas to Gordon Bottomley* (London, 1968), p. 282.
48 John Moore, *Letters*, p. 264.
49 Franklin Lushington (pseud. Mark Severn), *The Gambardier* (London, 1930), p. 128 [Thomas appears under the name Thomas Tyler].
50 Ibid., p. 129.
51 There are several conflicting reports of the time and manner of ET's death. Eleanor Farjeon in *The Last Four Years* (pp. 262–3) gives two versions. The first was told by a Sergeant in ET's Company: ' "At the end of the day when the battle was over we had the Huns on the run, and the plain was full of our men shouting and singing and dancing. We thought we had won the war! Mr. Thomas came up from the dug-out behind his gun and leaned in the opening filling his clay pipe. One of the Huns turned as he was running and

shot a stray shot, and Mr. Thomas fell. It was all over in an instant. I went out to the men and called, 'Men we've lost our best officer.' The cry went up, 'Not Mr. Thomas?' and there was no more shouting that day."'

Eleanor Farjeon comments: 'This was the story as nearly as I remember it in the Sergeant's own words. But my memory had misled me about the stray shot, it was a stray shell. When Helen came to know Edward's Captain, Franklin Lushington, he told her that as Edward stood by his dug-out lighting his pipe all the Germans had retreated, but a last shell they sent over passed so close to him that the blast of air stopped his heart. "He told me," Helen writes, "there was no wound and his beloved body was not injured. This was borne out by the fact that when the contents of his pockets were returned to me—a bundle of letters, a note-book and the Shakespeare Sonnets I had given him, they were all strangely creased as though subject to some terrible pressure, most strange to see. There was no wound or disfigurement at all."'

Mrs. Myfanwy Thomas writes to me: 'We have always understood that Franklin Lushington's letter [written on 10 April 1917 and quoted in full on pp. 263–4 of *The Last Four Years*] . . . was a true account of his death. A stray shell after a battle, in the evening, fell very near and the blast of it was the cause of death, his body unmarked. . . . The watch my father carried, which we have, has stopped at about 7.30, which one has imagined was the time.'

This account conflicts, however, with Franklin Lushington's second (later) version in *The Gambardier* (pp. 123–30). Immediately after the passage cited in note 49, Lushington continued: 'At seven o'clock next *morning* he was killed in the O.P. *by a direct hit through the chest*' (my italics).

John Moore (*Letters*, p. 266) follows this version with regard to the time of ET's death, but then reverts to Lushington's earlier version, claiming that ET was killed a few minutes after seven in the morning by a direct hit from a shell. This is substantiated by the opening of a letter from John M. Thorburn, a fellow officer with ET at the time of his death, to Helen Thomas. It is headed 'France, 9 April 1917': 'It is a great trial to me to write to inform you that your husband was killed this morning. As I have been very closely associated with him since we first met at Trowbridge, I thought it would be well to take upon myself the duty of letting you know of his death. It happened this morning, by shell fire, in the observation post.' The letter is now in the possession of Professor R. G. Thomas, to whom I am indebted for the above information.

6. The Road Not Taken

1 'How I Began', reprinted in *The Last Sheaf*, p. 15.
2 Loc. cit.
3 Ibid., p. 16.
4 Ibid., pp. 17–18.
5 A phrase he applied to Keats's first book of poems. See his *Keats* (London, 1916), p. 36.
6 *The Last Sheaf*, p. 18.
7 Ibid., p. 19.
8 'First Known when Lost', *CP*, p. 153.
9 John Moore, *Letters*, p. 26.
10 *The Last Sheaf*, p. 17.
11 F. R. Leavis, *New Bearings*, p. 69.
12 Quoted in Ian Hamilton (ed.), 'Introd.', *Selected Poetry and Prose of Alun Lewis* (London, 1966), p. 21.
13 John Freeman, 'Memoir', *The Tenth Muse* (London, 1917 edn.), p. i.
14 The phrase is from Ezra Pound's *Gaudier-Brzeska* (London, 1916), p. 103, used to describe his own poem 'In a Station of the Metro'.
15 F. R. Leavis, loc. cit.
16 *The Woodland Life* (London, 1897), pp. 19–20.
17 See John D. Gordan, *Bulletin of the New York Public Library*, p. 74.
18 *The Woodland Life*, p. 85.
19 F. R. Leavis, op. cit., p. 70.
20 *The Woodland Life*, pp. 85–6.
21 Ibid., pp. 86–7.
22 F. R. Leavis, loc. cit.
23 *Cloud Castle* (London, 1922), pp. 94–5.
24 *The Woodland Life*, p. 62.
25 *Horae Solitariae* (London, 1902), pp. 89–90.
26 *Oxford*, p. 110.
27 *Rose Acre Papers* (London, 1910 edn.), pp. 93–5.
28 *Oxford*, pp. 114–6.
29 *Horae Solitariae*, p. 125.

30 *Cloud Castle*, p. 130.
31 *The South Country* (London, 1932 edn.), p. 6.
32 *Horae Solitariae*, pp. 180–1.
33 *Light and Twilight* (London, 1911), p. 72.
34 *Horae Solitariae*, p. 91.
35 *Oxford*, p. 14.
36 *Horae Solitariae*, p. 92.
37 *Oxford*, p. 8.
38 John Moore, *Letters*, p. 37.
39 *Beautiful Wales*, pp. 82–3.
40 Gordon Bottomley, *The Welsh Review*, p. 173.
41 H. Coombes, *Edward Thomas*, p. 182.
42 John Moore, *Letters*, p. 197.
43 Ibid., p. 282.
44 Ibid., pp. 288–9.
45 Ibid., p. 121.
46 Norman Douglas, *Looking Back*, pp. 174–5.
47 See his Preface to *The American*. James is, of course, describing a more unconscious act than Thomas.
48 'March', *CP*, p. 124.
49 *Beautiful Wales*, pp. 100–2.
50 'Rain', *CP*, p. 84.
51 *Beautiful Wales*, p. 131.
52 *Horae Solitariae*, pp. 6–7.
53 'There was nowhere any sign of decay or change. . . . All things expressed a calm and certainly immortal bliss.' *Light and Twilight*, p. 145.
54 'I felt entirely free there and alone and without responsibility . . .' *Rest and Unrest* (London, 1910), p. 149.
55 '. . . to live upon that green grass, to race upon that pale sand, to swim in that sapphire water . . .' *Light and Twilight*, p. 65.
56 *Beautiful Wales*, p. 94.
57 Ibid., p. 77.
58 *The Heart of England* (London, 1906), pp. 62–3.
59 Ibid., p. 72.
60 Ibid., p. 141.
61 Ibid., pp. 63–4.
62 Ibid., pp. 108–9.
63 *Rest and Unrest*, p. 63.

64 *The Icknield Way* (London, 1929 edn.), pp. 266–7.
65 *The Country* (London, 1913), pp. 21–2.
66 Ibid., p. 6.
67 *Beautiful Wales*, pp. 73–5.
68 *The Heart of England*, pp. 73–4.
69 R. P. Eckert, *A Biography*, pp. 214–5.
70 John Moore, *Letters*, p. 159.
71 *Light and Twilight*, p. 1.
72 ET to Edward Garnett, 1909, *ACL*.
73 *The South Country*, p. 45.
74 Ibid., p. 20.
75 *Light and Twilight*, p. 133.
76 *The South Country*, p. 50.
77 *Rest and Unrest*, pp. 128–9.
78 Ibid., pp. 140–3.
79 'Unfathomable Sea! whose waves are years . . .
Who shall put forth on thee,
Unfathomable Sea?'
('Time')
'Of frozen floods, unfathomable deeps . . .'
('Mont Blanc')
Thomas quoted the opening line of 'Time' in recalling his youthful appetite for Shelley in *The Happy-Go-Lucky Morgans*, p. 293.
80 *Rose Acre Papers*, pp. 95–100 (my italics).
81 *Beautiful Wales*, p. 133 (my italics).
82 *The Heart of England*, p. 59 (my italics).
83 *The South Country*, pp. 24–5 (my italics).
84 *Light and Twilight*, pp. 75–6 (my italics).

7. Critic As Artist

1 Alun Lewis, [review of] *The Trumpet and Other Poems*, *Horizon*, vol. III, no. 13 (Jan. 1941), 80.
2 *Horae Solitariae*, p. 125.
3 *The South Country*, p. 136.
4 Ibid., p. 82.
5 *Richard Jefferies*, p. 336.
6 *Feminine Influence on the Poets* (London, 1910), p. 85.
7 *Maurice Maeterlinck* (London, 1911), p. 27.
8 *Algernon Charles Swinburne* (London, 1912), pp. 94–6.

9 *Walter Pater*, p. 213.
10 Ibid., p. 189.
11 Thomas included this passage from the *Defence of Poetry* in his *This England* anthology, which was contemporary with 'Words'.
12 *Walter Pater*, pp. 198–9.
13 *Lafcadio Hearn* (London, 1912), pp. 73–4.
14 The typescript of 'March' is included in ET's letters to Frost in *DCL*; the MS is in *LML*.
15 H. Coombes, *Edward Thomas*, p. 198.
16 *Swinburne*, p. 20.
17 *Walter Pater*, p. 125.
18 *Swinburne*, p. 22.
19 *Walter Pater*, p. 215.
20 Quoted in Elizabeth S. Sergeant, *Robert Frost: The Trial by Existence* (New York, 1961), p. 113.
21 T. S. Eliot, 'The Music of Poetry', *The Partisan Review*, vol. IX, no. 6 (Nov.–Dec. 1942), 459.
22 *Richard Jefferies*, p. 321.
23 T. S. Eliot, op. cit., p. 457.
24 'A New Poet', *The Daily News and Leader*, 22 July 1914, p. 7.
25 See chap. 4, note 27.
26 *Swinburne*, p. 198.
27 *Walter Pater*, p. 104.
28 Ibid., pp. 85, 153.
29 *Swinburne*, pp. 159–60.
30 Ibid., pp. 119–20.
31 Ibid., pp. 158–62.
32 *Walter Pater*, pp. 97–104.
33 *Lafcadio Hearn*, p. 40.
34 'Introd.', *Rural Rides* (London, 1912), pp. x–xi.
35 *Swinburne*, p. 171.
36 Julian Thomas, 'Introd.', *The Childhood*, p. 8.
37 *The Country*, pp. 8–9.
38 *Walter Pater*, p. 68.
39 Ibid., pp. 73–4.
40 *Lafcadio Hearn*, pp. 51–2.
41 'Reviewers make me out a very fine chap,' he wrote to Berridge on 14 Sept. 1902, 'so I am forced to the extreme of humility. You should have seen *The Athenaeum*.'

42 *The Athenaeum*, 30 Aug. 1902, pp. 285–6.
43 *Walter Pater*, pp. 95–6.
44 'Introd.', *Rural Rides*, p. ix.
45 *George Borrow*, pp. 162, 321–2.
46 *The Heart of England*, p. 66.
47 MacDonald Emslie, 'Spectatorial Attitudes', *A Review of English Literature*, vol. V, no. 1 (Jan. 1964), 67. Emslie's article contains a detailed analysis of 'The Watchers'.
48 John Moore, *Letters*, p. 253 (my italics).
49 *Swinburne*, pp. 77–84.
50 During the course of the book he also approached his contemporaries for help. 'It has just occurred to me you might answer an important question I have just been putting to three other poets,' he wrote to Berridge on 14 April 1910. 'It is to help me in my book on Women and Poets. I want to find out as many different ways as possible of establishing a relation between "reality" and a poem to or about an individual woman. I want to know how and when poets write such poems, whether in the quiet of the end, of satiety, of anticipation, or of an interval in love's progress, or etc. . . . Well can you help me? Can you single out any poem of which you feel able to tell me the circumstances under which it was written and what relation it bears to "reality" *if any*, and if none then the nature of the fancy or whatever you think it might be called. If you can do this I will . . . ensure that nobody but myself has any suspicion of the authorship of the remarks, if I use them in any way.'

Some of his friends' replies were included in *Feminine Influence*, pp. 45–7. One of them may be identified as that of W. H. Davies, who gave the origin of three of his poems: 'A Lovely Woman', 'Love's Birth' and 'Love's Coming'.
51 *Feminine Influence*, p. 251.
52 Ibid., p. 300.
53 Ibid., pp. 94–5.
54 Ibid., p. 147.
55 Ibid., pp. 33–4.
56 Ibid., pp. 285–94.
57 Ibid., pp. 92–3.
58 Ibid., p. 179.
59 *Light and Twilight*, p. 56.
60 Ibid., p. 121.

61 Ibid., p. 173.
62 Helen Thomas, *World Without End*, p. 117.
63 *A Bibliography of Modern Poetry*, vol. II, no. 12 (June 1920).
64 *George Borrow*, p. 318 (my italics).
65 *Richard Jefferies*, p. 57.
66 Ibid., p. 187.

8. Like Exiles Home

1 'The White House', *LML*. Illegible in two places indicated.
2 *The Isle of Wight* (London, 1911), p. 29.
3 'Old Man's Beard', *LML*.
4 F. R. Leavis, *New Bearings*, p. 69.
5 *The Icknield Way*, pp. 278–83.
6 John Moore, *Letters*, p. 326.
7 *Light and Twilight*, pp. 54–5.
8 Alun Lewis, *Horizon*, p. 86.
9 *Beautiful Wales*, p. 94.
10 Gordon Bottomley, *The Welsh Review*, p. 173.
11 'The Figure a Poem Makes', *Complete Poems of Robert Frost* (London, 1959), p. 20.
12 R. P. Eckert, *A Biography*, p. 147.
13 John Moore, *Letters*, p. 199.
14 Edward Garnett (ed.), 'Introd.', *Selected Poems* (Newtown, Montgomeryshire, 1927), p. xiii.
15 H. Coombes, *Edward Thomas*, p. 244.
16 C. Day Lewis, 'The Poetry of Edward Thomas', *Essays by Divers Hands*, vol. XXVIII (London, 1956), p. 78.
17 Vernon Scannell, *Edward Thomas* (London, 1963), p. 13.
18 Harold Roy Brennan, 'The Poet of the Countryside: Edward Thomas', *The Cardinal*, vol. I, no. 4 (Jan.–Feb. 1926), 25.
19 Louis Mertins, *Robert Frost*, p. 126.
20 Radcliffe Squires, *The Major Themes of Robert Frost* (Michigan, 1963), pp. 12–14.
21 *Selected Letters of Robert Frost*, pp. 262–3.
22 Quoted in Harold Roy Brennan, op. cit., p. 18.
23 *In Pursuit of Spring*, p. 178.
24 Gordon Bottomley, *The Welsh Review*, p. 172.
25 *Letters from W. H. Hudson to Edward Garnett*, pp. 134–5.
26 Alun Lewis, *Letters from India* (Cardiff, 1946), p. 61.

27 *The Last Sheaf*, p. 221.
28 John Moore, *Letters*, p. 211 (my italics).
29 'ET's Letters to W. H. Hudson', *London Mercury*, p. 440.
30 *Selected Letters of Robert Frost*, p. 193.
31 Quoted in R. J. Stonesifer, *W. H. Davies*, p. 239, n. 39.
32 John Lehmann, 'Edward Thomas', *The Open Night* (London, 1952), p. 80.
33 C. Day Lewis, *The Buried Day* (London, 1960), p. 97.
34 *The South Country*, p. 7.
35 *Beautiful Wales*, p. 174.
36 Thomas used this excerpt from Yeats's play as his epigraph to *The South Country*.
37 *Keats*, p. 45.
38 Ibid., p. 63.
39 *The Happy-Go-Lucky Morgans*, p. 115.
40 C. Day Lewis, *Essays by Divers Hands*, p. 82.
41 *The South Country*, pp. 132–3.
42 *The Heart of England*, p. 18.
43 John Moore, *Letters*, p. 326.
44 R. J. Stonesifer, *W. H. Davies*, p. 116.
45 'ET's Letters to W. H. Hudson', *London Mercury*, p. 441.
46 F. R. Leavis, *Revaluation* (London, 1956 edn.), p. 246.
47 Quoted in Lawrance Thompson, 'Introd.', *Selected Letters of Robert Frost*, p. vii.
48 *Selected Letters of Robert Frost*, pp. 45–6.
49 John Moore, *Letters*, p. 172.
50 'You mustn't give away the fact that The Other Man is rather a lie,' he wrote to Berridge on 3 May 1914. His commissioned prose was not, however, the medium for intimate revelation and his meetings with his *alter ego* (pp. 119, 140, 218) never amount to anything.
51 *Selected Letters of Robert Frost*, pp. 189–90.
52 Details concerning Frost's explanation of 'The Road Not Taken' are drawn from Lawrance Thompson's 'Introd.' to the *Selected Letters of Robert Frost*, pp. xiv–xvi.

Thomas himself appeared dubious about such an interpretation. 'I doubt if you can get anybody to see the fun of the thing without showing them and advising which kind of laugh they are to turn on,' he wrote to Frost on 11 July 1915, *DCL*.

9. Roads to France

1 Athalie Bushnell, 'Edward Thomas', *The Poetry Review*, vol. XXXVIII, no. 4 (1947), 251.
2 H. Coombes, *Edward Thomas*, pp. 187–8.
3 John H. Johnston, *English Poetry of the First World War* (London, 1964), p. 128.
4 Bernard Bergonzi, *Heroes' Twilight* (London, 1965), p. 85.
5 Brian Gardner (ed.), *Up The Line To Death* (London, 1964), p. 182 (my italics).
6 I. M. Parsons (ed.), *Men Who March Away* (London, 1965), p. 16.
7 Loc. cit.
8 'I don't take the cigarette out of my mouth when I write Deceased over their letters. But one day I will write Deceased over many books.' Quoted in Edmund Blunden's 'Memoir' to *The Poems of Wilfred Owen* (London, 1960 edn.), p. 36.
9 'War Poetry', *Poetry and Drama*, vol. II, no. 8 (Dec. 1914), 341–5.
10 Helen Thomas, *World Without End*, p. 165.
11 'Anthologies and Reprints', *Poetry and Drama*, vol. II, no. 8 (Dec. 1914), 384.
12 *The Last Sheaf*, p. 109.
13 'Preface', *This England*.
14 John Moore, *Letters*, p. 223.
15 'Introd.', *Rural Rides*, pp. vii–x.
16 *This England*, p. 97.
17 Ibid., pp. 93–4.
18 'Introd.', *Words and Places* (London, 1911), p. ix.
19 *A Literary Pilgrim in England* (London, 1917), p. 24.
20 *Richard Jefferies*, p. 11.
21 *The Icknield Way*, p. 3.
22 Quoted in Edmund Blunden's 'Memoir', pp. 34–5.
23 See *This England*, pp. 68–9.
24 In *The Last Sheaf* (p. 139), Thomas related how many people were beginning to 'scent a new reality' in old prophecies and expressions as a result of the war and invasion scares.
25 *The Last Sheaf*, p. 136.
26 Ibid., p. 137 (my italics).
27 Ibid., p. 108.

28 *The Letters of Charles Sorley* (London, 1919), p. 97.
29 *Richard Jefferies*, pp. 208–9.
30 C. Day Lewis, *Essays by Divers Hands*, p. 76.
31 Vernon Scannell, *Edward Thomas*, p. 20.
32 Quoted in Edmund Blunden's 'Memoir', p. 29.
33 *Selected Letters of Robert Frost*, p. 184.
34 John Moore, *Letters*, p. 330.
35 D. W. Harding, 'A Note on Nostalgia', *Scrutiny*, vol. I, no. 1 (May 1932), 8.
36 Ibid., p. 13.
37 Ibid., p. 15.
38 Ibid., p. 17.
39 *Light and Twilight*, pp. 164–5.
40 Eleanor Farjeon, *The Last Four Years*, p. 12.
41 Ibid., p. 191.
42 Ibid., pp. 188, 205.
43 D. W. Harding, op. cit., p. 18.
44 ET to Edward Garnett, 24 June 1915, *ACL*.
45 ET to Edward Garnett, 25 June 1915, *ACL*.
46 *The South Country*, pp. 4–5.
47 John Moore, *Letters*, p. 236.
48 I. M. Parsons, *Men Who March Away*, p. 20.
49 Ibid., p. 21.
50 H. N. Fairchild, *Religious Trends in English Poetry*, vol. V (New York and London, 1962), p. 339 (my italics).
51 Ibid., p. 340.
52 *Rose Acre Papers*, p. 105.
53 *Selected Letters of Robert Frost*, p. 217.

BIBLIOGRAPHY

1. EDWARD THOMAS'S PUBLISHED WORKS

I. Prose

The Woodland Life (William Blackwood and Sons, London, 1897).
Horae Solitariae (Duckworth, London, 1902).
Oxford (A. & C. Black, London, 1903).
Rose Acre Papers (S. C. Brown Langham, London, 1904).
Beautiful Wales (A. & C. Black, London, 1905).
The Heart of England (J. M. Dent, London, 1906).
Richard Jefferies (Hutchinson, London, 1909).
The South Country (J. M. Dent, London, 1909).
Rest and Unrest (Duckworth, London, 1910).
Rose Acre Papers (Duckworth, London, 1910).
Feminine Influence on the Poets (Martin Secker, London, 1910).
Windsor Castle (Blackie and Son, London, 1910).
The Isle of Wight (Blackie and Son, London, 1911).
Light and Twilight (Duckworth, London, 1911).
Maurice Maeterlinck (Methuen, London, 1911).
Celtic Stories (The Clarendon Press, Oxford, 1911).
The Tenth Muse (Martin Secker, London, 1911).
Algernon Charles Swinburne (Martin Secker, London, 1912).
George Borrow (Chapman & Hall, London, 1912).
Lafcadio Hearn (Constable, London, 1912).
Norse Tales (The Clarendon Press, Oxford, 1912).
The Icknield Way (Constable, London, 1913).
The Country (B. T. Batsford, London, 1913).
The Happy-Go-Lucky Morgans (Duckworth, London, 1913).
Walter Pater (Martin Secker, London, 1913).
In Pursuit of Spring (Thomas Nelson and Sons, London, 1914).
Four-and-Twenty Blackbirds (Duckworth, London, 1915).
The Life of the Duke of Marlborough (Chapman & Hall, London, 1915).
Keats (T. C. & E. C. Jack, London, 1916).

A Literary Pilgrim in England (Methuen, London, 1917).
Cloud Castle (Duckworth, London, 1922).
Essays of To-day and Yesterday (George G. Harrap, London, 1926).
Chosen Essays (The Gregynog Press, Newtown, Montgomeryshire, 1926).
The Last Sheaf (Jonathan Cape, London, 1928).
The Childhood of Edward Thomas (Faber and Faber, London, 1938).
The Friend of the Blackbird [written in October 1911] (The Pear Tree Press, Flansham, Sussex, 1938).
The Prose of Edward Thomas, edited by Roland Gant (The Falcon Press, London, 1948).

II. Editions and Anthologies

The Poems of John Dyer (T. Fisher Unwin, London, 1903).
The Bible in Spain, by George Borrow (J. M. Dent, London, 1906).
The Pocket Book of Poems and Songs for the Open Air (E. Grant Richards, London, 1907).
British Country Life in Spring and Summer (Hodder and Stoughton, London, 1907).
British Country Life in Autumn and Winter (Hodder and Stoughton, London, 1908).
The Temple and A Priest to the Temple, by George Herbert (J. M. Dent, London, 1908).
Some British Birds (Hodder and Stoughton, London, 1908).
British Butterflies and Other Insects (Hodder and Stoughton, London, 1908).
The Plays and Poems of Christopher Marlowe (J. M. Dent, London, 1909).
The Hills and the Vale, by Richard Jefferies (Duckworth, London, 1909).
Words and Places, by Isaac Taylor (J. M. Dent, London, 1911).
Rural Rides, by William Cobbett (J. M. Dent, London, 1912).
The Pocket George Borrow (Chatto and Windus, London, 1912).
The Zincali, by George Borrow (J. M. Dent, London, 1914).
This England: An Anthology from her Writers (Oxford Univ. Press, London, 1915).
The Flowers I Love (T. C. & E. C. Jack, London, 1916).

III. The Poetry

(i) Poems published during Thomas's lifetime. The first appeared under the pseudonym Llewelyn the Bard, the remainder under Edward Eastaway:

'Eluned', *Beautiful Wales*, pp. 82–3.

'House and Man' and 'Interval', *Root and Branch*, vol. I, no. 4 (1915), 59–60.

'Haymaking' and 'The Manor Farm', *This England*, pp. 111–12.

Six Poems (The Pear Tree Press, Flansham, Sussex, 1916).

'Lob' and 'Words', *Form*, vol. I, no. 1 (April 1916), 33–4.

'Old Man', 'The Word' and 'The Unknown', *Poetry* (Chicago), vol. IX (Feb. 1917), 247–50.

18 poems appeared in *An Annual of New Poetry* (Constable, London, 1917), pp. 35–60.

(ii) The main collections and selections of the poetry, published posthumously:

Poems (Selwyn & Blount, London, 1917).

Last Poems (Selwyn & Blount, London, 1918).

Collected Poems [with a foreword by Walter de la Mare] (Selwyn & Blount, London, 1920).

This edition contains 136 poems: 64 from *Poems*, 71 from *Last Poems*, and 'Up in the Wind', first published in *In Memoriam: Edward Thomas* (The Morland Press, London, 1919).

Edward Thomas, The Augustan Books of Poetry, edited by Edward Thompson (Ernest Benn, London, 1926).

Selected Poems, edited by Edward Garnett (The Gregynog Press, Newtown, Montgomeryshire, 1927).

Two Poems (Ingpen & Grant, London, 1927).

The first publication of 'The Lane' and 'The Watchers'.

Collected Poems (Ingpen & Grant, London, 1928).

This edition contains 140 poems: 136 from the first edition (1920), with *Two Poems*, and the first publication of 'No One So Much As You' and 'The Wind's Song'.

Collected Poems (Faber and Faber, London, 1936).

The Trumpet and Other Poems (Faber and Faber, London, 1940).

Collected Poems [fifth impression] (Faber and Faber, London, 1949).

This edition contains 141 poems: 140 from the first Faber imprint (1936) with the first publication of 'P.H.T.'

Selected Poems, edited by Robin Skelton (Hutchinson, London, 1962).

Selected Poems, edited by R. S. Thomas (Faber and Faber, London, 1965).

The Green Roads, edited by Eleanor Farjeon (The Bodley Head, London, 1965).

Collected Poems [ninth impression] (Faber and Faber, London, 1965).

'The Poetry of Edward Thomas', a large selection of the poems read and introduced by Helen Thomas, was recorded at Bridge Cottage, Newbury, in 1965.

2. UNPUBLISHED MATERIAL

The main sources of unpublished material are given below. The remainder have been mentioned in the notes.

I. Correspondence

1900–13 (Berg Collection of the New York Public Library): 23 letters from Emily and Gordon Bottomley to Helen and Edward Thomas. The major collection of Thomas-Bottomley correspondence (1902–17) is deposited in the library of the Univ. College of South Wales and Monmouthshire. A number of the letters were included in John Moore's *The Life and Letters of Edward Thomas* (London, 1939). 182 of the 238 letters and postcards have recently been edited by R. G. Thomas and appear in *Letters from Edward Thomas to Gordon Bottomley* (London, 1968).

1901–17 (Mr. Christian Berridge): 76 letters from ET to Jesse Berridge. Extracts from the letters appeared in John Moore's *Letters*.

1906–17 (Academic Center Library, Univ. of Texas): 85 letters from ET to Edward Garnett. Extracts from the letters had previously appeared in *The Athenaeum*, no. 4694 (16 April 1920), pp. 501–3, and no. 4695 (23 April 1920), pp. 534–6.

1908–11 (Yale Univ. Library): 19 letters from W. H. Davies to ET.

1909–14 (Lockwood Memorial Library, State Univ. of New York at Buffalo): 39 letters from ET to Harold Monro (1909–14); one letter from Helen Thomas to Monro (undated); 14 letters from ET to Holbrook Jackson (1912–14).

1913–17 (Dartmouth College Library, New Hampshire): 60 letters from ET to Robert Frost, and one letter from Roger Ingpen to Frost. Enclosed in this group are copies of 19 of ET's poems, most of which are undated typescripts. They are: 'The Other', 'Interval', 'After Rain', 'The Hollow Wood', 'The Mountain Chapel', 'Old Man', 'November', 'March', 'The Sign-Post', 'An Old Song' (1), 'An Old Song' (2), 'Birds' Nests', 'The Manor Farm', 'The New Year', 'The Source', 'The Penny Whistle', 'Fifty Faggots', 'Sedge-Warblers' and 'Words'.

II. Manuscripts

A MS notebook in Lockwood Memorial Library covers the period 16 Nov.–7 Dec. 1914 and marks ET's transition from prose to poetry. It contains the prose sketches 'The White House' and 'Old Man's Beard', and versions of 'Up in the Wind', 'November', 'March', 'Old Man' and 'The Sign-Post'.

Additional MS 44990 is a manuscript book containing 62 of ET's poems, dated 24 Dec. 1914–23 May 1915. It was presented to the Dept. of MSS of the British Museum by Helen Thomas in 1938, in connection with the unveiling of the memorial to her husband at Steep. See H. I. Bell, 'Autograph Poems of Edward Thomas', *British Museum Quarterly*, vol. XII (Jan. 1938), 11–13.

Don. d. 28 is an exercise book containing 67 of ET's poems, dated 25 June 1915–24 Dec. 1916. It was presented to the Bodleian on 16 June 1932. Don. e. 10, a private anthology entitled 'A Golden Book', was presented in March 1935. The Bodleian also acquired the collection of books, MSS, and letters of the late R. P. Eckert in 1967.

The largest single collection of ET's MSS, both published and unpublished, is that of the Berg Collection. Among the more significant items consulted for this study were the following:

(i) 5 MS poems: 'The Unknown Bird', 'The Mill-Pond', 'The Gypsy', ' Man and Dog' and 'Ambition'.

(ii) 'Olivia Patterson', a novelette in collaboration with E. S. P. Haynes of 87 pages and 10 chapters of which four are signed by ET and a fifth is in his hand, a total of 38 pages.

(iii) 'Addenda to Autobiography', eleven autobiographical sketches.

(iv) Miscellaneous essays, correspondence, and early notebook poetry.

For a more detailed description of their holdings, see John D. Gordan, 'New in the Berg Collection', *Bulletin of the New York Public Library*, vol. LXVIII, no. 2 (Feb. 1964), 73–7.

3. OTHERS

I. Bibliography

Eckert, R. P., *Edward Thomas: A Biography and a Bibliography* (London, 1937). A detailed bibliography to the year 1937. Several notable omissions and a selection of the work published since 1937 are given below.

II. Biography

Abbott, Claude Colleer, and Bertram, Anthony (eds.), *Poet and Painter. Being the Correspondence between Gordon Bottomley and Paul Nash 1910–1946* (London, 1955).

Abercrombie, Mrs. Lascelles, 'Memories of a Poet's Wife', *The Listener*, 15 Nov. 1956, pp. 793–4.

Bax, Clifford, *Some I Knew Well* (London, 1951).

Bentley, E. C., *Those Days* (London, 1940).

Bottomley, Gordon, 'A Note on Edward Thomas', *The Welsh Review*, vol. IV, no. 3 (Sept. 1945), 166–78.

Davies, Anthony, 'Edward Thomas and his Father', *John O' London's*, 28 Oct. 1949.

Eckert, R. P., *Edward Thomas: A Biography and a Bibliography* (London, 1937).

Farjeon, Eleanor, *Magic Casements* (London, 1941).

'Edward Thomas and Robert Frost', *London Magazine*, May 1954, pp. 50–61.

Edward Thomas: The Last Four Years (London, 1958).

Fletcher, John Gould, *Life is my Song* (New York, 1937).

Guthrie, James, *To the Memory of Edward Thomas* (Flansham, Sussex, 1937).

'Edward Thomas in Sussex', *Sussex County Magazine*, Sept. 1939, pp. 591–3.

Haynes, E. S. P., *The Lawyer: A Conversation Piece* (London, 1951).

Hockey, Lawrence, 'Edward Thomas and W. H. Davies', *The Welsh Review*, vol. VII, no. 2 (1948), 81–91.

Jepson, Edgar, *Memories of an Edwardian and Neo-Georgian* (London, 1938).

Lushington, Franklin (pseud. Mark Severn), *The Gambardier* (London, 1930).

MacAlister, Sir Ian, 'I Knew Edward Thomas', *The Listener*, 5 Jan. 1939, pp. 32–3.

Moore, John, *The Life and Letters of Edward Thomas* (London, 1939).

Nevinson, H. W., 'Fame Too Late', *Life and Letters To-day*, March 1940, pp. 269–73.

Rhys, Ernest, *Letters From Limbo* (London, 1936).

Wales England Wed (London, 1940).

Robson, W. W., 'Edward Thomas', *The Lincoln Imp*, vol. XII, no. 2 (1948), 39–42.

'Edward Thomas's "Roads"', *The Times Literary Supplement*, 23 March 1962, p. 208.

Snaith, Stanley, 'A Note on Edward Thomas and "Eluned"', *Listen*, vol. III, no. 1 (Winter 1958), 15–18.

Thomas, Helen, *As It Was* and *World Without End* (London, 1956).

'Melting the Shyness of William Morris', *The Times*, 16 Jan. 1963, p. 10.

'Two Pieces of Advice from D. H. Lawrence', *The Times*, 13 Feb. 1963, p. 12.

'The Discovery of W. H. Davies', *The Times*, 27 March 1963, p. 12,

'Poets' Holiday in the Shadow of War', *The Times*, 3 Aug. 1963, p. 8.

'A Memory of W. H. Hudson', *The Times*, 27 Aug. 1965, p. 10.

Thomas, R. G. (ed.), *Letters from Edward Thomas to Gordon Bottomley* (London, 1968).

'Edward Thomas, Poet and Critic', *Essays and Studies* (1968), pp. 118–36.

Thompson, Lawrance (ed.), *Selected Letters of Robert Frost* (London. 1965).

III. Criticism

Ashton, Theresa, 'Edward Thomas: From Prose to Poetry', *The Poetry Review*, vol. XXVIII, no. 6 (1937), 449–55.

Bushnell, Athalie, 'Edward Thomas', *The Poetry Review*, vol. XXXVIII, no. 4 (1947), 241–52.

Burrow, John, 'Keats and Edward Thomas', *Essays in Criticism*, vol. VII, no. 4 (Oct. 1957), 404–15.

Cooke, W., 'Roads to France: The War Poetry of Edward Thomas', *Stand*, vol. IX, no. 3 (Spring 1968), 11–17.

Coombes, H., 'The Poetry of Edward Thomas', *Essays in Criticism*, vol. III, no. 2 (April 1953), 191–200.

Edward Thomas (London, 1956).

Short note, *Essays in Criticism*, vol. VIII, no. 2 (April 1958), 227–8.

'Hardy, De la Mare, and Edward Thomas', *Pelican Guide to English Literature*, vol. VII (Middlesex, 1961).

Cox, C. B., and Dyson, A. E., [analysis of] 'The Sign-Post', *Modern Poetry: Studies in Practical Criticism* (London, 1967 edn.), pp. 48–51.

Danby, John F., 'Edward Thomas', *Critical Quarterly*, vol. I, no. 4 (Winter 1959), 308–17.

Emslie, MacDonald, 'Spectatorial Attitudes' [analysis of 'The Watchers'], *A Review of English Literature*, vol. V, no. 1 (Jan. 1964), 66–9.

Harding, D. W., 'A Note on Nostalgia', *Scrutiny*, vol. I, no. 1 (May 1932), 8–19.

Harding, Joan, 'Dylan Thomas and Edward Thomas', *Contemporary Review*, vol. 192 (Sept. 1957), 150–4.

Jacobs, R. A., 'Regrets and Wishes', *English Journal*, vol. LIV (1965), 569–70.

Lawrence, Ralph, 'Edward Thomas in Perspective', *English*, vol. XII, no. 71 (Summer 1959), 177–83.

Lea, F. A., 'On Patriotism and Edward Thomas', *Adelphi*, Aug. 1938, pp. 323–5.

Lehmann, John, 'Edward Thomas', *The Open Night* (London, 1952).

Leavis, F. R., *New Bearings in English Poetry* (London, 1932).

'Imagery and Movement', *Scrutiny*, vol. XIII, no. 2 (Sept. 1945), 133–4.

Lewis, C. Day, 'The Poetry of Edward Thomas', *Essays by Divers Hands* [transactions of the Royal Society of Literature], vol. XXVIII (London, 1956).

Mathias, Roland, 'Edward Thomas', *Anglo-Welsh Review*, vol. X, no. 26 (1960), 23–37.

Rajan, B., 'Georgian Poetry: A Retrospect', *The Critic*, vol. I, no. 2 (Autumn 1947), 11–12.

Reeves, James, *The Critical Sense* [analysis of 'The Owl'] (London, 1963 edn.), pp. 79–82.

Scannell, Vernon, 'Content With Discontent', *London Magazine*, Jan. 1962, pp. 44–51.

Edward Thomas [Writers and their Work, no. 163] (London, 1962).

Weygandt, C., 'Realists of the Countryside', *Time of Yeats* (New York and London, 1937).

Wright, H. G., 'The Sense of the Past in Edward Thomas', *Welsh Outlook* (Sept. 1932), pp. 250–3.

IV. Recent Background Studies

Bergonzi, Bernard, *Heroes' Twilight* (London, 1965).

Fairchild, H. N., *Religious Trends in English Poetry*, vol. V (New York and London, 1962).

Gardner, Brian (ed.), *Up The Line To Death* (London, 1964).

Grant, Joy, *Harold Monro and the Poetry Bookshop* (London, 1967).

Hassall, Christopher, *Edward Marsh, Patron of the Arts* (London, 1959).
Rupert Brooke: A Biography (London, 1964).

Hastings, Michael, *The Handsomest Young Man in England* (London, 1967).

Heilbrun, Carolyn G., *The Garnett Family* (London, 1961).

Hutchins, Patricia, *Ezra Pound's Kensington* (London, 1965).

Johnston, John H., *English Poetry of the First World War* (London, 1964).

Jones, A. R., *The Life and Opinions of Thomas Ernest Hulme* (London, 1960).

Mertins, Louis, *Robert Frost: Life and Talks—Walking* (Norman, Oklahoma, 1965).

Norman, Charles, *Ezra Pound* (New York, 1960).

Parsons, I. M. (ed.), *Men Who March Away* (London, 1965).

Reeves, James (ed.), *Georgian Poetry* (Middlesex, 1962).

Ross, Robert H., *The Georgian Revolt* (London, 1967).

Sergeant, Elizabeth S., *Robert Frost: The Trial by Existence* (New York, 1961).

Stead, C. K., *The New Poetic* (London, 1964).

Stonesifer, Richard J., *W. H. Davies: A Critical Biography* (London, 1963).

Thompson, Lawrance, *Robert Frost: The Early Years 1874–1915* (London, 1967).

Thorpe, Michael, *Siegfried Sassoon* (London, 1966).

Welland, D. S. R., *Wilfred Owen: A Critical Study* (London, 1960).

INDEX

INDEX

INDEX